APPLICATIONS FOR ENROLLMENT OF SEMINOLE NEWBORN ACT OF 1905

VOLUME II

TRANSCRIBED BY

JEFF BOWEN

NATIVE STUDY
Gallipolis, Ohio
USA

Originally published:
Baltimore, Maryland
2012

Reprinted by:

Native Study LLC
Gallipolis, OH
www.nativestudy.com
2020

Library of Congress Control Number: 2020916646

ISBN: 978-1-64968-053-2

Made in the United States of America.

Other Books and Series by Jeff Bowen

1901-1907 Native American Census Seneca, Eastern Shawnee, Miami, Modoc, Ottawa, Peoria, Quapaw, and Wyandotte Indians (Under Seneca School, Indian Territory)

1932 Census of The Standing Rock Sioux Reservation with Births And Deaths 1924-1932

Census of The Blackfeet, Montana, 1897- 1901 Expanded Edition

Eastern Cherokee by Blood, 1906-1910, Volumes I thru XIII

Choctaw of Mississippi Indian Census 1929-1932 with Births and Deaths 1924-1931 Volume I

Choctaw of Mississippi Indian Census 1933, 1934 & 1937, Supplemental Rolls to 1934 & 1935 with Births and Deaths 1932-1938, and Marriages 1936-1938 Volume II

Eastern Cherokee Census Cherokee, North Carolina 1930-1939 Census 1930-1931 with Births And Deaths 1924-1931 Taken By Agent L. W. Page Volume I

Eastern Cherokee Census Cherokee, North Carolina 1930-1939 Census 1932-1933 with Births And Deaths 1930-1932 Taken By Agent R. L. Spalsbury Volume II

Eastern Cherokee Census Cherokee, North Carolina 1930-1939 Census 1934-1937 with Births and Deaths 1925-1938 and Marriages 1936 & 1938 Taken by Agents R. L. Spalsbury And Harold W. Foght Volume III

Seminole of Florida Indian Census, 1930-1940 with Birth and Death Records, 1930-1938

Texas Cherokees 1820-1839 A Document For Litigation 1921

Choctaw By Blood Enrollment Cards 1898-1914 Volumes I thru XVII

Starr Roll 1894 (Cherokee Payment Rolls) Districts: Canadian, Cooweescoowee, and Delaware Volume One

Starr Roll 1894 (Cherokee Payment Rolls) Districts: Flint, Going Snake, and Illinois Volume Two

Starr Roll 1894 (Cherokee Payment Rolls) Districts: Saline, Sequoyah, and Tahlequah; Including Orphan Roll Volume Three

Other Books and Series by Jeff Bowen

Cherokee Intruder Cases Dockets of Hearings 1901-1909 Volumes I & II

Indian Wills, 1911-1921 Records of the Bureau of Indian Affairs
Books One thru Seven;

Native American Wills & Probate Records 1911-1921

Turtle Mountain Reservation Chippewa Indians 1932 Census with Births & Deaths, 1924-1932

Chickasaw By Blood Enrollment Cards 1898-1914 Volume I thru V

Cherokee Descendants East An Index to the Guion Miller Applications Volume I
Cherokee Descendants West An Index to the Guion Miller Applications Volume II (A-M)
Cherokee Descendants West An Index to the Guion Miller Applications Volume III (N-Z)

Applications for Enrollment of Seminole Newborn Freedmen, Act of 1905

Eastern Cherokee Census, Cherokee, North Carolina, 1915-1922, Taken by Agent James E. Henderson   *Volume I (1915-1916)*
                                 Volume II (1917-1918)
                                 Volume III (1919-1920)
                                 Volume IV (1921-1922)

Complete Delaware Roll of 1898

Eastern Cherokee Census, Cherokee, North Carolina, 1923-1929, Taken by Agent James E. Henderson   *Volume I (1923-1924)*
                                 Volume II (1925-1926)
                                 Volume III (1927-1929)

Applications for Enrollment of Seminole Newborn Act of 1905 Volume I

Visit our website at **www.nativestudy.com** to learn more about these
and other books and series by Jeff Bowen

This series is dedicated to the descendants of the
Seminole newborn listed in these applications.

DEPARTMENT OF THE INTERIOR.

Commissioner to the Five Civilized Tribes.

NOTICE.

Opening of Land Office at Wewoka,

IN THE SEMINOLE NATION, INDIAN TERRITORY.

Notice is hereby given that on Monday, September 4, 1905, the Commissioner to the Five Civilized Tribes will establish a land office at Wewoka, in the Seminole Nation, Indian Territory, for the purpose of allowing citizens and freedmen of the Seminole Nation to select allotments of land for their minor children enrolled under the Act of Congress approved March 3, 1905 (33 Stat. L 1060), and for the further purpose of allowing citizens and freedmen of the Seminole Nation, whose allotments are incomplete, to select additional land in order to bring the value of their allotments up to the standard of $309.09, as nearly as may be practicable.

Each child whose enrollment in accordance with the Act of March 3, 1905, has been duly approved by the Secretary of the Interior, is entitled to receive an alllotment of forty acres without regard to the character or value of the land selected.

Selection of allotments for minor children must be made by their citizen or freedmen parents or by a duly appointed guardian, or curator, or by a duly appointed administrator.

TAMS BIXBY,
Commissioner.

Muskogee, Indian Territory,
July 29, 1905.

This particular notice makes mention of the Act of 1905. The Creek and Seminole were closely related tribes. Both tribes' notices were like similar in nature.

INTRODUCTION

The *Applications for Enrollment of Seminole Newborn Act of 1905*, National Archive film M-1301, Rolls 401-402, are found under the heading of Applications for Enrollment of the Commission to the Five Civilized Tribes. For this series, I have transcribed the application forms filled out by individuals applying for enrollment in the Five Civilized Tribes under the Dawes Commission. These applications contain considerably more information than is stated on the census cards found in series M-1186. M-1301 (Seminole by Birth) possesses its own numerical sequence, separate from M-1186. To find each party's roll number you would have to reference M-1186.

"On May 1, 1905, as previously announced, an office was opened for the enrollment of children at Wewoka, Indian Territory the tribal capital. The office was maintained until midnight June 2, and applications for the enrollment of 414 children received. Of this number, 270 were the children by blood of the Seminole Nation and 144 were the children of Seminole freedmen. Two hundred applications of the former class have been approved by the Commission and the names of the applicants included upon a schedule transmitted for departmental approval on June 28. The remaining applications will be passed upon as rapidly as possible, so that the work of making allotments to such children may be taken up and completed in the near future."[1]

"The language used in the 1905 act excluded some children who probably had a legitimate right to enrollment because it specified that a parent had to be enrolled, thereby excluding all the people whose applications were still pending. A subsequent report on enrollment concluded that this was 'probably an unintentional defect in the law,' but the Commission followed its standard practice of strictly following the letter of the legislation."[2]

"Of the applications acted on by the Department the percentages approved are as follows: Creeks 30, Choctaws 9, Chickasaws 13, Cherokees 23, and Seminoles 22 per cent. The remainder were disapproved."[3]

---

[1] Interestingly enough, this particular film's title stated that there were 181 applications. It was found during the transcription process that under some application numbers there was more than one applicant's name included, increasing the total to 260 applicants, 88 Seminole newborns that were not assigned their own number.
Annual Reports of The Department of the Interior For the Fiscal Year Ended June 30, 1905, p. 607.

[2] The Dawes Commission and the Allotment of the Five Civilized Tribes, 1893-1914 by Kent Carter, p.63

[3] Annual Reports of The Department of the Interior For the Fiscal Year Ended June 30, 1905, p. 138.

The Commission had started enrolling Seminoles immediately following the tribe's acceptance of the agreement in 1898. Intermarried citizenship was not recognized as most citizens were fullblood Indians or freedmen. The Seminole rolls were found to be free of complication and corruption so it was found that the work was simple and able to be completed quickly. The newborn process for the Seminole, while thorough, was still less taxing during the enrollment period compared to other tribes who were larger and had more complications because of controversial non-acceptance of new treaties. Groups like the Creek had the organization called the "Snakes" and the Cherokee had the "Keetoowah", who were mostly full-bloods and fiercely stood up against the new allotment system not wanting any changes from the old treaties, realizing they were going to lose more of their freedoms as well as millions of acres of land.

Besides the applications themselves, researchers will find the identities of other individuals within these applications--doctors, lawyers, mid-wives, and other relatives--that may help with your genealogical research. Since the Creek and Seminole tribes were so closely related, this two-volume series will complement my recently completed fourteen-volume Creek newborn series.

Jeff Bowen
Gallipolis, Ohio
NativeStudy.com

Sem NB 109   Father's Roll 1144
BIRTH AFFIDAVIT.   Mother's Roll 1145

DEPARTMENT OF THE INTERIOR.
COMMISSION TO THE FIVE CIVILIZED TRIBES.

IN RE APPLICATION FOR ENROLLMENT, as a citizen of the   Seminole   Nation, of
William McCulla   , born on the 21   day of Dec , 1901

Name of Father: McCulla   a citizen of the Seminole Nation.
Name of Mother: Rosanna McCulla   a citizen of the Seminole Nation.

Postoffice   Keokuk Falls I.T.

Child present

AFFIDAVIT OF MOTHER.

UNITED STATES OF AMERICA, Indian Territory,
   Western   DISTRICT.

     I,   Rosanna McCulla   , on oath state that I am 32   years of age and a citizen by   blood   , of the   Seminole   Nation; that I am the lawful wife of McCulla   , who is a citizen, by blood   of the   Seminole   Nation; that a male   child was born to me on 21 day of   Dec   , 1901; that said child has been named   William McCulla   , and was living March 4, 1905.

                                   her
                     Rosanna x McCulla
Witnesses To Mark: mark
   Chas E Webster
   Frank C. Sabourin

   Subscribed and sworn to before me this 2 day of   May   , 1905.

                           Chas E Webster
                           Notary Public.

AFFIDAVIT OF ATTENDING ~~PHYSICIAN OR MID-WIFE~~.

UNITED STATES OF AMERICA, Indian Territory,
   Western   DISTRICT.

                          am the husband of
     I,   McCulla   , a   , on oath state that I attended on Mrs.   Rosanna
McCulla   , ~~wife of~~   and   on the 21 day of Dec   , 1901; that there was born to her on said date a   male   child; that said child was living March 4, 1905, and is said to have been named William McCulla

1

   his

                                 McCulla   x

Witnesses To Mark: mark
   { Chas E Webster
   { Frank C. Sabourin

Subscribed and sworn to before me this 2 day of   May   , 1905.

                                  Chas E Webster
                                  Notary Public.

Sem NB 110
BIRTH AFFIDAVIT.

DEPARTMENT OF THE INTERIOR.
COMMISSION TO THE FIVE CIVILIZED TRIBES.

IN RE APPLICATION FOR ENROLLMENT, as a citizen of the   Seminole   Nation, of
Lucinda Wolf   , born on the   20th   day of ~~Aug~~. Oct.   , 1902

Name of Father: Jackson Wolf   ([#]1149)   a citizen of the   Seminole   Nation.
Name of Mother: Milla Wolf   ([#]1150)   a citizen of the Nation.

                           Postoffice   Wewoka, I.T.

(Child present)

AFFIDAVIT OF MOTHER.

UNITED STATES OF AMERICA, Indian Territory, }
    Western   **DISTRICT.**

    I,   Milla Wolf   , on oath state that I am 39   years of age and a citizen by
blood   , of the   Seminole   Nation; that I am the lawful wife of   Jackson Wolf   ,
who is a citizen, by blood   of the   Seminole   Nation; that a   female
child was born to me on 20th   day of   Oct   , 1902; that said child has been named
Lucinda Wolf   , and was living March 4, 1905.

                               her
                          Milla x Wolf
Witnesses To Mark: mark
   { Ed. Merrick
   { Frank C. Sabourin

Subscribed and sworn to before me this 2nd day of May , 1905.

Seal

Edward Merrick
Notary Public.

AFFIDAVIT OF ATTENDING PHYSICIAN OR MID-WIFE.

UNITED STATES OF AMERICA, Indian Territory,
Western DISTRICT.

I, Melinda Tiger , a midwife , on oath state that I attended on Mrs. Milla Wolf , wife of Jackson Wolf on the 20th day of Oct , 1902; that there was born to her on said date a female child; that said child was living March 4, 1905, and is said to have been named Lucinda Wolf

her
Melinda x Tiger
mark

Witnesses To Mark:
Frank C. Sabourin
Edward Merrick

Subscribed and sworn to before me this 2nd day of May , 1905.

Seal

Edward Merrick
Notary Public.

Sem NB 110
BIRTH AFFIDAVIT.

DEPARTMENT OF THE INTERIOR.
COMMISSION TO THE FIVE CIVILIZED TRIBES.

IN RE APPLICATION FOR ENROLLMENT, as a citizen of the Seminole Nation, of Sissy Wolf , born on the 18 day of Sept. , 1904

Name of Father: Jackson Wolf #1149 a citizen of the Seminole Nation.
Name of Mother: Milla Wolf #1150 a citizen of the Seminole Nation.

Postoffice Wewoka, I.T.

(Child present)

AFFIDAVIT OF MOTHER.

UNITED STATES OF AMERICA, Indian Territory, ⎫
    Western   DISTRICT. ⎭

    I,   Milla Wolf   , on oath state that I am   39   years of age and a citizen by blood   , of the   Seminole   Nation; that I am the lawful wife of   Jackson Wolf   , who is a citizen, by   blood   of the   Seminole   Nation; that a   female child was born to me on   18th   day of   Sept   , 1904; that said child has been named Sissy Wolf   , and was living March 4, 1905.

her

Milla x Wolf

mark

Witnesses To Mark:
  ⎧ Edward Merrick
  ⎩ Frank C. Sabourin

    Subscribed and sworn to before me this 2nd   day of   May   , 1905.

Edward Merrick

Notary Public.

_____

Husband

AFFIDAVIT OF ~~ATTENDING PHYSICIAN OR MID-WIFE~~.

UNITED STATES OF AMERICA, Indian Territory, ⎫
    Western   DISTRICT. ⎭

    I,   Jackson Wolf   , ~~a~~——— , on oath state that I attended on Mrs.   Milla Wolf   my , wife ~~of~~——— on the 18th   day of   Sept   , 1904; that there was born to her on said date a   female   child; that said child was living March 4, 1905, and is said to have been named Sissy Wolf

her

Melinda x Tiger

mark

Witnesses To Mark:
  ⎧ Frank C. Sabourin
  ⎩ Edward Merrick

    Subscribed and sworn to before me this 2nd   day of   May   , 1905.

Edward Merrick

Notary Public.

Sem NB 111
BIRTH AFFIDAVIT.

DEPARTMENT OF THE INTERIOR.
COMMISSION TO THE FIVE CIVILIZED TRIBES.

IN RE APPLICATION FOR ENROLLMENT, as a citizen of the   Seminole   Nation, of
Winey Harjoche   , born on the 5   day of Jan , 1901

Name of Father: Foas Harjoche   1158   a citizen of the Seminole   Nation.
Name of Mother: Putty Harjoche   1159   a citizen of the Seminole   Nation.

Postoffice   Little I.T.

(Child present)

AFFIDAVIT OF MOTHER.

UNITED STATES OF AMERICA, Indian Territory, ⎱
     Western   **DISTRICT.** ⎰

I, Putty Harjoche   , on oath state that I am about 35 years of age and a citizen
by   blood   , of the   Seminole   Nation; that I am the lawful wife of   Foas
Harjoche   , who is a citizen, by   blood   of the   Seminole   Nation; that a
Female   child was born to me on   5   day of Jan   , 1901, that said child has been
named   Winey Harjoche   , and is now living.

her
Putty x Harjoche
Witnesses To Mark: mark
⎰ Chas E Webster
⎱ A. B. Davis

Subscribed and sworn to before me this 24   day of   May   , 1905.

Chas E Webster
Notary Public.

AFFIDAVIT OF ATTENDING PHYSICIAN OR MID-WIFE.

UNITED STATES OF AMERICA, Indian Territory, ⎱
     Western   **DISTRICT.** ⎰

I,   Foas Harjoche   , a   , on oath state that I attended on Mrs.   Putty
Harjoche   , ~~wife of~~ my wife   on the   5 day of Jan , 1901; that there was born
to her on said date a   Female   child; that said child is now living and is said to have
been named Winey Harjoche   his
Foas x Harjoche
mark

5

Witnesses To Mark:
   { Chas E Webster
     A. B. Davis

     Subscribed and sworn to before me this 24   day of   May   , 1905.

                          Chas E Webster
                          Notary Public.

Sem NB 111
BIRTH AFFIDAVIT.

DEPARTMENT OF THE INTERIOR.
COMMISSION TO THE FIVE CIVILIZED TRIBES.

IN RE APPLICATION FOR ENROLLMENT, as a citizen of the   Seminole   Nation, of
Rosanna Harjoche   , born on the   10   day of   May , 1904

Name of Father: Foas Harjoche   1158   a citizen of the Seminole   Nation.
Name of Mother: Putty Harjoche   1159   a citizen of the   Seminole   Nation.

                   Postoffice   Little I.T.

(Child present)

AFFIDAVIT OF MOTHER.

UNITED STATES OF AMERICA, Indian Territory, ⎤
     Western   **DISTRICT.** ⎦

     I, Putty Harjoche   , on oath state that I am about 35 years of age and a citizen
by   blood   , of the   Seminole   Nation; that I am the lawful wife of   Foas
Harjoche   , who is a citizen, by   blood   of the   Seminole   Nation; that a
Female   child was born to me on   10 day of May   , 1904, that said child has
been named   Rosanna Harjoche   , and is now living.

                          her
                  Putty x Harjoche
Witnesses To Mark: mark
   { Chas E Webster
     A. B. Davis

     Subscribed and sworn to before me this 24   day of   May   , 1905.

                          Chas E Webster
                          Notary Public.

Applications for Enrollment of Seminole Newborn
Act of 1905   Volume II

AFFIDAVIT OF ATTENDING PHYSICIAN OR MID-WIFE.

UNITED STATES OF AMERICA, Indian Territory,
 Western   DISTRICT.

I, Foas Harjoche   , a   , on oath state that I attended on Mrs.   Putty
Harjoche   , wife of   my wife   on the   10 day of May , 1904; that there was
born to her on said date a   Female   child; that said child is now living and is said to
have been named Rosanna Harjoche   his
                                         Foas x Harjoche
                                              mark

Witnesses To Mark:
  Chas E Webster
  A. B. Davis

Subscribed and sworn to before me this 24   day of   May   , 1905.

                                   Chas E Webster
                                   Notary Public.

                                                      Seminole
                                                      NB 112

                    Muskogee, Indian Territory, July 3, 1905.

Chittoe Harjoche,
     Wewoka, Indian Territory.

Dear Sir:

On May 4, 1905, you appeared before the Commission to the Five Civilized
Tribes and made application for the enrollment of your son, Abler Harjoche, as a citizen
by blood of the Seminole Nation, and at that time the affidavits of yourself and wife as to
the birth of said child on December 18, 1904, were taken.

You are advised that it will be necessary for you to furnish this office with the
affidavits of two disinterested parties who know of the birth of said child, when he was
born and whether or not he was living on March 4, 1905.

It also appears that said child is dead, and for the purpose of making his death a matter of record there is inclosed herewith blank for proof of death, which you are requested to have filled out, properly executed and returned to this office.

In having these affidavits executed be careful to see that all blanks are properly filled, all names written in full and that the Notary Public, before whom the affidavits are executed attaches his name and seal to each affidavit. In case any signature is by mark, it must be attested by two disinterested parties witnesses thereto.

Please give this matter your prompt attention.

Respectfully,

LM-3-2.   Commissioner.

DEPARTMENT OF THE INTERIOR.
COMMISSION TO THE FIVE CIVILIZED TRIBES.

In the matter of the death of   Abler Harjoche   a citizen of the   Seminole Nation, who formerly resided at or near   Wewoka   , Ind. Ter., and died on the   12   day of   March   , 1905

AFFIDAVIT OF RELATIVE.

UNITED STATES OF AMERICA, Indian Territory,
      Western   DISTRICT.

I,   Chittoe Harjoche   , on oath state that I am   53   years of age and a citizen by blood , of the Seminole Nation; that my postoffice address is   Wewoka   , Ind. Ter.; that I am   the father   of Abler Harjoche   who was a citizen, by   blood   , of the Seminole   Nation and that said   Abler Harjoche   died on the   12   day of March   , 1905

Chittoe Harjoche

Witnesses To Mark:
      John W Willmott

Subscribed and sworn to before me this 11th day of   July , 1905.

Com exp Oct 5-1905   John W. Willmott
                                                                     Notary Public.

8

AFFIDAVIT OF ACQUAINTANCE.

UNITED STATES OF AMERICA, Indian Territory, ⎫
Western   DISTRICT. ⎭

      I, Thomas Hawkins , on oath state that I am 58   years of age, and a citizen by blood   of the Seminole   Nation; that my postoffice address is   Wewoka   , Ind. Ter.; that I was personally acquainted with   Abler Harjoche   who was a citizen, by blood   , of the   Seminole   Nation; and that said   Abler Harjoche   died on the   12 day of   March   , 1905

his
Thomas Hawkins x
mark

Witnesses To Mark:
   ⎧ John W. Willmott
   ⎩ Cansur Tiger

    Subscribed and sworn to before me this 11ᵗʰ day of   July , 1905.

Com exp Oct   John W. Willmott
  5-1905   Notary Public.

Sem NB 112
BIRTH AFFIDAVIT.

DEPARTMENT OF THE INTERIOR.
COMMISSION TO THE FIVE CIVILIZED TRIBES.

    IN RE APPLICATION FOR ENROLLMENT, as a citizen of the   Seminole   Nation, of Jennie Harjoche   , born on the 10   day of Nov , 1903

Name of Father: Chittoe Harjoche   1166   a citizen of the   Seminole   Nation.
Name of Mother: Leah Harjoche   1167   a citizen of the   Seminole   Nation.

Postoffice   Wewoka

(Child present)
AFFIDAVIT OF MOTHER.

UNITED STATES OF AMERICA, Indian Territory, ⎫
Western   DISTRICT. ⎭

    I,   Leah Harjoche   , on oath state that I am 33   years of age and a citizen by   blood   , of the   Seminole   Nation; that I am the lawful wife of   Chittoe Harjoche   , who is a citizen, by blood   of the   Seminole   Nation; that a Female   child was born to me on   10   day of   Nov   , 1903; that said child has been named   Jennie Harjoche   , and was living March 4, 1905.

<table>
<tr><td>Witnesses To Mark:
{ Chas E Webster
  Frank C. Sabourin</td><td>her
Leah x Harjoche
mark</td></tr>
</table>

Subscribed and sworn to before me this 4 day of   May   , 1905.

Chas E Webster
Notary Public.

AFFIDAVIT OF ATTENDING PHYSICIAN OR MID-WIFE.

UNITED STATES OF AMERICA, Indian Territory,
   Western   DISTRICT.

I, Chittoe Harjoche   , a medicine man   , on oath state that I attended on Mrs. Leah Harjoche   , ~~wife of~~ my wife   on the 10 day of Nov   , 1903; that there was born to her on said date a   female   child; that said child was living March 4, 1905, and is said to have been named Jennie Harjoche

<table>
<tr><td>Witnesses To Mark:
{ Chas E Webster
  Frank C. Sabourin</td><td>his
Chittoe x Harjoche
mark</td></tr>
</table>

Subscribed and sworn to before me this 4 day of   May   , 1905.

Chas E Webster
Notary Public.

Sem NB 112
BIRTH AFFIDAVIT.

DEPARTMENT OF THE INTERIOR.
COMMISSION TO THE FIVE CIVILIZED TRIBES.

IN RE APPLICATION FOR ENROLLMENT, as a citizen of the   Seminole   Nation, of Abler Harjoche   , born on the 18 day of Dec , 1904

Name of Father: Chittoe Harjoche   a citizen of the   Seminole   Nation.
Name of Mother: Leah Harjoche   a citizen of the   Seminole   Nation.

Postoffice   Wewoka Ind Ter

10

Applications for Enrollment of Seminole Newborn
Act of 1905   Volume II

AFFIDAVIT OF MOTHER.

UNITED STATES OF AMERICA, Indian Territory, ⎤
    Western   DISTRICT. ⎦

I, Martha Tiger , on oath state that I am 30 years of age and a citizen by blood , of the Seminole Nation; that I am ~~the lawful wife of~~ not related to Leah Harjoche , who is a citizen, by blood of the Seminole Nation; ~~that a~~ to whom a male child was born ~~to me~~ on 18" day of December , 1904; that said child has been named Abler Harjoche , and was living March 4, 1905.

her
Martha Tiger x
mark

Witnesses To Mark:
{ John H. Willmott
{ Cansur Tiger

Subscribed and sworn to before me this 11th day of July , 1905.

My Com exp   John W. Willmott
  Oct 5-1905   Notary Public.

AFFIDAVIT OF ATTENDING PHYSICIAN OR MID-WIFE.

UNITED STATES OF AMERICA, Indian Territory, ⎤
      Western   DISTRICT. ⎦

personally know

I, Thomas Hawkins , a Seminole citizen , on oath state that I ~~attended~~ ~~on~~ Mrs. Leah Harjoche , wife of Chittoe Harjoche both Seminoles by blood ~~on the   day of   , 1~~ ;to said Leah Harjoche on the 18" December 1904 that there was born to her ~~on said date~~ a male child; that said child was living March 4, 1905, and is said to have been named Abler Harjoche that I am not related to any of the above named parties

his
Thomas x Hawkins
mark

Witnesses To Mark:
{ John H. Willmott
{ Cansur Tiger

Subscribed and sworn to before me this 11th day of July , 1905.

My Com exp   John W. Willmott
  Oct 5-1905   Notary Public.

Sem NB 112
BIRTH AFFIDAVIT.

DEPARTMENT OF THE INTERIOR.
COMMISSION TO THE FIVE CIVILIZED TRIBES.

IN RE APPLICATION FOR ENROLLMENT, as a citizen of the   Seminole   Nation, of
Abler Harjoche   , born on the 18   day of   Dec   , 1904

Name of Father: Chittoe Harjoche   1166   a citizen of the   Seminole   Nation.
Name of Mother: Leah Harjoche   1167   a citizen of the   Seminole   Nation.

Postoffice   Wewoka

AFFIDAVIT OF MOTHER.

UNITED STATES OF AMERICA, Indian Territory,
    Western   DISTRICT.

I,   Leah Harjoche   , on oath state that I am   33   years of age and a citizen
by   blood   , of the   Seminole   Nation; that I am the lawful wife of   Chittoe
Harjoche   , who is a citizen, by blood   of the   Seminole   Nation; that a
Male   child was born to me on 18   day of   Dec   , 1904; that said child has been
named   Abler Harjoche   , and was living March 4, 1905. and died March 12-1905
                                                her
                                  Leah x Harjoche
Witnesses To Mark: mark
    Chas E Webster
    Frank C. Sabourin

Subscribed and sworn to before me this 4 day of   May   , 1905.

Chas E Webster
Notary Public.

AFFIDAVIT OF ATTENDING PHYSICIAN OR MID-WIFE.

UNITED STATES OF AMERICA, Indian Territory,
    Western   DISTRICT.

I,   Chittoe Harjoche   , a medicine man   , on oath state that I attended on
Mrs. Leah Harjoche   , ~~wife of~~ my wife   on the 18 day of   Dec   , 1904;
that there was born to her on said date a   Male   child; that said child was living
March 4, 1905, and died March 12, 1905 and is said to have been named Abler Harjoche

12

	his
	Chittoe x Harjoche
Witnesses To Mark:	mark
⎰ Chas E Webster	
⎱ Frank C. Sabourin	

Subscribed and sworn to before me this 4 day of   May   , 1905.

Chas E Webster
Notary Public.

Abler Harjoche now dead ~~See death affidavit~~.

Seminole
NB-113.

Muskogee, Indian Territory June 29, 1905.

Commission to the Five Civilized Tribes,
Creek Enrollment Division.

Gentlemen:

On May 15, 1905 there was filed with the Commission application for the enrollment of Marchee Buck, born March 28, 1903, as a citizen by blood of the Seminole Nation. It is stated in said application that the father of said child is Joe Buck, a citizen by blood of the Creek Nation, and that his mother is Liley Buck, a citizen by blood of the Seminole Nation.

You are requested to inform the Seminole Enrollment Division as to whether any application has been made to the Commission for the enrollment of said Marchee Buck as a citizen of the Creek Nation and if so what disposition, if any, has been made of such application.

Respectfully,

Chairman.

13

HGH

DEPARTMENT OF THE INTERIOR.
COMMISSION TO THE FIVE CIVILIZED TRIBES.

Sem. NB. 113.

Muskogee, Indian Territory, July 10, 1905.

Seminole Enrollment Division,
       General Office.

Gentlemen:

     Receipt is acknowledged of your communication of June 29, 1905 (Sem. NB. 113), in which you ask if application has been made for enrollment as a citizen of the Creek Nation for March[sic] Buck, child of Joe Buck, a citizen of the Creek Nation, and Liley Buck, a citizen by blood of the Seminole Nation.

     In reply you are advised that the records of this office have been examined and it does not appear that application has been made for the enrollment of said March Buck, as a citizen of the Creek Nation.

                  Respectfully,
                      Tams Bixby   Commissioner.

Sem NB 113
BIRTH AFFIDAVIT.

DEPARTMENT OF THE INTERIOR.
COMMISSION TO THE FIVE CIVILIZED TRIBES.

IN RE APPLICATION FOR ENROLLMENT, as a citizen of the   Seminole   Nation, of Marchee Buck   , born on the 28   day of March , 1903

Name of Father: Joe Buck   a citizen of the   Creek   Nation.
Name of Mother: Liley Buck   1176   a citizen of the Seminole   Nation.

                    Postoffice   Wewoka, IT

(Child present)

AFFIDAVIT OF MOTHER.

UNITED STATES OF AMERICA, Indian Territory, ⎫
    Western   DISTRICT. ⎭

     I, Liley Buck   , on oath state that I am about 28 years of age and a citizen by blood   , of the   Seminole   Nation; that I am the lawful wife of   Joe Buck   , who is a citizen, by   blood   of the   Creek   Nation; that a   male   child was

born to me on   28   day of   March   , 1903, that said child has been named
Marchee Buck   , and is now living.

her
Liley x Buck
mark

Witnesses To Mark:
   { Chas E Webster
   { Frank C. Sabourin

Subscribed and sworn to before me this   15   day of   May   , 1905.

Chas E Webster
Notary Public.

AFFIDAVIT OF ATTENDING PHYSICIAN OR MID-WIFE.

UNITED STATES OF AMERICA, Indian Territory,
     Western   **DISTRICT.**

   I,   Joe Buck   , a   , on oath state that I attended on Mrs.   Liley Buck   ,
~~wife of~~   my wife   on the   28   day of   March , 1903; that there was born to her on
said date a   male   child; that said child is now living and is said to have been named
Marchee Buck

his
Joe x Buck
mark

Witnesses To Mark:
   { Chas E Webster
   { Frank C. Sabourin

Subscribed and sworn to before me this   15   day of   May   , 1905.

Chas E Webster
Notary Public.

Sem NB 114
BIRTH AFFIDAVIT.

DEPARTMENT OF THE INTERIOR.
COMMISSION TO THE FIVE CIVILIZED TRIBES.

IN RE APPLICATION FOR ENROLLMENT, as a citizen of the   Seminole   Nation, of
Amos Tiger   , born on the 6th   day of December   , 1904

Name of Father: Chepon Tiger   (1201)   a citizen of the   Seminole   Nation.
Name of Mother: Louisa Tiger   (1202)   a citizen of the   Seminole   Nation.

Postoffice   Wcwoka IT

Child present

AFFIDAVIT OF MOTHER.

UNITED STATES OF AMERICA, **Indian Territory,**
     Western   **DISTRICT.**

I,   Louisa Tiger   , on oath state that I am 24 years of age and a citizen by
blood   , of the   Seminole   Nation; that I am the lawful wife of   Chepon Tiger
, who is a citizen, by   blood   of the   Seminole   Nation; that a   male   child
was born to me on 6th   day of   December   , 1904, that said child has been named
Amos Tiger   , and is now living.

her
Louisa x Tiger
mark

Witnesses To Mark:
   Frank C. Sabourin
   Chas E Webster

Subscribed and sworn to before me this 15th   day of   May   , 1905.

Chas E Webster
Notary Public.

AFFIDAVIT OF ATTENDING PHYSICIAN OR MID-WIFE.

UNITED STATES OF AMERICA, **Indian Territory,**   Midwife sick
     Western   **DISTRICT.**

helped
I,   Chepon Tiger   , ~~a~~   , on oath state that I attended on Mrs.   Louisa
Tiger, ~~wife of~~   my wife   on the 6   day of Dec   , 1904; that there was born to her
on said date a   male   child; that said child is now living and is said to have been
named Amos Tiger   his

Chepon x Tiger
mark

Witnesses To Mark:
  { Chas E Webster
  { A. B. Davis

    Subscribed and sworn to before me this 31 day of   May   , 1905.

                               Chas E Webster
                               Notary Public.

Sem NB 115
BIRTH AFFIDAVIT.

DEPARTMENT OF THE INTERIOR.
COMMISSION TO THE FIVE CIVILIZED TRIBES.

IN RE APPLICATION FOR ENROLLMENT, as a citizen of the   Seminole   Nation, of
Jeffie Harjo   , born on the 12 day of   March , 1903

Name of Father: Sammah Harjo   (241)   a citizen of the Seminole   Nation.
Name of Mother: Mollea Harjo   (1217)   a citizen of the Seminole   Nation.
                  nee McGirt
                      Postoffice   Sasakwa, I.T.

AFFIDAVIT OF MOTHER.

UNITED STATES OF AMERICA, Indian Territory, }
    Western   **DISTRICT.** }

    I, Mollea Harjo nee McGirt   , on oath state that I am 18 years of age
and a citizen by   blood   , of the Seminole Nation; that I am the lawful wife of
Sammah Harjo   , who is a citizen, by blood   of the   Seminole   Nation;
that a   male   child was born to me on 12   day of   March   , 1903; that said
child has been named   Jeffie Harjo   , and was living March 4, 1905.
                               her
                     Mollea x Harjo
Witnesses To Mark: mark
  { Chas E Webster
  { Frank C. Sabourin

17

Applications for Enrollment of Seminole Newborn
Act of 1905   Volume II

Subscribed and sworn to before me this 18 day of   May   , 1905.

Chas E Webster
Notary Public.

AFFIDAVIT OF ATTENDING PHYSICIAN OR MID-WIFE.

UNITED STATES OF AMERICA, Indian Territory,
Western   DISTRICT. }

I,   Elsie McGirt   , a   midwife   , on oath state that I attended on Mrs. Mollca Harjo   , wife of   Sammah Harjo   on the 12 day of   March   , 1903; that there was born to her on said date a   male   child; that said child was living March 4, 1905, and is said to have been named Jeffie Harjo

her
Elsie x McGirt
mark

Witnesses To Mark:
{ Chas E Webster
{ Frank C. Sabourin

Subscribed and sworn to before me this 18 day of   May   , 1905.

Chas E Webster
Notary Public.

Father on roll as Sammah #241

Sem NB 116
BIRTH AFFIDAVIT.
DEPARTMENT OF THE INTERIOR.
COMMISSION TO THE FIVE CIVILIZED TRIBES.

IN RE APPLICATION FOR ENROLLMENT, as a citizen of the   Seminole   Nation, of Lillie Lena   , born on the 23   day of August   , 1901

Name of Father: Charley Lena   (1230)   a citizen of the Seminole   Nation.
Name of Mother: Martha Lena   (1231)   a citizen of the   Seminole   Nation.

Postoffice   Wewoka IT

18

Child present

AFFIDAVIT OF MOTHER.

UNITED STATES OF AMERICA, Indian Territory, ⎱
    Western   **DISTRICT.** ⎰

     I,   Martha Lena   , on oath state that I am 30 years of age and a citizen by blood   , of the   Seminole   Nation; that I am the lawful wife of   Charley Lena , who is a citizen, by   blood   of the   Seminole   Nation; that a   female child was born to me on 23rd day of August   , 1901, that said child has been named   Lillie Lena   , and is now living.

her
Martha x Lena
mark

Witnesses To Mark:
  ⎰ Frank C. Sabourin
  ⎱ Chas E Webster

     Subscribed and sworn to before me this 15 day of   May   , 1905.

Chas E Webster
Notary Public.

Father

AFFIDAVIT OF ATTENDING PHYSICIAN OR MID-WIFE.

UNITED STATES OF AMERICA, Indian Territory, ⎱
    Western   **DISTRICT.** ⎰

     I, Charley Lena   , ———, on oath state that I attended on Mrs. Martha Lena, my wife ~~of~~——— on the 23 day of August , 1901; that there was born to her on said date a   female   child; that said child is now living and is said to have been named Lillie Lena

Charley Lena

Witnesses To Mark:
  ⎰

     Subscribed and sworn to before me this 15 day of   May   , 1905.

Chas E Webster
Notary Public.

Sem NB 116
BIRTH AFFIDAVIT.

DEPARTMENT OF THE INTERIOR.
COMMISSION TO THE FIVE CIVILIZED TRIBES.

IN RE APPLICATION FOR ENROLLMENT, as a citizen of the   Seminole   Nation, of
Losenda Lena   , born on the 1ˢᵗ day of October   , 1904

Name of Father: Charley Lena   (1230)   a citizen of the Seminole   Nation.
Name of Mother: Martha Lena   (1231)   a citizen of the Seminole   Nation.

Postoffice   Wewoka IT

Child present

AFFIDAVIT OF MOTHER.

UNITED STATES OF AMERICA, Indian Territory,
      Western   **DISTRICT.**

      I,   Martha Lena   , on oath state that I am 30 years of age and a citizen by
blood   , of the   Seminole   Nation; that I am the lawful wife of   Charley Lena ,
who is a citizen, by   blood   of the   Seminole   Nation; that a   female
child was born to me on   1ˢᵗ   day of   October   , 1904, that said child has been
named   Losenda Lena   , and is now living.

                                   her
                         Martha x Lena
Witnesses To Mark: mark
   ⎰ Frank C. Sabourin
   ⎱ Chas E Webster

      Subscribed and sworn to before me this 15   day of   May   , 1905.

                              Chas E Webster
                                 Notary Public.

AFFIDAVIT OF ATTENDING PHYSICIAN OR MID-WIFE.

UNITED STATES OF AMERICA, Indian Territory,
      Western   **DISTRICT.**

      I,   Charley Lena   , ~~a~~ , on oath state that I attended on Mrs. Martha Lena,
my wife ~~of~~ on the   1ˢᵗ   day of   October , 1904; that there was born to her on
said date a   female   child; that said child is now living and is said to have been
named   Losenda Lena

                              Charley Lena

20

Witnesses To Mark:

{

Subscribed and sworn to before me this   15 day of   May   , 1905.

Chas E Webster
Notary Public.

Land Division.
D. 45//-20. Encl.
WHA-GH. 8-20-20.

In re correction of
record as to sex of
Lillie Lena, Seminole
New Born 141.

August 20, 1920.

Mr. Barney McKellop,
Acting Field Clark,
Wewoka, Okla.

Dear Mr. McKellop:

It appears from the approved roll of new Born Seminoles that the above mentioned enrollee is enrolled as a female.

From an oil and gas lease filed at this office covering the land allotted to said Lillie Lena, it appears that this person is a male an several affidavits were filed to establish this fact.

The case was reported to the Indian Office with the end in view of having the rolls corrected to show that Lillie Lena is a male instead of a female.

By Indian Office letter of August 10, 1920, this office was requested to secure additional evidence and make further report in the matter.

You are requested to secure testimony from the parents of said enrollee showing that said Lillie Lena is a male and the identical person enrolled as a Seminole New Born at No. 141, and the reason for the long delay in bringing the matter to the attention of this office, it now being fifteen years since Lillie Lena was enrolled. You are also requested to obtain, if possible, testimony from the doctor or midwife who was present at the time of the birth of the enrollee, and also from the Notary Public before whom Martha Lena and Charley Lena executed their birth affidavit of May 15, 1905, in which the sex of the enrollee was designated as a female; also, if possible, the testimony of the witnesses to mark of said Martha Lena in her said affidavit.

21

For your information and guidance in securing the testimony, there are enclosed herewith copies of the enrollment card of said Lillie Lena and the birth affidavit filed in connection with the case.

Kindly obtain this testimony as soon as possible, as it is desired for use in connection with making a report in the matter to the Indian Office.

Sincerely yours,

Superintendent for the
Five Civilized Tribes.

REFER IN REPLY TO THE FOLLOWING: 5-1100   ADDRESS ONLY THE
                                                        COMMISSIONER OF INDIAN AFFAIRS

DEPARTMENT OF THE INTERIOR
OFFICE OF INDIAN AFFAIRS
WASHINGTON

Land-Probate-FCT
  6147-1920
  51346-1920
    J E D
In re alleged error on
Seminole roll concerning   AUG 10 1920
description of sex of
Lillie Lena, Newborn
Roll No. 141.

DEPARTMENT
R E C E I V E D
AUG 13 1920
No.   4588
Supt. Five Civilized Tribes

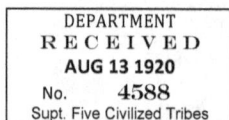

Mr. Gabe E. Parker,
    Superintendent for the
        Five Civilized Tribes.

My dear Mr. Parker:

Reference is made herein to your report of January 17, 1920, and to the supplemental report of June 14, 1920, of the Acting Superintendent for the Five Civilized Tribes, in regard to an alleged error on the final roll of newborn citizens by blood of the Seminole Indian Nation in the matter of the application for the enrollment of designation of the sex of Lillie Lena, Roll No. 141.

It appears from said roll that the above named enrollee was designated thereon as a female. It further appears that said designation was in keeping with the information contained on the census card of said enrollee, and in accordance with the birth affidavits submitted by the enrollee's father and mother on May 15, 1905, in said case.

With the above mentioned report there were submitted an affidavit executed on December 6, 1919, by the father of the enrollee and one executed January 9, 1920, by the mother of the enrollee, which affidavits, together with the affidavits of certain other

22

persons received therewith, were to the effect that said enrollee is a male. In view thereof, you recommended the correction of the above named Seminole roll so as to show thereon the sex of Lillie Lena as male instead of female.

It appears from your report that the alleged error as to the designation of the sex of the enrollee was brought to your attention through papers received by you in connection with an oil and gas lease covering the land of said Lillie Lena. The Office is unable to identify the oil and gas lease referred to or said papers as having been received in this Office.

In view of the fact that the land is apparently of value by reason of oil and gas prospects and in view of the log period of time which has elapsed since the date of the enrolment of said Lillie Lena, the Office believes that a thorough investigation should be made to determine the identity of the enrollee. In connection therewith, an explanation should be obtained from the enrollee and from the father and mother of said enrollee, as to the reason for the long delay in bringing the matter to the attention of your Office, it now being fifteen years since the enrollment of said Lillie Lena.

Testimony in the case should also be obtained if possible from the doctor or midwife, who was present at the time of the birth of the enrollee and also from the notary before whom Martha Len and Charley Lena executed their affidavits of May 15, 1905, in which the sex of the enrollee was designated as female. The testimony of the witnesses to the mark of said Martha Lena on her above mentioned affidavit should also be obtained if possible.

The Office will be pleased to received your further report in this matter at the earliest practicable date and to receive therewith the papers which you mention as having been filed in connection with the oil and gas lease, and to receive therewith also such further evidence as may be obtained in the case. Upon receipt of your further report in the matter, prompt action will be taken thereon.

Very truly yours,
EB Meritt
Acting Commissioner.

8 Rz '7.

(The above letter given again.)

_(Information typed
here is very
difficult to read.)_

August 22, 1920.

The Honorable,
    The Commissioner of Indian Affairs.

23

Applications for Enrollment of Seminole Newborn
Act of 1905   Volume II

Dear Mr. Commissioner:

(Illegible) to Indian Office letter of the *(illegible)*, you are advised that I have directed a field employee of this office to secure the additional information desired, and when it is received further report will be made in the matter.

Sincerely yours,

Superintendent for the
Five Civilized Tribes.

Land-F.T.   JULy[sic] 12 1921
6147--20
70463-20
OGP

| DEPARTMENT |
| R E C E I V E D |
| **JUL 18 1921** |
| ENCL. To |
| No.   **4360** |
| Supt. Five Civilized Tribes |

Error on citizenship roll
as to designation of sex:
Lillie Lena.

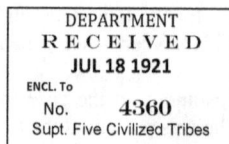

The Honorable
    The Secretary of the Interior

Sir:

I have the honor to transmit herewith a report of January 17, 1920 from the Superintendent for the Five Civilized Tribes, and other papers relative to an error appearing on the final approved roll of citizens by blood of the Seminole Nation in reference to the designation of the sex of Lillie Lena, whose name appears opposite No. 141 on said roll. It appears that Lillie Lena was designated on said roll as a female and should have been designated as a male.

The Office therefore recommends that the letter "F" appearing in the sex column opposite the name of Lillie Lena at No. 141 on the final approved roll of citizens by blood of the Seminole Nation be cancelled and that the letter "M" be substituted therefore, and that this Office and the Superintendent for the Five Civilized Tribes be authorized to make a similar correction upon the copies of the rolls in their possession.

Respectfully,
(Signed) E. B. Meritt,
Assistant Commissioner.

Approved: July 12, 1921
    (Signed) E. M. GOODWIN,
    Assistant Secretary.

24

Applications for Enrollment of Seminole Newborn
Act of 1905   Volume II

Land-F.T.
70463-20
OOP

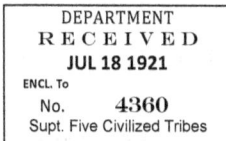

Mr. Victor M. Locke, Jr.,   JUL 15 1921
    Supt. Five Civilized Tribes.

My dear Mr. Locke:

    Referring to a report of January 17, 1920 from the Superintendent for the Five Civilized Tribes relative to an error appearing on the final approved roll of citizens by blood of the Seminole Nation in reference to the designation of the sex of Lillie Lena, whose name appears opposite No. 141 on said roll, you are advised that the Department on July 12, 1921, authorized a correction to be made in said roll by the cancellation of the letter "F" appearing in the sex column opposite the name of said Lillie Lena on the above mentioned roll, and the substitution of the letter "M" therefor.

    A copy of Office letter of July 12, 1921, approved by the Department on the same date, is inclosed for your information and guidelines.

Very truly yours,
EB Meritt
Assistant Commissioner.

7-13-CMS

Sem NB 117
BIRTH AFFIDAVIT.

DEPARTMENT OF THE INTERIOR.
COMMISSION TO THE FIVE CIVILIZED TRIBES.

    IN RE APPLICATION FOR ENROLLMENT, as a citizen of the   Seminole   Nation, of
Almon Harjochee   , born on the   9th   day of   May   , 1902

Name of Father: Tony Harjochee   (I-187)   a citizen of the   Seminole   Nation.
Name of Mother: Yanah (Grant) Harjochee (1247) a citizen of the   Seminole   Nation.

Postoffice   Sasakwa IT

25

(Mother home sick with child)

AFFIDAVIT OF ~~MOTHER~~. Father

UNITED STATES OF AMERICA, Indian Territory, ⎫
    Western   **DISTRICT.** ⎭

    I, Tony Harjochee , on oath state that I am 35 years of age and a citizen by blood , of the Seminole Nation; that I am the lawful husband ~~wife~~ of Yanah Harjochee (nee Grant) , who is a citizen, by blood of the Seminole Nation; that a male child was born to ~~me~~ her on 9th day of May , 1902; that said child has been named Almon Harjochee , and was living March 4, 1905.

Tony Harjochee

Witnesses To Mark:
{

    Subscribed and sworn to before me this 2nd day of May , 1905.

⟨Seal⟩   Edward Merrick
                                  Notary Public.

AFFIDAVIT OF ATTENDING PHYSICIAN OR MID-WIFE.

UNITED STATES OF AMERICA, Indian Territory, ⎫
    Western   **DISTRICT.** ⎭

    I, Lydia Harjochee , a midwife , on oath state that I attended on Mrs. Yanah Harjochee , wife of Tony Harjochee on the 9 day of May , 1902; that there was born to her on said date a male child; that said child was living March 4, 1905, and is said to have been named ~~Lydia Harjochee~~ Almon Harjochee

her
Lydia x Harjochee
mark

Witnesses To Mark:
  { Frank C. Sabourin
  { Edward Merrick

    Subscribed and sworn to before me this 2 day of May , 1905.

⟨Seal⟩   Edward Merrick
                                  Notary Public.

Sem NB 116
BIRTH AFFIDAVIT.

DEPARTMENT OF THE INTERIOR.
COMMISSION TO THE FIVE CIVILIZED TRIBES.

IN RE APPLICATION FOR ENROLLMENT, as a citizen of the   Seminole   Nation, of
Losenda Lena   , born on the 1st day of October , 1904

Name of Father: Charley Lena   (1230)   a citizen of the Seminole   Nation.
Name of Mother: Martha Lena   (1231)   a citizen of the Seminole   Nation.

Postoffice   Wewoka IT

Child present

AFFIDAVIT OF MOTHER.

UNITED STATES OF AMERICA, Indian Territory,
    Western   DISTRICT.

I,   Martha Lena   , on oath state that I am 30 years of age and a citizen by
blood   , of the   Seminole   Nation; that I am the lawful wife of   Charley Lena ,
who is a citizen, by   blood   of the   Seminole   Nation; that a   female
child was born to me on   1st day of   October   , 1904, that said child has been
named   Losenda Lena   , and is now living.

                                    her
                            Martha x Lena
Witnesses To Mark: mark
    Frank C. Sabourin
    Chas E Webster
    Subscribed and sworn to before me this 15   day of   May   , 1905.

                        Chas E Webster
                        Notary Public.

AFFIDAVIT OF ATTENDING ~~PHYSICIAN OR MID-WIFE~~.

UNITED STATES OF AMERICA, Indian Territory,
    Western   DISTRICT.

I,   Charley Lena   , ~~a~~ , on oath state that I attended on Mrs. Martha Lena,
my wife ~~of~~ on the   1st day of   October , 1904; that there was born to her on
said date a   female   child; that said child is now living and is said to have been
named   Losenda Lena

                        Charley Lena

Witnesses To Mark:

Applications for Enrollment of Seminole Newborn
Act of 1905 Volume II

Subscribed and sworn to before me this 15 day of   May   , 1905.

Chas E Webster
Notary Public.

Blank 731.

Seminole Roll. Citizens By Blood.

New Born.

Act of Congress Approved March 3rd, 1905. (Public No. 212.)

No.	Name	Age	Sex	Blood	Card No.
142	Lena, Losenda	1	F	Full	116

C. L. Ellis,
Dist. Supt. in Charge.

BY   E.C. Funk   CLERK

IN CHARGE   Seminole   RECORDS

DATE   9/10/28
___
D8

Blank 744

DEPARTMENT OF THE INTERIOR
United States Indian Service
Five Civilized Tribes
Muskogee, Oklahoma.

This is to certify that I am the officer having the custody of the records pertaining to the enrollment of the members of the members of the Choctaw, Chickasaw, Cherokee, Creek and Seminole tribes of Indians, and the disposition of the land of said tribes, and the following described papers, attached hereto, are true and correct copies of the entire enrollment record on file in this office in connection with the application of

Losenda Lena

28

Roll No. 142-NB for enrollment as New Born Citizen of the Seminole Nation:

Census Card #116: Birth Affidavit and a Copy of Approved Roll No. 142

C. L. Ellis,
Dist. Supt. in Charge.

BY   E.C. Funk   **CLERK**

IN CHARGE   Seminole   **RECORDS**

DATE   9/10/28   ___
D8

Sem NB 118
BIRTH AFFIDAVIT.

DEPARTMENT OF THE INTERIOR.
COMMISSION TO THE FIVE CIVILIZED TRIBES.

IN RE APPLICATION FOR ENROLLMENT, as a citizen of the   Seminole   Nation, of
Bennie Johnson   , born on the   4   day of   March   , 1901

Name of Father: Silas Johnson   1248   a citizen of the   Seminole   Nation.
Name of Mother: Lowine Johnson   1249   a citizen of the   Seminole   Nation.

Postoffice   Wewoka, I.T.

29

<u>Child</u> <u>sick</u>

AFFIDAVIT OF MOTHER.

UNITED STATES OF AMERICA, Indian Territory, ⎫
    Western   **DISTRICT.** ⎭

      I,   Lowine Johnson   , on oath state that I am 35 years of age and a citizen by   blood   , of the   Seminole   Nation; that I am the lawful wife of   Silas Johnson   , who is a citizen, by blood   of the   Seminole   Nation; that a male   child was born to me on   4   day of   March   , 1901; that said child has been named   Bennie Johnson   , and was living March 4, 1905.

her
Lowine x Johnson

Witnesses To Mark: mark
    ⎧ Chas E Webster
    ⎩ Frank C. Sabourin

      Subscribed and sworn to before me this 8 day of   May   , 1905.

Chas E Webster
Notary Public.

AFFIDAVIT OF ATTENDING PHYSICIAN OR MID-WIFE.

UNITED STATES OF AMERICA, Indian Territory, ⎫
    Western   **DISTRICT.** ⎭

      I,   Silas Johnson   , ~~a~~   , on oath state that I attended on Mrs.   Lowine Johnson   , ~~wife of~~   my wife   on the 4 day of   March   , 1901; that there was born to her on said date a   male   child; that said child was living March 4, 1905, and is said to have been named   Bennie Johnson

Silas Johnson

Witnesses To Mark:

    ⎧

      Subscribed and sworn to before me 8 day of   May   , 1905.

Chas E Webster
Notary Public.

Sem NB 119
BIRTH AFFIDAVIT.

DEPARTMENT OF THE INTERIOR.
COMMISSION TO THE FIVE CIVILIZED TRIBES.

IN RE APPLICATION FOR ENROLLMENT, as a citizen of the   Seminole   Nation, of
Sally Factor   , born on the 8   day of April   , 1903

Name of Father: Buckner Factor   1261   a citizen of the Seminole   Nation.
Name of Mother: Winey Factor   1262   a citizen of the Seminole   Nation.

Postoffice   Wewoka, I.T.

Child present

AFFIDAVIT OF MOTHER.

UNITED STATES OF AMERICA, Indian Territory,
    Western   DISTRICT.

    I,   Winey Factor   , on oath state that I am 26 years of age and a citizen by
blood   , of the   Seminole   Nation; that I am the lawful wife of Buckner Factor,
who is a citizen, by   blood   of the   Seminole   Nation; that a   Female
child was born to me on 8   day of April   , 1903, that said child has been named
Sally Factor   , and is now living.   her
                                                   Winey x Factor
Witnesses To Mark: mark
  ⎰ Chas E Webster
  ⎱ Frank C. Sabourin
    Subscribed and sworn to before me this 13 day of   May   , 1905.

Chas E Webster
Notary Public.

AFFIDAVIT OF ATTENDING PHYSICIAN OR MID-WIFE.

UNITED STATES OF AMERICA, Indian Territory,
    Western   DISTRICT.

    I,   Carlarna   , a   midwife   , on oath state that I attended on Mrs.   Winey
Factor   , wife of   Buckner Factor   on the 8   day of April , 1903; that there was
born to her on said date a   Female   child; that said child is now living and is said to
have been named Sally Factor   her
                                                 Carlarna x
Witnesses To Mark: mark
  ⎰ Chas E Webster
  ⎱ Frank C. Sabourin

31

Subscribed and sworn to before me this 13 day of   May   , 1905.

Chas E Webster
Notary Public.

Sem NB 119
BIRTH AFFIDAVIT.

DEPARTMENT OF THE INTERIOR.
COMMISSION TO THE FIVE CIVILIZED TRIBES.

IN RE APPLICATION FOR ENROLLMENT, as a citizen of the   Seminole   Nation, of
Amos Factor   , born on the   10   day of   June   , 1900

Name of Father: Buckner Factor   1261   a citizen of the   Seminole   Nation.
Name of Mother: Winey Factor   1262   a citizen of the   Seminole   Nation.

Postoffice   Wewoka, I.T.

(Child present)

AFFIDAVIT OF MOTHER.

UNITED STATES OF AMERICA, Indian Territory,
     Western   **DISTRICT.**

I,   Winey Factor   , on oath state that I am 26 years of age and a citizen by
blood   , of the   Seminole   Nation; that I am the lawful wife of   Buckner Factor,
who is a citizen, by   blood   of the   Seminole   Nation; that a   Male   child
was born to me on   10   day of   Jan   , 1900, that said child has been named   Amos
Factor   , and is now living.

her
Winey x Factor
mark

Witnesses To Mark:
    Chas E Webster
    Frank C. Sabourin

Subscribed and sworn to before me this 13 day of   May   , 1905.

Chas E Webster
Notary Public.

Applications for Enrollment of Seminole Newborn
Act of 1905   Volume II

AFFIDAVIT OF ATTENDING PHYSICIAN OR MID-WIFE.

UNITED STATES OF AMERICA, Indian Territory, ⎱
     Western   **DISTRICT.** ⎰

I, Carlarna , a midwife , on oath state that I attended on Mrs. Winey Factor , wife of Buckner Factor on the 10 day of Jan , 1900; that there was born to her on said date a Male child; that said child is now living and is said to have been named Amos Factor

                                                  her
                                     Carlarna   x

Witnesses To Mark: mark
    ⎰ Chas E Webster
    ⎱ Frank C. Sabourin

Subscribed and sworn to before me this 13 day of May , 1905.

                                Chas E Webster
                                Notary Public.

Sem NB 120
BIRTH AFFIDAVIT.
DEPARTMENT OF THE INTERIOR.
COMMISSION TO THE FIVE CIVILIZED TRIBES.

IN RE APPLICATION FOR ENROLLMENT, as a citizen of the   Seminole   Nation, of
Lily Davis   , born on the ▬▬day of July , 1900

Name of Father: Jimmie Davis   a citizen of the Creek   Nation.
Name of Mother: Lowesa   (1290)   a citizen of the Seminole   Nation.

             Postoffice   Wewoka, IT

33

Applications for Enrollment of Seminole Newborn
Act of 1905   Volume II

Child present

AFFIDAVIT OF MOTHER.

UNITED STATES OF AMERICA, Indian Territory, ⎱
    Western   DISTRICT. ⎰

      I,   Lowesa   , on oath state that I am   27   years of age and a citizen by blood   , of the   Seminole   Nation; that I am the lawful wife of   Jimmie Davis   , who is a citizen, by blood   of the   Creek   Nation; that a   male   child was born to me on ——— day of   July   , 1900; that said child has been named   Lily Davis, and was living March 4, 1905.

her

Lowesa x

mark

Witnesses To Mark:
  ⎰ Frank C. Sabourin
  ⎱ Chas E Webster

      Subscribed and sworn to before me this 8ᵗʰ day of   May   , 1905.

Chas E Webster

Notary Public.

AFFIDAVIT OF ATTENDING PHYSICIAN OR MID-WIFE.

UNITED STATES OF AMERICA, Indian Territory, ⎱
    Western   DISTRICT. ⎰

saw

     I, Mut-ho-ya   , a   , on oath state that I ~~attended on~~ Mrs. Lowesa   , wife of Jimmie Davis   on the ——day of July   , 1900; that there was born to her on said date a   male   child; that said child was living March 4, 1905, and is said to have been named Lily Davis

his

Mut-ho-ya x

mark

Witnesses To Mark:
  ⎰ Frank C. Sabourin
  ⎱ Chas E Webster

      Subscribed and sworn to before me 8 day of   May   , 1905.

Chas E Webster

Notary Public.

Seminole
NB-120.

Muskogee, Indian Territory June 29, 1903.

Commission to the Five Civilized Tribes,
    Creek Enrollment Division.

Gentlemen:

On May 8, 1905 there was filed with the Commission application for the enrollment of Lily Davis, born in July 1900, as a citizen by blood of the Seminole Nation. It is stated in said application that said child is a son of Jimmie Davis, a citizen by blood of the Creek Nation, and Lowesa, a citizen by blood of the Seminole Nation.

You are requested to advise the Seminole Enrollment Division as to whether any application has been made to the Commission for the enrollment of said Lily Davis as a citizen of the Creek Nation and if so what disposition, if any, has been made of such application.

Respectfully,

Chairman.

———————

HGH

DEPARTMENT OF THE INTERIOR.
COMMISSION TO THE FIVE CIVILIZED TRIBES.

Muskogee, Indian Territory, July 11, 1905.

Seminole Enrollment Division,
    General Office.

Gentlemen:

Receipt is acknowledged of your communication of June 29, 1905, (Sem. NB.120), in which you ask if application for enrollment as a citizen of the Creek Nation has been made for Lilly Davis, child of Jimmie Davis, a citizen of the Creek Nation, and Lowesa, a citizen by blood of the Seminole Nation.

In reply you are advised that the records of this office have been examined and it does not appear that application has been made for the enrollment of said Lilly Davis, as a citizen of the Creek Nation.

Respectfully,

Tams Bixby   Commissioner.

Sem NB 121
BIRTH AFFIDAVIT.

DEPARTMENT OF THE INTERIOR.
COMMISSION TO THE FIVE CIVILIZED TRIBES.

IN RE APPLICATION FOR ENROLLMENT, as a citizen of the   Seminole   Nation, of
Eliza Lowe   , born on the   17   day of   April , 1904

Name of Father: Tom Lowe   1595   a citizen of the Seminole   Nation.
Name of Mother: Lizzie Lowe   1593   a citizen of the Seminole   Nation.
                    nee Bowlegs
                            Postoffice   Wewoka IT

(Child present)

AFFIDAVIT OF MOTHER.

UNITED STATES OF AMERICA, Indian Territory, ⎤
     Western   DISTRICT. ⎦

I, Lizzie Lowe   , on oath state that I am about 28 years of age and a citizen by
blood   , of the   Seminole   Nation; that I am the lawful wife of   Tom Lowe   ,
who is a citizen, by   blood   of the   Seminole   Nation; that a   Female
child was born to me on   17   day of   April   , 1904, that said child has been named
Eliza Lowe   , and is now living.

                                        Lizzie Lowe

Witnesses To Mark:

   {

     Subscribed and sworn to before me this   22   day of   May   , 1905.

                            Chas E Webster
                                Notary Public.

AFFIDAVIT OF ATTENDING PHYSICIAN OR MID-WIFE.

UNITED STATES OF AMERICA, Indian Territory, ⎤
     Western   DISTRICT. ⎦

I, Lucy Cosar   , a   midwife   , on oath state that I attended on Mrs. Lizzie
Lowe   , wife of Tom Lowe   on the   17   day of   April , 1904; that there was
born to her on said date a   Female   child; that said child is now living and is said to
have been named Eliza Lowe   her
                            Lucy x Cosar
                               mark

36

Witnesses To Mark:
{ Chas E Webster
{ Frank C. Sabourin

Subscribed and sworn to before me this 22 day of   May   , 1905.

Chas E Webster
Notary Public.

Sem NB 121
BIRTH AFFIDAVIT.

DEPARTMENT OF THE INTERIOR.
COMMISSION TO THE FIVE CIVILIZED TRIBES.

IN RE APPLICATION FOR ENROLLMENT, as a citizen of the   Seminole   Nation, of
Mary Lowe   , born on the 31   day of   July , 1902

Name of Father: Tom Lowe   1595   a citizen of the Seminole   Nation.
Name of Mother: Lizzie Lowe   1293[sic] a citizen of the Seminole   Nation.
nee Bowlegs
Postoffice   Wewoka IT

(Child present)

AFFIDAVIT OF MOTHER.

UNITED STATES OF AMERICA, Indian Territory, }
Western   **DISTRICT.**

I, Lizzie Lowe   , on oath state that I am about 28 years of age and a citizen by
blood   , of the   Seminole   Nation; that I am the lawful wife of   Tom Lowe   ,
who is a citizen, by   blood   of the   Seminole   Nation; that a   Female
child was born to me on   31   day of   July   , 1902, that said child has been named
Mary Lowe   , and is now living.

Lizzie Lowe

Witnesses To Mark:
{

Subscribed and sworn to before me this 22   day of   May   , 1905.

Chas E Webster
Notary Public.

Applications for Enrollment of Seminole Newborn
Act of 1905   Volume II

AFFIDAVIT OF ATTENDING PHYSICIAN OR MID-WIFE.

UNITED STATES OF AMERICA, Indian Territory,
     Western   DISTRICT.

    I, Lucy Cosar   , a midwife   , on oath state that I attended on Mrs. Lizzie Lowe   , wife of Tom Lowe   on the   31   day of   July , 1902; that there was born to her on said date a   Female   child; that said child is now living and is said to have been named Mary Lowe

her
Lucy x Cosar
mark

Witnesses To Mark:
  { Chas E Webster
  { Frank C. Sabourin

    Subscribed and sworn to before me this 22 day of   May   , 1905.

Chas E Webster
Notary Public.

Sem NB 122
BIRTH AFFIDAVIT.

DEPARTMENT OF THE INTERIOR.
COMMISSION TO THE FIVE CIVILIZED TRIBES.

IN RE APPLICATION FOR ENROLLMENT, as a citizen of the   Seminole   Nation, of Janie Bowlegs   , born on the   23   day of   January   , 1905

Name of Father: David Bowlegs   #1295   a citizen of the   Seminole   Nation.
                         #1399
Name of Mother: Nancy Bowlegs (nee Wolf)   a citizen of the   "   Nation.

Postoffice   Mekusukey I.T.

38

Applications for Enrollment of Seminole Newborn
Act of 1905   Volume II

(Child present)

AFFIDAVIT OF MOTHER.

UNITED STATES OF AMERICA, Indian Territory, ⎫
   Western   DISTRICT. ⎭

      I,   Nancy Bowlegs   , on oath state that I am 26   years of age and a citizen by   blood   , of the   Seminole   Nation; that I am the lawful wife of   David Bowlegs   , who is a citizen, by blood   of the   Seminole   Nation; that a female   child was born to me on 23" day of   January   , 1905; that said child has been named   Janie Bowlegs   , and was living March 4, 1905.

her
Nancy x Bowlegs
mark

Witnesses To Mark:
  ⎰ Ed. Merrick
  ⎱ Frank C. Sabourin

      Subscribed and sworn to before me this 2nd day of   May   , 1905.

  ⟨ Seal ⟩   Edward Merrick
                         Notary Public.

AFFIDAVIT OF ATTENDING PHYSICIAN OR MID-WIFE.

UNITED STATES OF AMERICA, Indian Territory, ⎫
   Western   DISTRICT. ⎭

      I, David Bowlegs   , a̶——, on oath state that I attended on Mrs. Nancy Bowlegs   my   , wife o̶f̶——on the 23" day of January   , 1905; that there was born to her on said date a   female   child; that said child was living March 4, 1905, and is said to have been named Janie Bowlegs

David Bowlegs

Witnesses To Mark:

  ⎰

      Subscribed and sworn to before me this 2nd day of   May   , 1905.

  ⟨ Seal ⟩   Edward Merrick
                         Notary Public.

Applications for Enrollment of Seminole Newborn
Act of 1905   Volume II

Sem NB 123
BIRTH AFFIDAVIT.

DEPARTMENT OF THE INTERIOR.
COMMISSION TO THE FIVE CIVILIZED TRIBES.

IN RE APPLICATION FOR ENROLLMENT, as a citizen of the   Seminole   Nation, of
Nancy   , born on the   30   day of   Nov   , 1902

Name of Father: Sumka Lee   a citizen of the   Creek   Nation.
Name of Mother: Nellie   1299   a citizen of the   Seminole   Nation.

Postoffice   Paden I.T.

(Child present)

AFFIDAVIT OF MOTHER.

UNITED STATES OF AMERICA, Indian Territory,
   Western   DISTRICT.

I,   Nellie   , on oath state that I am   25   years of age and a citizen by
blood   , of the   Seminole   Nation; that I am the lawful wife of   Sumka Lee   ,
who is a citizen, by blood   of the   Creek   Nation; that a   Female   child
was born to me on   30   day of   Nov   , 1902; that said child has been named
Nancy   , and was living March 4, 1905.   her
                                         Nellie x
Witnesses To Mark: mark
    Chas E Webster
    Frank C. Sabourin

Subscribed and sworn to before me this 5 day of   May   , 1905.

Chas E Webster
Notary Public.

AFFIDAVIT OF ATTENDING PHYSICIAN OR MID-WIFE.

UNITED STATES OF AMERICA, Indian Territory,
   Western   DISTRICT.

I,   Bessie Foster   , a   midwife   , on oath state that I attended on Mrs.
Nellie   , wife of   Sumka Lee   on the   30   day of   Nov   , 1902; that there was
born to her on said date a   Female   child; that said child was living March 4, 1905,
and is said to have been named   Nancy   her
                            Bessie x Foster
                            mark

Applications for Enrollment of Seminole Newborn
Act of 1905   Volume II

Witnesses To Mark:
  { Chas E Webster
  { Frank C. Sabourin

Subscribed and sworn to before me 5 day of   May   , 1905.

Chas E Webster
Notary Public.

_____

Seminole
NB-123.

Muskogee, Indian Territory June 29, 1905

Commission to the Five Civilized Tribes,
Creek Enrollment Division.

Gentlemen:

On May 5, 1905 there was filed with the Commission application for the enrollment of Nancy as a citizen by blood of the Seminole Nation. It is stated in said application that said child is a daughter of Sumka Lee, a citizen by blood of the Creek Nation, and Nellie, a citizen by blood of the Seminole Nation.

You are requested to inform the Seminole Enrollment Division as to whether or not any application has been made to the Commission for the enrollment of said Nancy as a citizen of the Creek Nation and if so what disposition, if any, has been made of said application.

Respectfully,

Chairman.

_____

HGH

DEPARTMENT OF THE INTERIOR.
COMMISSION TO THE FIVE CIVILIZED TRIBES.

Muskogee, Indian Territory, July 10, 1905.

Seminole Enrollment Division,
General Office.

Gentlemen:

Receipt is acknowledged of your communication of June 29, 1905 (Sem. NB. 123), in which you ask if application for the enrollment as a citizen of the Creek Nation

41

has been made for Nancy, child of Sumka Lee, a citizen by blood of the Creek Nation, and Nellie, a citizen by blood of the Seminole Nation.

In reply you are advised that the records of this office have been examined and it does not appear that application has been made for the enrollment of said Nancy, as a citizen of the Creek Nation.

Respectfully,

Tams Bixby   Commissioner.

Sem NB 124
BIRTH AFFIDAVIT.

DEPARTMENT OF THE INTERIOR.
COMMISSION TO THE FIVE CIVILIZED TRIBES.

IN RE APPLICATION FOR ENROLLMENT, as a citizen of the   Seminole   Nation, of
Thompson Johnson   , born on the 22   day of   December , 1902

Name of Father: Paul Johnson   (1255)   a citizen of the Seminole   Nation.
                                     No. 1320
Name of Mother: Sissie Johnson (nee Sissie)   a citizen of the   Seminole   Nation.

Postoffice   Wewoka, I.T.

Child present

AFFIDAVIT OF MOTHER.

UNITED STATES OF AMERICA, Indian Territory,
    Western   DISTRICT.

I,   Sissie Johnson   , on oath state that I am 23   years of age and a citizen by   blood   , of the   Seminole   Nation; that I am the lawful wife of   Paul Johnson   , who is a citizen, by blood   of the   Seminole   Nation; that a male   child was born to me on 22   day of   December   , 1902; that said child has been named   Thompson Johnson   , and was living March 4, 1905.

Sissie Johnson

Witnesses To Mark:

Applications for Enrollment of Seminole Newborn
Act of 1905   Volume II

Subscribed and sworn to before me this 8th day of   May   , 1905.

Chas E Webster
Notary Public.

AFFIDAVIT OF ATTENDING PHYSICIAN OR MID-WIFE.

UNITED STATES OF AMERICA, Indian Territory, ⎫
  Western   DISTRICT. ⎭

I,   Sarah Larney   , a midwife   , on oath state that I attended on Mrs. Sissie Johnson   , wife of   Paul Johnson   on the 22 day of   December   , 1902; that there was born to her on said date a   male   child; that said child was living March 4, 1905, and is said to have been named   Thompson Johnson

her
Sarah x Larney
mark

Witnesses To Mark:
⎰ Frank C. Sabourin
⎱ Chas E Webster

Subscribed and sworn to before me 8th day of   May   , 1905.

Chas E Webster
Notary Public.

Sem NB 124
BIRTH AFFIDAVIT.

DEPARTMENT OF THE INTERIOR.
COMMISSION TO THE FIVE CIVILIZED TRIBES.

IN RE APPLICATION FOR ENROLLMENT, as a citizen of the   Seminole   Nation, of Jenetta Johnson   , born on the 8th day of   April , 1904

Name of Father: Paul Johnson   (1255)   a citizen of the   Seminole   Nation.
No. 1320
Name of Mother: Sissie Johnson (nee Sissie)   a citizen of the   Seminole   Nation.

Postoffice   Wewoka, I.T.

43

Applications for Enrollment of Seminole Newborn
Act of 1905 Volume II

AFFIDAVIT OF MOTHER.

UNITED STATES OF AMERICA, Indian Territory,
Western   DISTRICT.

I, Sissie Johnson   , on oath state that I am 23 years of age and a citizen by blood   , of the   Seminole   Nation; that I am the lawful wife of   Paul Johnson , who is a citizen, by   blood   of the   Seminole   Nation; that a   female child was born to me on   8ᵗʰ   day of   April   , 1904, that said child has been named Jenetta Johnson   , and is now living. died April 28, 1905

Sissie Johnson

Witnesses To Mark:

Subscribed and sworn to before me this 8ᵗʰ   day of   May   , 1905.

Chas E Webster
Notary Public.

AFFIDAVIT OF ATTENDING PHYSICIAN OR MID-WIFE.

UNITED STATES OF AMERICA, Indian Territory,
Western   DISTRICT.

I, Sarah Larney   , a   midwife   , on oath state that I attended on Mrs. Sissie Johnson   , wife of Paul Johnson   on the   8ᵗʰ   day of   April , 1904; that there was born to her on said date a   child; that said child is now living and is said to have been named Jenetta Johnson and died about two weeks ago.

her
Sarah x Larney
mark

Witnesses To Mark:
Frank C. Sabourin
Chas E Webster

Subscribed and sworn to before me this 8ᵗʰ   day of   May   , 1905.

Chas E Webster
Notary Public.

Sem NB 125
BIRTH AFFIDAVIT.

DEPARTMENT OF THE INTERIOR.
COMMISSION TO THE FIVE CIVILIZED TRIBES.

_____

IN RE APPLICATION FOR ENROLLMENT, as a citizen of the   Seminole   Nation, of
Wesley Tanyan   , born on the 15   day of   July , 1901

Name of Father: Nina Tanyan   (1342)   a citizen of the   Seminole   Nation.
Name of Mother: Sallie Tanyan   (1343)   a citizen of the   Seminole   Nation.

Postoffice   Wewoka I.T.

_____

AFFIDAVIT OF ATTENDING PHYSICIAN OR MID-WIFE.

UNITED STATES OF AMERICA, Indian Territory, ⎤
        Western   DISTRICT. ⎦

I,   Susie Posey   , a   mid-wife   , on oath state that I attended on Mrs.
Sallie Tanyan   , wife of   Nina Tanyan   on the 15 day of   July   , 1901;
that there was born to her on said date a   male   child; that said child was living
March 4, 1905, and is said to have been named Wesley Tanyan
                                                her
                                    Susie x Posey
                                               mark

Witnesses To Mark:
  ⎧ DH Smith
  ⎩ AG. Smith

Subscribed and sworn to before me 29   day of   May   , 1905.

                          W. W. Lucas
                                Notary Public.

_____

Sem NB 125
BIRTH AFFIDAVIT.

DEPARTMENT OF THE INTERIOR.
COMMISSION TO THE FIVE CIVILIZED TRIBES.

_____

IN RE APPLICATION FOR ENROLLMENT, as a citizen of the   Seminole   Nation, of
Wesley Tanyan   , born on the 15   day of   July , 1901

Name of Father: Nina Tanyan   (1342)   a citizen of the   Seminole   Nation.
Name of Mother: Sallie Tanyan   (1343)   a citizen of the   Seminole   Nation.

Applications for Enrollment of Seminole Newborn
Act of 1905   Volume II

Postoffice   Wewoka I.T.

_____

(Child present)

AFFIDAVIT OF MOTHER.

UNITED STATES OF AMERICA, Indian Territory,
Western   **DISTRICT.**

I,   Sallie Tanyan   , on oath state that I am   about 24   years of age and a citizen by   blood   , of the   Seminole   Nation; that I am the lawful wife of Nina Tanyan   , who is a citizen, by blood   of the   Seminole   Nation; that a   male   child was born to me on 15   day of July   , 1901; that said child has been named   Wesley Tanyan   , and was living March 4, 1905.

Sallie Tanyan

Witnesses To Mark:

Subscribed and sworn to before me this 20 day of   May   , 1905.

Chas E Webster
Notary Public.

_____

Sem NB 126
BIRTH AFFIDAVIT.

DEPARTMENT OF THE INTERIOR.
COMMISSION TO THE FIVE CIVILIZED TRIBES.

_____

IN RE APPLICATION FOR ENROLLMENT, as a citizen of the   Seminole   Nation, of Leister Harrison   , born on the 23   day of Aug , 1903

Name of Father: Willie Harrison   1348   a citizen of the Seminole Nation.
Name of Mother: Lydia Harrison   1349   a citizen of the Seminole Nation.

Postoffice   Wewoka, IT

_____

46

Child home with mother who is confined

AFFIDAVIT OF MOTHER.

Father   mother sick

UNITED STATES OF AMERICA, Indian Territory,⎤
     Western   **DISTRICT.** ⎦

I, Willie Harrison   , on oath state that I am about 29   years of age and a citizen by   blood   , of the   Seminole   Nation; that I am the lawful ~~wife~~ husband of Lydia Harrison   , who is a citizen, by   blood   of the   Seminole   Nation; that a   Female   child was born to ~~me~~ her on   23   day of   Aug   , 1903, that said child has been named   Leister Harrison   , and is now living.

his
Willie x Harrison
mark

Witnesses To Mark:
⎧ Chas E Webster
⎩ A. B. Davis

Subscribed and sworn to before me this   22   day of   May   , 1905.

Chas E Webster
Notary Public.

AFFIDAVIT OF ATTENDING PHYSICIAN OR MID-WIFE.

UNITED STATES OF AMERICA, Indian Territory,⎤
     Western   **DISTRICT.** ⎦

saw

I,   Thomas Harrison   , ~~a~~   , on oath state that I ~~attended on~~ Mrs. Lydia Harrison   , wife of   Willie Harrison   on the   23   day of Aug , 1903; that there was born to her on said date a   Female   child; that said child is now living and is said to have been named Leister Harrison

his
Thomas x Harrison
mark

Witnesses To Mark:
⎧ Chas E Webster
⎩ A. B. Davis

Subscribed and sworn to before me this 22   day of   May   , 1905.

Chas E Webster
Notary Public.

Sem NB 127
BIRTH AFFIDAVIT.

DEPARTMENT OF THE INTERIOR.
COMMISSION TO THE FIVE CIVILIZED TRIBES.

IN RE APPLICATION FOR ENROLLMENT, as a citizen of the   Seminole   Nation, of
Anna Davis   , born on the 26"   day of   June   , 1902

Name of Father: Robert Davis   (1365)   a citizen of the   Seminole   Nation.
Name of Mother: Rhoda   "   (1368)   a citizen of the   "   Nation.

Postoffice   Wewoka I.T.

(Child present)

AFFIDAVIT OF MOTHER.

UNITED STATES OF AMERICA, Indian Territory, ⎱
    Western   DISTRICT.   ⎰

I,   Rhoda Davis   , on oath state that I am   29   years of age and a citizen by
blood   , of the   Seminole   Nation; that I am the lawful wife of   Robert Davis ,
who is a citizen, by blood   of the   Seminole   Nation; that a   female
child was born to me on   26th day of   June   , 1902; that said child has been named
Anna Davis   , and was living March 4, 1905.

her
Rhoda x Davis
mark

Witnesses To Mark:
    ⎰ Edward Merrick
    ⎱ Frank C. Sabourin
        Subscribed and sworn to before me this 4th day of   May   , 1905.

⟨ Seal ⟩

Edward Merrick
        Notary Public.

AFFIDAVIT OF ATTENDING PHYSICIAN OR MID-WIFE.

UNITED STATES OF AMERICA, Indian Territory, ⎱
    Western   DISTRICT.   ⎰

I,   Passake   , a   midwife   , on oath state that I attended on Mrs.   Rhoda
Davis   , wife of Robert Davis   on the 26th day of   June   , 1902; that there
was born to her on said date a   female   child; that said child was living March 4,
1905, and is said to have been named Anna Davis

her
Passake
mark

Applications for Enrollment of Seminole Newborn
Act of 1905   Volume II

Witnesses To Mark:
  { Frank C. Sabourin
  { Edward Merrick

Subscribed and sworn to before me this 4th day of   May   , 1905.

< Seal >   Edward Merrick
                                     Notary Public.

Sem NB 128
BIRTH AFFIDAVIT.

DEPARTMENT OF THE INTERIOR.
COMMISSION TO THE FIVE CIVILIZED TRIBES.

IN RE APPLICATION FOR ENROLLMENT, as a citizen of the   Seminole   Nation, of
Solomon Pon-no-kee   , born on the 7th day of   Sept , 1900

Name of Father: Sefah (Pon-no-kee) #340   a citizen of the Seminole   Nation.
                              (1392)
Name of Mother: Susey Pon-no-kee (nee Micco) a citizen of the Seminole   Nation.

Postoffice   Maud ~~O.T.~~. O.T.

Child present

AFFIDAVIT OF MOTHER.

UNITED STATES OF AMERICA, Indian Territory, }
     Western   DISTRICT. }

I, Susey Pon-no-kee (nec Micco)   , on oath state that I am 23   years of
age and a citizen by   blood   , of the   Seminole   Nation; that I am the lawful
wife of   Sefah (Pon-no-kee)   , who is a citizen, by blood   of the   Seminole
Nation; that a   male   child was born to me on 7th   day of   Sept   , 1900; that
said child has been named   Solomon Pon-no-kee   , and was living March 4, 1905.
                                   her
                          Susey x Pon-no-kee
                                  mark

49

Applications for Enrollment of Seminole Newborn
Act of 1905 Volume II

Witnesses To Mark:
⎰ Frank C. Sabourin
⎱ Edward Merrick

Subscribed and sworn to before me this 2" day of   May   , 1905.

Edward Merrick
Notary Public.

AFFIDAVIT OF ATTENDING PHYSICIAN OR MID-WIFE.

UNITED STATES OF AMERICA, Indian Territory, ⎤
    Western   **DISTRICT.** ⎦

I, Sefah (Pon-no-kee)   , a———, on oath state that I attended on Mrs.
Susey Pon-no-kee   my   , wife of ————on the   7th day of   Sept   , 1900; that
there was born to her on said date a   male   child; that said child was living March 4,
1905, and is said to have been named   Solomon Pon-no-kee

his
Sefah x Pon-no-kee
Witnesses To Mark: mark
⎰ Frank C. Sabourin
⎱ Edward Merrick

Subscribed and sworn to before me this 2nd day of   May   , 1905.

Edward Merrick
Notary Public.

Sem NB 128
BIRTH AFFIDAVIT.
DEPARTMENT OF THE INTERIOR.
COMMISSION TO THE FIVE CIVILIZED TRIBES.

IN RE APPLICATION FOR ENROLLMENT, as a citizen of the   Seminole   Nation, of
Martha Pon-no-kee   , born on the   14   day of   Dec , 1902

Name of Father: Sefah (Pon-no-kee)   (340)   a citizen of the   Seminole   Nation.
Name of Mother: Susey Pon-no-kee (nee Micco) a citizen of the   Seminole   Nation.
O.
Postoffice   Maud ~~Ind~~. Ter

50

Child present

AFFIDAVIT OF MOTHER.

UNITED STATES OF AMERICA, Indian Territory, ⎫
   Western   DISTRICT. ⎭

    I, Susey Pon-no-kee (nee Micco)   , on oath state that I am   23   years of age and a citizen by   blood   , of the   Seminole   Nation; that I am the lawful wife of   Sefah (Pon-no-kee)   , who is a citizen, by blood   of the   Seminole Nation; that a   female   child was born to me on   14" day of   December   , 1902; that said child has been named   Martha Pon-no-kee   , and was living March 4, 1905.

her
Susey x Pon-no-kee
mark

Witnesses To Mark:
   ⎧ Frank C. Sabourin
   ⎩ Edward Merrick

    Subscribed and sworn to before me this 2nd   day of   May   , 1905.

Edward Merrick
Notary Public.

AFFIDAVIT OF ATTENDING PHYSICIAN OR MID-WIFE.

UNITED STATES OF AMERICA, Indian Territory, ⎫
   Western   DISTRICT. ⎭

    I, Sefah (Pon-no-kee)   , a————, on oath state that I attended on Mrs. Susey Pon-no-kee   my , wife of ————on the   14" day of December   , 1902; that there was born to her on said date a   female   child; that said child was living March 4, 1905, and is said to have been named   Martha Pon-no-kee

his
Sefah x Pon-no-kee
mark

Witnesses To Mark:
   ⎧ Frank C. Sabourin
   ⎩ Ed. Merrick

    Subscribed and sworn to before me this 2nd   day of   May   , 1905.

Edward Merrick
Notary Public.

Applications for Enrollment of Seminole Newborn
Act of 1905   Volume II

Sem NB 129
BIRTH AFFIDAVIT.

DEPARTMENT OF THE INTERIOR.
COMMISSION TO THE FIVE CIVILIZED TRIBES.

IN RE APPLICATION FOR ENROLLMENT, as a citizen of the   Seminole   Nation, of
Lula Burden   , born on the   19   day of   December , 1903

Name of Father: Lincoln Burden   (1396)   a citizen of the   Seminole   Nation.
Name of Mother: Betsey Burden   (1397)   a citizen of the   Seminole   Nation.

Postoffice   Tidmore, I.T.

Child present

AFFIDAVIT OF MOTHER.

UNITED STATES OF AMERICA, Indian Territory,
    Western   DISTRICT.

I, Betsey Burden   , on oath state that I am   30   years of age and a citizen
by   blood   , of the   Seminole   Nation; that I am the lawful wife of   Lincoln
Burden   , who is a citizen, by blood   of the   Seminole   Nation; that a
female   child was born to me on 19   day of   December   , 1903; that said child
has been named   Lula Burden   , and was living March 4, 1905.

                                        Betsey Burden
Witnesses To Mark:

Subscribed and sworn to before me this 4 day of   May   , 1905.

⟨ Seal ⟩   Edward Merrick
                                        Notary Public.

AFFIDAVIT OF ATTENDING PHYSICIAN OR MID-WIFE.

UNITED STATES OF AMERICA, Indian Territory,
    Western   DISTRICT.

I, Malinda Tiger   , a   midwife   , on oath state that I attended on Mrs.
Betsey Burden   , wife of   Lincoln Burden   on the 19   day of   December   ,
1903; that there was born to her on said date a   female   child; that said child was
living March 4, 1905, and is said to have been named   Lula Burden

                                        her
                            Malinda x Tiger
                                        mark

52

Witnesses To Mark:
    { Chas E Webster
    { A. B. Davis

Subscribed and sworn to before me 25   day of   May   , 1905.

Chas E Webster
Notary Public.

DEPARTMENT OF THE INTERIOR.

COMMISSION TO THE FIVE CIVILIZED TRIBES.

In the matter of the application for the enrollment of George Johnson as a citizen by blood of the Seminole Nation.

Thomas McGeisey, being duly sworn, testified as follows:

Q. What is your name?   A. Thomas McGeisey.
Q. Your age?   A. Forty-eight.
Q. What is your post-office? A. Wewoka.
Q. You now desire to make application for the enrollment of George Johnson, as a citizen of the Seminole Nation? A. Yes sir.
Q. What relation is he to you? A. None. No relation at all. I am band chief, no relation.
Q. What is the name of George Johnson's mother? A. Lizzie Johnson.
Q. A. citizen of the Seminole Nation? A. Yes sir.
Q. What is her post office address? A. Her post-office? I think it is Wetumka.

It appears from an examination of the records of the Commission that the name of Lizzie Johnson, the mother of George Johnson was listed on Indian card No. 427, as Lizzie Chupco, approved roll No. 1415.

Q. What is the reason that the mother of this child does not appear before this Commission and make application for the enrollment of the child? A. Because they belong to the snake gang of people, and also they live far off from here, and have no way to come, they are poor. I sent a letter, but they never came. John Johnson never came before the Commission. They think Dawes Commission gives land without seeing it. They don't know what land belongs to them.

Applications for Enrollment of Seminole Newborn
Act of 1905 Volume II

Q. Does the name of this child appear on your record as a citizen of the Seminole Nation? A. Yes sir.
Q. When was this child born? A. Some time in the month of December, last; I am told.
Q. When was the name placed upon your record? A. In the month of February last.
Q. Has the child ever drawn any annuities or headright paid by the Seminoles? A. Yes sir. The money has not been paid yet, but the mother sold his headright money to the merchants here.

William S. Webb, being duly sworn, states that he is a stenographer for the Commission to the Five Civilized Tribes, and that the above and foregoing is a true transcript of his stenographic notes taken in said case, in May, 1905.

William Webb

Subscribed and sworn to before me this 31st day of May, A. D. 1905.

John W. Willmott
Notary Public.

Sem NB 130

AFFIDAVIT OF MOTHER.

UNITED STATES OF AMERICA, Indian Territory,
   Western   DISTRICT.

I, Lizzie Johnson   , on oath state that I am 23 years of age and a citizen by blood   , of the   Seminole   Nation; that I ~~am~~ was the lawful wife of   Curtis Johnson   , who is a citizen, by   blood   of the   United States   ~~Nation~~; that a male   child was born to me on   day of   October   , 1904, that said child has been named   George Johnson   , and is now living.

her
Lizzie x Johnson
mark

Witnesses To Mark:
  { Jonas Monley
  { J. L. Gary

Subscribed and sworn to before me this 14th   day of   January   , 1907.

J. L. Gary
Notary Public.

54

AFFIDAVIT OF ATTENDING PHYSICIAN OR MID-WIFE.

UNITED STATES OF AMERICA, Indian Territory,
  Western   DISTRICT.

I,   Rebecca Hay   , a   acquaintance   , on oath state that I attended on Mrs. Lizzie Johnson   , wife of   Curt Johnson   on the   during the month   day of October , 1904; that there was born to her on said date a   male   child; that said child is now living and is said to have been named   George Johnson

Rebecca Hay

Witnesses To Mark:
{

Subscribed and sworn to before me this 7$^{\underline{th}}$ day of   January   , 1907.

J. L. Gary
Notary Public.

———————

Sem NB 130
BIRTH AFFIDAVIT.

DEPARTMENT OF THE INTERIOR.
COMMISSION TO THE FIVE CIVILIZED TRIBES.

———————

IN RE APPLICATION FOR ENROLLMENT, as a citizen of the   Seminole   Nation, of George Johnson   , born ~~on the~~   sometime in ~~day of~~ Dec   , 1904

Name of Father: ___ Johnson   a citizen of the   U. S.   Nation.
Name of Mother: Lizzie Johnson   1415   a citizen of the   Seminole   Nation.
                    nee Chupco
                    Postoffice   Wetumka, IT

———————

AFFIDAVIT OF ~~MOTHER~~.
Band Chief

UNITED STATES OF AMERICA, Indian Territory,
  Western   DISTRICT.

I,   Thomas McGeisey   , on oath state that I am   48   years of age and a citizen by   blood   , of the   Seminole   Nation; that I am acquainted with the lawful wife of ____ Johnson   , who is a citizen, ~~by~~   of the   U. S.   Nation; that a   male   child was born ~~to me on~~ to Lizzie Johnson nee Chupco   ~~day of~~ sometime in Dec   , 1904, that said child has been named   George Johnson   , and is now living.

Thomas McGeisey

55

Witnesses To Mark:

{

Subscribed and sworn to before me this 25 day of   May   , 1905.

Chas E Webster
Notary Public.

AFFIDAVIT OF ATTENDING PHYSICIAN OR MID-WIFE.

UNITED STATES OF AMERICA, Indian Territory,
Western   **DISTRICT.**

I,   J. L. Hay   , a   acquaintance   , on oath state that I ~~attended on~~ Mrs. Lizzie Johnson   , wife of   Kirk[sic] Johnson   on the during the month   day of October , 1904; that there was born to her on said date a   male   child; that said child is now living and is said to have been named   George Johnson

J. L. Hay

Witnesses To Mark:

{

Subscribed and sworn to before me this 7th day of   January   , 1907.

J. L. Gary
Notary Public.

Seminole
NB-130.

Muskogee, Indian Territory June 29, 1905

Lizzie Johnson (or Chupco),
     Wetumka, Indian Territory.

Dear Madam:

On May 25, 1905 Thomas McGeisey, band chief, appeared before the Commission and made application for the enrollment of your son, George Johnson, as a citizen by blood of the Seminole Nation.

You are advised that before the matter of the enrollment of said child can be finally determined it will be necessary for you to file with the Commission the affidavits of yourself and the attending physician or midwife as to the birth of said child. A blank for that purpose is inclosed herewith.

Applications for Enrollment of Seminole Newborn
Act of 1905   Volume II

In having the same executed be careful to see that all blanks are properly filled, all names written in full and that the notary public before whom the affidavits are acknowledged affixes his name and seal to each separate affidavit. In case any signature is by mark, it must be attested by two disinterested persons witnesses thereto.

Respectfully,

BC
Env.   Chairman.

NBS 130.

Muskogee, Indian Territory, November 7, 1905.

Thomas McGeisey,
    Wewoka, Indian Territory.

Dear Sir:

On May 25, 1905, you appeared before the Commission to the Five Civilized Tribes at Wewoka, Indian Territory, and made application for the enrollment of George Johnson, as a citizen by blood of the Seminole Nation.

You are advised that before the matter of the enrollment of said child can be finally determined it will be necessary for this office to be furnished with the affidavits of this mother and attending physician or midwife as to the birth of said child. A blank for that purpose is enclosed herewith.

Under date of June 29, 1905, this office addressed a letter to Lizzie Johnson, mother of said George Jonson, at Wetumka, Indian Territory, relative to the enrollment of this child, but the name was returned to this office unclaimed.

Respectfully,

B.C.   Commissioner.

Sem. N.B. 130

Muskogee, Indian Territory, December 29, 1905.

McKennon & Willmott,
        Attorneys for the Seminoles,
                Wewoka, Indian Territory.

Gentlemen:

On May 28, 1905, application was made to the Commission to the Five Civilized Tribes by Thomas McGeisey, of Wewoka, Indian Territory, for the enrollment of George

Johnson, born in the month of December, 1904, as a citizen of the Seminole Nation under the provisions of the act of Congress approved March 3, 1905.

It appears from such evidence as this office has been able to secure in reference to this child that he is the son of Lizzie Johnson whose name appears upon the roll of Seminole citizens opposite Number 1415 as Lizzie Chupco.

It is earnestly desired that there be secured at the earliest practicable date the affidavit of Lizzie Johnson, nee Chupco, to the birth of the child, George Johnson, as to whether said child was living on March 4, 1905. It is also desirable that there be secured the affidavits of two disinterested parties who know that the child is the child of Lizzie Johnson, nee Chupco, and that he is now and was living on March 4, 1905. Please give this matter your early attention.

Respectfully,

BC

Commissioner.

Department of the Interior.
Commissioner to the Five Civilized Tribes,
MUSKOGEE, IND. TER,

Lizzie Johnson,
Wetumka, Indian Territory.

AP

REFER IN REPLY TO THE FOLLOWING:

Sem N B 130

DEPARTMENT OF THE INTERIOR,
COMMISSIONER TO THE FIVE CIVILIZED TRIBES.

Muskogee, Indian Territory, *(Illegible)*, 29, 1906.

Lizzie Johnson,
Wetumka, Indian Territory.

Dear Madam:

You are hereby advised that a representation[sic] of the Commissioner to the Five Civilized Tribes will be in Wewoka, Indian Territory, Friday and Saturday, January 4 and 5, 1907, for the purpose of hearing testimony in Seminole enrollment cases and you and the physician or midwife who was in attendance at the birth of your child, George Johnson, should appear at that place on one of those days for the purpose of testifying relative to the right of said child to enrollment. In the event there was no physician or midwife in attendance you should present the testimony of two disinterested witnesses who know of the birth of said child the,[sic] date thereof, the names of his parents, and that he was still living March 4, 1905.

Respectfully,
Tams Bixby   Commissioner.

Department of the Interior.
Commissioner to the Five Civilized Tribes,
MUSKOGEE, IND. TER,

Lizzie Johnson,
Wetumka, Indian Territory.

AP

REFER IN REPLY TO THE FOLLOWING:

Sem-NB-130.

**DEPARTMENT OF THE INTERIOR,
COMMISSIONER TO THE FIVE CIVILIZED TRIBES.**

Muskogee, Indian Territory, April 16, 1907.

Lizzie Johnson,
Wetumka, Indian Territory.

Dear Madam:

You are hereby advised that on March 4, 1907, the Secretary of the Interior approved the enrollment of your minor child, George Johnson, as a new born Seminole Indian, and is name appears on the final roll of such citizens of the Seminole Nation opposite No. 243.

Respectfully,
Tams Bixby
Commissioner.

Applications for Enrollment of Seminole Newborn
Act of 1905   Volume II

Sem NB 131
BIRTH AFFIDAVIT.

DEPARTMENT OF THE INTERIOR.
COMMISSION TO THE FIVE CIVILIZED TRIBES.

IN RE APPLICATION FOR ENROLLMENT, as a citizen of the   Seminole   Nation, of
Lucindy Brown   , born on the 2" day of July , 1904

Name of Father: Simon Brown   (I-1401)   a citizen of the Seminole   Nation.
Name of Mother: Wisey Brown   (I-1402)   a citizen of the Seminole   Nation.

Postoffice   Maud, I.T.

(Child present)

AFFIDAVIT OF MOTHER.

UNITED STATES OF AMERICA, Indian Territory,
Western   DISTRICT.

I,   Wisey Brown   , on oath state that I am 20   years of age and a citizen by
blood   , of the   Seminole   Nation; that I am the lawful wife of   Simon Brown   ,
who is a citizen, by blood   of the   Seminole   Nation; that a   female
child was born to me on   2"   day of   July   , 1904; that said child has been named
Lucindy Brown   , and was living March 4, 1905.

Wisey Brown
Witnesses To Mark:

Subscribed and sworn to before me this 2" day of   May   , 1905.

⟨ Seal ⟩   Edward Merrick
                                      Notary Public.

AFFIDAVIT OF ATTENDING PHYSICIAN OR MID-WIFE.

UNITED STATES OF AMERICA, Indian Territory,
Western   DISTRICT.

I, Lizzie Johnson   , a   midwife   , on oath state that I attended on Mrs.
Wisey Brown   , wife of   Simon Brown   on the 2" day of   July   , 1904;
that there was born to her on said date a   female   child; that said child was living
March 4, 1905, and is said to have been named Lucindy Brown

Lizzie Johnson

60

Witnesses To Mark:

{

Subscribed and sworn to before me this 2" day of   May   , 1905.

⬡ Seal

Edward Merrick
Notary Public.

Sem NB 131
BIRTH AFFIDAVIT.

DEPARTMENT OF THE INTERIOR.
COMMISSION TO THE FIVE CIVILIZED TRIBES.

IN RE APPLICATION FOR ENROLLMENT, as a citizen of the   Seminole   Nation, of
George Brown   , born on the 2" day of May , 1901

Name of Father: Simon Brown   (#1401)   a citizen of the Seminole   Nation.
Name of Mother: Wisey Brown   (#1402)   a citizen of the Seminole   Nation.

Postoffice   Maud, Ind.Ter.

(Child present)

AFFIDAVIT OF MOTHER.

UNITED STATES OF AMERICA, Indian Territory,
     Western   **DISTRICT.**

I,   Wisey Brown   , on oath state that I am   20   years of age and a citizen by
blood   , of the   Seminole   Nation; that I am the lawful wife of   Simon Brown   ,
who is a citizen, by blood   of the   Seminole   Nation; that a   male   child
was born to me on   2"   day of   May   , 1901; that said child has been named
George Brown   , and was living March 4, 1905.

Wisey Brown

Witnesses To Mark:

{

Subscribed and sworn to before me this 2" day of   May   , 1905.

⬡ Seal

Edward Merrick
Notary Public.

61

Applications for Enrollment of Seminole Newborn
Act of 1905   Volume II

AFFIDAVIT OF ATTENDING PHYSICIAN OR MID-WIFE.

UNITED STATES OF AMERICA, Indian Territory,
  Western   DISTRICT.

   I, Lizzie Johnson   , a midwife   , on oath state that I attended on Mrs.
Wisey Brown   , wife of Simon Brown   on the 2" day of   May   , 1901;
that there was born to her on said date a   male   child; that said child was living
March 4, 1905, and is said to have been named George Brown

                                   Lizzie Johnson
Witnesses To Mark:

   Subscribed and sworn to before me this 2" day of   May   , 1905.

   Seal   Edward Merrick
                                          Notary Public.

Sem NB 132
BIRTH AFFIDAVIT.
DEPARTMENT OF THE INTERIOR.
COMMISSION TO THE FIVE CIVILIZED TRIBES.

IN RE APPLICATION FOR ENROLLMENT, as a citizen of the   Seminole   Nation, of
Joseph Hawkins   , born on the 26 day of Jany , 1903

Name of Father: Thomas Hawkins (#1375)   a citizen of the   Seminole   Nation.
Name of Mother: Sally Harjo   (#1425)   a citizen of the   "   Nation.

                 Postoffice   Wewoka, Ind. Ter.

Applications for Enrollment of Seminole Newborn
Act of 1905   Volume II

(Child present)   Father, Mother dead
AFFIDAVIT <s>OF MOTHER</s>.

UNITED STATES OF AMERICA, Indian Territory, ⎱
   Western   DISTRICT. ⎰

    I,   Thomas Hawkins   , on oath state that I am   56   years of age and a
citizen by   blood   , of the   Seminole   Nation; that I <s>am</s> was the lawful <s>wife</s>
husband of   Sally Harjo Hawkins, deceased   , who <s>is</s> was a citizen, by blood
of the   Seminole   Nation; that a   male   child was born to <s>me</s> her on   26th
day of   January   , 1903; that said child has been named   Joseph Hawkins   , and
was living March 4, 1905.   his
                                     Thomas x Hawkins
Witnesses To Mark: mark
   ⎰ Ed. Merrick
   ⎱ Frank C. Sabourin

    Subscribed and sworn to before me this 5th   day of   May   , 1905.

⬡ Seal

                            Edward Merrick
                            Notary Public.

AFFIDAVIT OF ATTENDING PHYSICIAN OR MID-WIFE.

UNITED STATES OF AMERICA, Indian Territory, ⎱
   Western   DISTRICT. ⎰

    I,   Mima Tiger   , a   midwife   , on oath state that I attended on Mrs.
Sally Hawkins   , wife of Thomas Hawkins   on the 26th day of   January   ,
1903; that there was born to her on said date a   male   child; that said child was living
March 4, 1905, and is said to have been named Joseph Hawkins
                                 her
                           Mima x Tiger
Witnesses To Mark: mark
   ⎰ Ed. Merrick
   ⎱ Frank C. Sabourin

    Subscribed and sworn to before me this 5th   day of   May   , 1905.

⬡ Seal

                            Edward Merrick
                            Notary Public.

Applications for Enrollment of Seminole Newborn
Act of 1905 Volume II

Sem NB 133
BIRTH AFFIDAVIT.

DEPARTMENT OF THE INTERIOR.
COMMISSION TO THE FIVE CIVILIZED TRIBES.

IN RE APPLICATION FOR ENROLLMENT, as a citizen of the   Seminole   Nation, of
J Robb Brown   , born on the 9 day of Oct , 1901

Name of Father: E.J. Brown Jr.   a citizen of the   U. S.   ~~Nation~~.
Name of Mother: Emma Brown   a citizen of the   Seminole   Nation.
                        (Nee Marthla 1428)
                                   Postoffice   Keokuk Falls, O.T.

AFFIDAVIT OF MOTHER.
                        Okla.
UNITED STATES OF AMERICA, ~~Indian~~ Territory, ⎱
  Pottawatomie County   ~~DISTRICT.~~ ⎰

    I,   Emma Brown   , on oath state that I am   28   years of age and a citizen by
blood   , of the   Seminole   Nation; that I am the lawful wife of   E. J. Brown Jr ,
who is a citizen, ~~by~~ of U. S.   ~~of the~~   ~~Nation~~; that a   male   child was
born to me on 9th   day of   Oct   , 1901; that said child has been named   J. Robb
Brown   , and was living March 4, 1905.
                                            Emma Brown
Witnesses To Mark:
    ⎰ H D Owen
    ⎱ J W Edwards

    Subscribed and sworn to before me this 9 day of   May   , 1905.
Com Ex Mar 13. 07
                                   JE Thompson
                                        Notary Public.

AFFIDAVIT OF ATTENDING PHYSICIAN OR MID-WIFE.
                        Okla.
UNITED STATES OF AMERICA, ~~Indian~~ Territory, ⎱
  Pottawatomie County   ~~DISTRICT.~~ ⎰

    I,   Peache Martha   , a MidWife   , on oath state that I attended on Mrs.
Emma Brown   , wife of E.J. Brown Jr   on the 9 day of   Oct   , 1901; that
there was born to her on said date a   male   child; that said child was living March 4,
1905, and is said to have been named J. Robb Brown
                                            her
                             Peache Martha   x
                                            mark

64

Witnesses To Mark:
{ H D Owen
{ J W Edwards

Subscribed and sworn to before me this   9 day of   May   , 1905.
Com Ex Mar 13. 07

JE Thompson
Notary Public.

Sem NB 133
BIRTH AFFIDAVIT.

DEPARTMENT OF THE INTERIOR.
COMMISSION TO THE FIVE CIVILIZED TRIBES.

IN RE APPLICATION FOR ENROLLMENT, as a citizen of the   Seminole   Nation, of
Leo D Brown   , born on the   17   day of   July   , 1904

Name of Father: E.J. Brown Jr.   a citizen of the   U. S.   ~~Nation~~.
Name of Mother: Emma Brown   a citizen of the   Seminole   Nation.
(nee Marthla 1428)
Postoffice   Keokuk Falls, O.T.

Child present at filing of application.
AFFIDAVIT OF MOTHER.
Okla.
UNITED STATES OF AMERICA, ~~Indian~~ Territory, ⎤
Pottawatomie County   ~~DISTRICT.~~ ⎦

I,   Emma Brown   , on oath state that I am   28   years of age and a citizen by
Blood   , of the   Seminole   Nation; that I am the lawful wife of   E. J. Brown Jr ,
who is a citizen, ~~by~~   of the   U. S.   Nation; that a   Male   child was
born to me on   17   day of   July   , 1904; that said child has been named   Leo D.
Brown   , and was living March 4, 1905.

Emma Brown

Witnesses To Mark:
{ H D Owen
{ J W Edwards

Subscribed and sworn to before me this   9 day of   May   , 1905.
Com Ex Mar 13. 07

JE Thompson
Notary Public.

Applications for Enrollment of Seminole Newborn
Act of 1905   Volume II

Okla.

UNITED STATES OF AMERICA, ~~Indian~~ Territory,
Pottawatomie County   ~~DISTRICT.~~

I,   Peache Martha   , a MidWife   , on oath state that I attended on Mrs. Emma Brown   , wife of E.J. Brown Jr   on the 17 day of   July   , 1904; that there was born to her on said date a   Male   child; that said child was living March 4, 1905, and is said to have been named Leo D Brown

her

Peache Martha   x

mark

Witnesses To Mark:
  H D Owen
  J W Edwards

Subscribed and sworn to before me this 9 day of   May   , 1905.

JE Thompson

Notary Public.

Com Ex Mar 13. 07

Sem NB 133

IN RE APPLICATION FOR ENROLLMENT, as a citizen of the   Seminole   Nation, of E John Brown   , born on the 17 day of July   , 1904

Name of Father: E.J. Brown Jr.   a citizen of the   U. S.   Nation.
Name of Mother: Emma Brown   a citizen of the   Seminole   Nation.

(Nee Marthla 1428)

Postoffice   Keokuk Falls, O.T.

Okla.

UNITED STATES OF AMERICA, ~~Indian~~ Territory,
Pottawatomie County   ~~DISTRICT.~~

I,   Emma Brown   , on oath state that I am   28   years of age and a citizen by Blood   , of the   Seminole   Nation; that I am the lawful wife of   E. J. Brown Jr , who is a citizen, ~~by~~   of the   U. S.   ~~Nation~~; that a   Male   child was born to me on 17   day of   July   , 1904; that said child has been named   E John Brown   , and was living March 4, 1905.

Emma Brown

66

Witnesses To Mark:
{ H D Owen
{ J W Edwards

Subscribed and sworn to before me this 9 day of   May   , 1905.
Com Ex Mar 13. 07

JE Thompson
Notary Public.

AFFIDAVIT OF ATTENDING PHYSICIAN OR MID-WIFE.
Okla.
UNITED STATES OF AMERICA, ~~Indian~~ Territory, ⎫
Pottawatomie County   ~~DISTRICT.~~ ⎬

I,   Peache Martha   , a   Mid wife   , on oath state that I attended on Mrs.
Emma Brown   , wife of E.J. Brown Jr   on the 17 day of   July   , 1904;
that there was born to her on said date a   Male   child; that said child was living
March 4, 1905, and is said to have been named E John Brown

her
Peache Martha   x
mark

Witnesses To Mark:
{ H D Owen
{ J W Edwards

Subscribed and sworn to before me this 9 day of   May   , 1905.

JE Thompson
Com Ex Mar 13. 07   Notary Public.

Sem NB 134
BIRTH AFFIDAVIT.

DEPARTMENT OF THE INTERIOR.
COMMISSION TO THE FIVE CIVILIZED TRIBES.

IN RE APPLICATION FOR ENROLLMENT, as a citizen of the   Seminole   Nation, of
Waldrond Camp   , born on the 25 day of Sept , 1900

Name of Father: John Hayecha	1445	a citizen of the Seminole Nation.
Name of Mother: Nitey	1446	a citizen of the Seminole Nation.

Postoffice   Wewoka IT

(Child present)

AFFIDAVIT OF MOTHER.

UNITED STATES OF AMERICA, Indian Territory,
    Western   DISTRICT.

    I,   Nitey   , on oath state that I am   about 25   years of age and a citizen by
blood   , of the   Seminole   Nation; that I am the lawful wife of   John Hayecha   ,
who is a citizen, by blood   of the   Seminole   Nation; that a   Male   child
was born to me on   25   day of   Sept   , 1900; that said child has been named
Waldrond Camp   , and is now living.

her
Nitey   x
mark

Witnesses To Mark:
    Chas E Webster
    A. B. Davis

Subscribed and sworn to before me this 22 day of   May   , 1905.

Chas E Webster
Notary Public.

AFFIDAVIT OF ATTENDING PHYSICIAN OR MID-WIFE.

UNITED STATES OF AMERICA, Indian Territory,
    Western   DISTRICT.

    I,   John Hayecha   , ~~a~~   , on oath state that I attended on Mrs. Nitey   ,
~~wife of~~   my wife   on the 25 day of   Sept   , 1900; that there was born to her on
said date a   male   child; that said child is now living, and is said to have been named
Waldrond Camp

his
John x Hayecha
Witnesses To Mark: mark
  { Chas E Webster
  { A. B. Davis

Subscribed and sworn to before me this 22 day of   May   , 1905.

Chas E Webster

Notary Public.

Sem NB 134
BIRTH AFFIDAVIT.

DEPARTMENT OF THE INTERIOR.
COMMISSION TO THE FIVE CIVILIZED TRIBES.

IN RE APPLICATION FOR ENROLLMENT, as a citizen of the   Seminole   Nation, of
Willie Camp   , born on the 2 day of   Feb , 1902

Name of Father: John Hayecha   1445   a citizen of the Seminole   Nation.
Name of Mother: Nitey   1446   a citizen of the Seminole   Nation.

Postoffice   Wewoka

(Child present)

AFFIDAVIT OF MOTHER.

UNITED STATES OF AMERICA, Indian Territory, ⎤
    Western   **DISTRICT.** ⎦

    I,   Nitey   , on oath state that I am   about 25   years of age and a citizen by
blood   , of the   Seminole   Nation; that I am the lawful wife of   John Hayecha   ,
who is a citizen, by blood   of the   Seminole   Nation; that a   Male   child
was born to me on 2 day of   Feb.   , 1902; that said child has been named   Willie
Camp   , and is now living.   her
                                             Nitey x
Witnesses To Mark: mark
  { Chas E Webster
  { A. B. Davis

Subscribed and sworn to before me this 22 day of   May   , 1905.

Chas E Webster
Notary Public.

69

AFFIDAVIT OF ATTENDING PHYSICIAN OR MID-WIFE.

UNITED STATES OF AMERICA, Indian Territory, ⎫
    Western   DISTRICT. ⎬
                          ⎭

I, John Hayecha   , a   , on oath state that I attended on Mrs. Nitey   ,
~~wife of~~   my wife   on the 2 day of   Feb   , 1902; that there was born to her on
said date a   Male   child; that said child is now living, and is said to have been named
Willie Camp   his
                                  John x Hayecha
Witnesses To Mark: mark
   ⎧ Chas E Webster
   ⎩ A. B. Davis

Subscribed and sworn to before me this 22 day of   May   , 1905.

                               Chas E Webster

                               Notary Public.

                                     Seminole
                                       NB-135.

                    Muskogee, Indian Territory June 29, 1905.

Commission to the Five Civilized Tribes,
              Creek Enrollment Division.

Gentlemen:

    On May 22, 1905 there was filed with the Commission application for the
enrollment of Charley Williams, born September 9, 1904, as a citizen by blood of the
Seminole Nation. It is stated in said application that said child is a son of Joney
Williams, a citizen by blood of the Creek Nation and Wisey Wakkie, a citizen by blood
of the Seminole Nation.

    You are requested to advise the Seminole Enrollment Division as to whether any
application has been made to the Commission for the enrollment of said Charley

Williams as a citizen of the Creek Nation and if so what disposition, if any, has been made of such application.

Respectfully,

Chairman.

HGH

DEPARTMENT OF THE INTERIOR.
COMMISSION TO THE FIVE CIVILIZED TRIBES.

Muskogee, Indian Territory, July 10, 1905.

Seminole Enrollment Division,
General Office.

Gentlemen:

Receipt is acknowledged of your communication of June 29, 1905, in which you state that application has been made for the enrollment of Charley Williams, born September 9, 1904, a citizen by blood of the Seminole Nation. You also state that it appears that said child was the son of Joney Williams, a citizen by blood of the Creek Nation, and Wisey Wakkie, a citizen by blood of the Seminole Nation, and ask if application has been made for the enrollment of said Charley Williams, as a citizen of the Creek Nation.

In reply you are advised that the records of this office have been examined and it does not appear that application has been made for the enrollment of said Charley Williams, as a citizen of the Creek Nation.

Respectfully,

Tams Bixby   Commissioner.

Sem NB 135
BIRTH AFFIDAVIT.

DEPARTMENT OF THE INTERIOR.
COMMISSION TO THE FIVE CIVILIZED TRIBES.

IN RE APPLICATION FOR ENROLLMENT, as a citizen of the   Seminole   Nation, of Charley Williams   , born on the 9 day of Sept , 1904

Name of Father: Joney Williams   a citizen of the   Creek   Nation.
Name of Mother: Wisey Wakkie   1453   a citizen of the   Seminole   Nation.

. Postoffice   Wewoka I.T.

71

Applications for Enrollment of Seminole Newborn
Act of 1905   Volume II

(Child present)

UNITED STATES OF AMERICA, Indian Territory,
Western   DISTRICT.

I,   Wisey Wakkie   , on oath state that I am about 30 years of age and a citizen by   blood   , of the   Seminole   Nation; that I am not the lawful wife of Joney Williams   , who is a citizen, by   blood   of the   Creek   Nation; that a male   child was born to me on 9   day of   Sept   , 1904, that said child has been named   Charley Williams   , and is now living.

her
Wisey x Wakkie
mark

Witnesses To Mark:
  Chas E Webster
  A. B. Davis

Subscribed and sworn to before me this 22   day of   May   , 1905.

Chas E Webster
Notary Public.

UNITED STATES OF AMERICA, Indian Territory,
Western   DISTRICT.

I,   Nitey   , a   midwife   , on oath state that I attended on Mrs.   Wisey Wakkie   , ~~wife of~~   on the   9   day of   Sept , 1904; that there was born to her on said date a   male   child; that said child is now living and is said to have been named Charley Williams

her
Nitey x
mark

Witnesses To Mark:
  Chas E Webster
  A. B. Davis

Subscribed and sworn to before me this 22   day of   May   , 1905.

Chas E Webster
Notary Public.

Sem NB 136
BIRTH AFFIDAVIT.

DEPARTMENT OF THE INTERIOR.
COMMISSION TO THE FIVE CIVILIZED TRIBES.

IN RE APPLICATION FOR ENROLLMENT, as a citizen of the   Seminole   Nation, of
Wesley Harjo   , born on the —–day of   August   , 1902

Name of Father: Pachos Harjo   (1455)   a citizen of the   Seminole   Nation.
Name of Mother: Jennie Harjo   (1456)   a citizen of the   Seminole   Nation.

Postoffice   Wewoka IT

AFFIDAVIT OF MOTHER.

UNITED STATES OF AMERICA, Indian Territory, ⎫
      Western   DISTRICT.   ⎰

      I, Jennie Harjo   , on oath state that I am 36   years of age and a citizen by
blood   , of the   Seminole   Nation; that I am the lawful wife of   Pachos Harjo ,
who is a citizen, by   blood   of the   Seminole   Nation; that a   male   child
was born to me on ——–day of August   , 1902, that said child has been named
Wesley Harjo   , and is now living.   her
                                                                Jennie x Harjo
Witnesses To Mark: mark
      ⎰ Frank C. Sabourin
      ⎱ Chas E Webster

      Subscribed and sworn to before me this 12 day of   May   , 1905.

                                          Chas E Webster
                                          Notary Public.

                                          Band Officer
AFFIDAVIT OF ~~ATTENDING PHYSICIAN OR MID-WIFE~~.

UNITED STATES OF AMERICA, Indian Territory, ⎫   No Midwife or attendant
      Western   DISTRICT.   ⎰
                                                       saw
      I,   Mut-ho-ya   , ~~a~~   , on oath state that I ~~attended on~~ Mrs.   Jennie Harjo ,
wife of   Pachos Harjo   on the —— day of   August , 1902; the day after the birth of
Wesley Harjo   that there was born to her on said date a   male   child; that said child
is now living and is said to have been named Wesley Harjo
                                                       his
                                          Mut-ho-ya   x
                                                       mark

73

Witnesses To Mark:
⎰ Frank C. Sabourin
⎱ Chas E Webster

Subscribed and sworn to before me this 12 day of   May   , 1905.

Chas E Webster
Notary Public.

Sem NB 137
BIRTH AFFIDAVIT.

DEPARTMENT OF THE INTERIOR.
COMMISSION TO THE FIVE CIVILIZED TRIBES.

IN RE APPLICATION FOR ENROLLMENT, as a citizen of the   Seminole   Nation, of
Joseph Cully   , born on the 8   day of Sept   , 1900

Name of Father: William Cully   (144)   a citizen of the Seminole   Nation.
Name of Mother: Nora Cully   a citizen of the Seminole   Nation.
nee McGiesey
Postoffice   Wewoka I.T.

Child present

AFFIDAVIT OF MOTHER.

UNITED STATES OF AMERICA, Indian Territory, ⎱
    Western   DISTRICT. ⎰

I,   Nora Cully   , on oath state that I am   25   years of age and a citizen by
blood   , of the   Seminole   Nation; that I am the lawful wife of   William Cully ,
who is a citizen, by blood   of the   Seminole   Nation; that a   male   child
was born to me on   8th   day of   Sept   , 1900; that said child has been named
Joseph Cully   , and was living March 4, 1905.

Nora Cully

Applications for Enrollment of Seminole Newborn
Act of 1905   Volume II

Witnesses To Mark:

{

Subscribed and sworn to before me this 1st day of   May   , 1905.

Chas E Webster
Notary Public.

_____

Husband

UNITED STATES OF AMERICA, Indian Territory,
    Western   DISTRICT.   }

am the husband of
I,   William Cully   , ~~a~~   , on oath state that I ~~attended on~~ Mrs. Nora
Cully   , ~~wife of~~ and was present   on the 8th day of   Sept   , 1900; that
there was born to her on said date a   male   child; that said child was living March 4,
1905, and is said to have been named Joseph Cully

William Cully

Witnesses To Mark:

{

Subscribed and sworn to before me 1st day of   May   , 1905.

Chas E Webster
Notary Public.

_____

Sem NB 137
BIRTH AFFIDAVIT.

DEPARTMENT OF THE INTERIOR.
COMMISSION TO THE FIVE CIVILIZED TRIBES.

_____

IN RE APPLICATION FOR ENROLLMENT, as a citizen of the   Seminole   Nation, of
George Cully   , born on the 1st day of Octo , 1902

Name of Father: William Cully   (144)   a citizen of the Seminole   Nation.
Name of Mother: Nora Cully   a citizen of the Seminole   Nation.
                nee McGiesey
                Postoffice   Wewoka I.T.

_____

(Child present)

AFFIDAVIT OF MOTHER.

UNITED STATES OF AMERICA, Indian Territory,
Western DISTRICT.

I, Nora Cully nee McGeisey , on oath state that I am 25 years of age and a citizen by blood , of the Seminole Nation; that I am the lawful wife of William Cully , who is a citizen, by blood of the Seminole Nation; that a male child was born to me on 1st day of Octo , 1902; that said child has been named George Cully , and was living March 4, 1905.

Nora Cully

Witnesses To Mark:

Subscribed and sworn to before me this 1st day of May , 1905.

Chas E Webster
Notary Public.

AFFIDAVIT OF ~~ATTENDING PHYSICIAN OR MID-WIFE~~. Grandfather

UNITED STATES OF AMERICA, Indian Territory,
Western DISTRICT.

I, Thomas McGeisey , ~~a~~ , on oath state that I ~~attended on~~ am the father of Mrs. Nora Cully , ~~wife of~~ and that on the 1st day of Octo , 1902; that there was born to her on said date a male child; that said child was living March 4, 1905, and is said to have been named George Cully

Thomas McGeisey

Witnesses To Mark:

Subscribed and sworn to before me 1st day of May , 1905.

Chas E Webster
Notary Public.

Applications for Enrollment of Seminole Newborn
Act of 1905   Volume II

Sem NB 138
BIRTH AFFIDAVIT.

DEPARTMENT OF THE INTERIOR.
COMMISSION TO THE FIVE CIVILIZED TRIBES.

IN RE APPLICATION FOR ENROLLMENT, as a citizen of the   Seminole   Nation, of
Lela Porter   , born on the 4 day of Feby , 1905

Name of Father: Selba   1804   a citizen of the Seminole Nation.
Name of Mother: Minnie Porter   1492   a citizen of the Seminole Nation.

Postoffice   Sasakwa IT

Child present

AFFIDAVIT OF MOTHER.

UNITED STATES OF AMERICA, Indian Territory,
     Western   **DISTRICT.**

    I,   Minnie Porter   , on oath state that I am 20 years of age and a citizen by
blood   , of the   Seminole   Nation; that I am the lawful wife of   Selba   ,
who is a citizen, by blood   of the   Seminole   Nation; that a   Female
child was born to me on 4   day of   Feby   , 1905; that said child has been named
Lela Porter   , and was living March 4, 1905.

Minnie Porter

Witnesses To Mark:

{

    Subscribed and sworn to before me this 3 day of   May   , 1905.

Chas E Webster
Notary Public.

AFFIDAVIT OF ATTENDING PHYSICIAN OR MID-WIFE.

UNITED STATES OF AMERICA, Indian Territory,
     Western   **DISTRICT.**

    I,   Mary Condella   , a   midwife   , on oath state that I attended on Mrs.
Minnie Porter   , wife of   Selba   on the 4 day of Feby   , 1905; that there
was born to her on said date a   Female   child; that said child was living March 4,
1905, and is said to have been named   Lela Porter

Mary Condella

Witnesses To Mark:

{

Subscribed and sworn to before me   3 day of   May   , 1905.

Chas E Webster
Notary Public.

Sem NB 139
BIRTH AFFIDAVIT.

DEPARTMENT OF THE INTERIOR.
COMMISSION TO THE FIVE CIVILIZED TRIBES.

IN RE APPLICATION FOR ENROLLMENT, as a citizen of the   Seminole   Nation, of
Fannie Joseph   , born on the   16 day of   Feb , 1905

Name of Father: Abler Harjo	1311	a citizen of the Seminole	Nation.
Name of Mother: Mary Joseph	1500	a citizen of the Seminole	Nation.

Postoffice   Irene, I.T.

(Child present)

AFFIDAVIT OF MOTHER.

UNITED STATES OF AMERICA, Indian Territory,
    Western   **DISTRICT.**

    I,   Mary Joseph   , on oath state that I am   about 25   years of age and a
citizen by   blood   , of the   Seminole   Nation; that I am not the lawful wife of
Abler Harjo   , who is a citizen, by blood   of the   Seminole   Nation; that
a   Female   child was born to me on 16   day of   Feb   , 1905; that said child
has been named   Fannie Joseph   , and was living March 4, 1905.

Mary Joseph
Witnesses To Mark:
{ Chas E Webster
  Frank C. Sabourin

78

Applications for Enrollment of Seminole Newborn
Act of 1905   Volume II

Subscribed and sworn to before me this 9 day of   May   , 1905.

Chas E Webster
Notary Public.

AFFIDAVIT OF ATTENDING PHYSICIAN OR MID-WIFE.

UNITED STATES OF AMERICA, Indian Territory,
Western   DISTRICT.

I,   Medisse Joseph   , a midwife   , on oath state that I attended on ~~Mrs.~~
Mary Joseph   , ~~wife of~~ my daughter   on the 16 day of   Feb   , 1905; that
there was born to her on said date a   Female   child; that said child was living March
4, 1905, and is said to have been named   Fannie Joseph

her
Medisse x Joseph
mark

Witnesses To Mark:
Chas E Webster
Frank C. Sabourin

Subscribed and sworn to before me this 9 day of   May   , 1905.

Chas E Webster
Notary Public.

Sem NB 140
BIRTH AFFIDAVIT.

DEPARTMENT OF THE INTERIOR.
COMMISSION TO THE FIVE CIVILIZED TRIBES.

IN RE APPLICATION FOR ENROLLMENT, as a citizen of the   Seminole   Nation, of
Elsie Yahola   , born on the 3" day of Mch   , 1900

Name of Father: Jesse Yahola   ($^{\#}$1269)   a citizen of the Seminole   Nation.
Name of Mother: Amey Yahola   ($^{\#}$1515)   a citizen of the   "   Nation.

Postoffice   Tate IT.

Applications for Enrollment of Seminole Newborn
Act of 1905 Volume II

(Child present)

AFFIDAVIT OF MOTHER.

UNITED STATES OF AMERICA, Indian Territory, ⎱
    Western   **DISTRICT.** ⎰

    I, Amey Yahola (formerly Thlocco)   , on oath state that I am 26 years of age and a citizen by   blood   , of the   Seminole   Nation; that I am the lawful wife of   Jesse Yahola   , who is a citizen, by blood   of the   Seminole Nation; that a   female   child was born to me on   3" day of   March   , 1900; that said child has been named Elsie Yahola   , and was living March 4, 1905.

her
Amey x Yahola
mark

Witnesses To Mark:
  ⎰ Edward Merrick
  ⎱ Frank C. Sabourin

    Subscribed and sworn to before me this 4th day of   May   , 1905.

⟨ Seal ⟩   Edward Merrick
                          Notary Public.

AFFIDAVIT OF ATTENDING PHYSICIAN OR MID-WIFE.

UNITED STATES OF AMERICA, Indian Territory, ⎱
    Western   **DISTRICT.** ⎰

    I, Jennie Tiger   , a midwife , on oath state that I attended on Mrs. Amey Yahola   , wife of Jesse Yahola   on the 3" day of Mch   , 1900; that there was born to her on said date a   female   child; that said child was living March 4, 1905, and is said to have been named Elsie Yahola

her
Jennie x Tiger
mark

Witnesses To Mark:
  ⎰ Edward Merrick
  ⎱ Frank C. Sabourin

    Subscribed and sworn to before me this 4th day of   May   , 1905.

⟨ Seal ⟩   Edward Merrick
                          Notary Public.

Sem NB 141
BIRTH AFFIDAVIT.

DEPARTMENT OF THE INTERIOR.
COMMISSION TO THE FIVE CIVILIZED TRIBES.

IN RE APPLICATION FOR ENROLLMENT, as a citizen of the   Seminole   Nation, of
Cheparney   , born on the 6th day of   April , 1901
Mother
Name of ~~Father~~: Martha   (1520)   a citizen of the   Seminole   Nation.
Father
Name of ~~Mother~~: Ponluste   (1519)   a citizen of the   Seminole   Nation.

Postoffice   Wewoka

Child at home
AFFIDAVIT OF MOTHER.

UNITED STATES OF AMERICA, Indian Territory,
     Western   **DISTRICT.**

I,   Martha   , on oath state that I am 34 years of age and a citizen by   blood   ,
of the   Seminole   Nation; that I am the lawful wife of   Ponlus te   , who is a
citizen, by   blood   of the   Seminole   Nation; that a   male   child was born
to me on   6th day of   April   , 1901, that said child has been named   Cheparney   ,
and is now living.

her
Martha x
mark

Witnesses To Mark:
    Frank C. Sabourin
    Chas E Webster

Subscribed and sworn to before me this 11th day of   May   , 1905.

Chas E Webster
Notary Public.

AFFIDAVIT OF ATTENDING PHYSICIAN OR MID-WIFE.

UNITED STATES OF AMERICA, Indian Territory,
     Western   **DISTRICT.**

I,   Ponluste   , e   , on oath state that I attended on Mrs. Martha   my ,
wife ~~of~~   on the   6th day of April   , 1901; that there was born to her on said date
a   male   child; that said child is now living and is said to have been named
Cheparney

Witnesses To Mark:

Ponluste   his x   mark

{ Frank C. Sabourin
{ Chas E Webster

Subscribed and sworn to before me this 11th   day of   May   , 1905.

Chas E Webster
Notary Public.

Sem NB 141
BIRTH AFFIDAVIT.

DEPARTMENT OF THE INTERIOR.
COMMISSION TO THE FIVE CIVILIZED TRIBES.

IN RE APPLICATION FOR ENROLLMENT, as a citizen of the   Seminole   Nation, of
Johnny   , born on the   3rd   day of   July , 1902

Name of Father: Ponluste   (1519)   a citizen of the   Seminole   Nation.
Name of Mother: Martha   (1520)   a citizen of the   Seminole   Nation.

Postoffice   Wewoka IT

Child present

AFFIDAVIT OF MOTHER.

UNITED STATES OF AMERICA, Indian Territory,
   Western   **DISTRICT.**

   I, Martha   , on oath state that I am 34 years of age and a citizen by   blood   ,
of the   Seminole   Nation; that I am the lawful wife of   Ponluste   , who is a
citizen, by   blood   of the   Seminole   Nation; that a   male   child was born
to me on   3rd   day of   July   , 1902, that said child has been named   Johnny   ,
and is now living.

Martha   her x   mark

Witnesses To Mark:
{ Frank C. Sabourin
{ Chas E Webster

Subscribed and sworn to before me this 11th   day of   May   , 1905.

Chas E Webster
Notary Public.

AFFIDAVIT OF ATTENDING PHYSICIAN OR MID-WIFE.

UNITED STATES OF AMERICA, Indian Territory,
    Western   DISTRICT.

    I, Ponlus te   , e   , on oath state that I attended on Mrs. Martha   my , wife of —— on the 3rd day of July , 1902; that there was born to her on said date a   male   child; that said child is now living and is said to have been named Johnny

his
Ponluste x

Witnesses To Mark: mark
    { Frank C. Sabourin
    { Chas E Webster

    Subscribed and sworn to before me this 11th day of May   , 1905.

Chas E Webster
Notary Public.

NBS 141

Muskogee, Indian Territory, November 7, 1905.

Ponluste,
    Wewoka, Indian Territory.

Dear Sir:

    On May 11, 1905, you and your wife, Martha, appeared before the Commission to the Five Civilized Tribes at Wewoka, Indian Territory, and made application for the enrollment of your minor children, Cheparney, born April 6, 1901, and Johnny, born July 3, 1902.

    Under date of June 20, 1905, you were advised that it would be necessary for you to furnish this office with the affidavits of two disinterested parties, who know the circumstances attending the birth of this child.[sic]

    You are again requested to give this matter your immediate attention as, until the affidavits requested are furnished, this office can not determine the rights to enrollment as citizens of the Seminole Nation of said children.

Respectfully,
    Commissioner.

Applications for Enrollment of Seminole Newborn
Act of 1905   Volume II

Seminole-NB-142.

Muskogee, Indian Territory, June 29, 1905.

Ponluste,
     Wewoka, Indian Territory.

Dear Sir:

On May 11, 1905, you and your wife, Martha, appeared before the Commission and made application for the enrollment of your son, Cheparney, born April 6, 1901, as a citizen by blood of the Seminole Nation, and at that time submitted your affidavits as to the birth of said child.

You are advised that it will be necessary for you to furnish the Commission with the affidavits of two disinterested persons who know your son, Cheparney, know the circumstance attending his birth, when he was born and whether he was living on March 4, 1905.

You should give this matter your immediate attention, as until the affidavits requested are furnished the Commission cannot determine the rights of said child as a citizen by blood of the Seminole Nation.

Respectfully,

Chairman.

(The letter below belongs with NB-146)

Sem. N.B. 146

Muskogee, Indian Territory, December 29, 1905.

McKennon & Willmott,
     Attorneys for the Seminoles,
          Wewoka, Indian Territory.

Gentlemen:

On May 1, 1905, application was made to the Commission to the Five Civilized Tribes for the enrollment of Simma Micco, born September 4, 1902, son of Tallahassee Micco and Mulleana Micco, Seminole roll Numbers 1589 and 1599, respectively, at which time the residence of these persons was given as Keokuk Falls, Oklahoma.

It is necessary, in the matter of the application for the enrollment of application for the enrolment of Simma Micco, that this office be supplied with the affidavits of at least two disinterested person who know of the birth of this child, that he is the child of Tallahassee and Mulleana Micco and that he was living on March 4, 1905. Several efforts have been made to secure this evidence from the parents which have proved ineffective and you are requested to give this matter early attention in order that this child may be enrolled as a Seminole citizen under the provisions of the act of Congress approved March 3, 1905.

Respectfully,

Commissioner.

Department of the Interior.
Commissioner to the Five Civilized Tribes,
MUSKOGEE, IND. TER,

Ponluste,
Wewoka, Indian Territory.

AP

REFER IN REPLY TO THE FOLLOWING:
Sem NB-141

DEPARTMENT OF THE INTERIOR,
COMMISSIONER TO THE FIVE CIVILIZED TRIBES.

Muskogee, Indian Territory, March 2, 1907.

Ponluste,
Wewoka, Indian Territory.

Dear Sir:

You are hereby advised that on February 12, 1907, the Secretary of the Interior approved the enrollment of your child, Cheparney as a New Born Citizen of the Seminole Nation, under the Act of Congress approved March 3, 1905, and his name appears upon the roll of such citizens enrolled under said Act, opposite No. 235.

Respectfully,
Tams Bixby   Commissioner.

Department of the Interior.
Commissioner to the Five Civilized Tribes,
MUSKOGEE, IND. TER,

Ponluste,
Wewoka, Indian Territory.

AP

REFER IN REPLY TO THE FOLLOWING:

Sem-NB-141.

DEPARTMENT OF THE INTERIOR,
COMMISSIONER TO THE FIVE CIVILIZED TRIBES.

Muskogee, Indian Territory, April 15, 1907.

Ponluste,
Wewoka, Indian Territory.

Dear Sir:

You are hereby advised that on February 12, 1907, the Secretary of the Interior approved the enrollment of your child, Cheparney as a new born Seminole Indian, and his name appears on the final roll of such citizens of the Seminole Nation opposite No. 235.

Respectfully,
Tams Bixby   Commissioner.

Sem NB 142
BIRTH AFFIDAVIT.

DEPARTMENT OF THE INTERIOR.
COMMISSION TO THE FIVE CIVILIZED TRIBES.

IN RE APPLICATION FOR ENROLLMENT, as a citizen of the   Seminole   Nation, of
Oscar Chupcogee   , born on the   7   day of   November   , 1902

Name of Father: Billy Chupcogee   279   a citizen of the   Seminole   Nation.
Name of Mother: Hulleah   1386   a citizen of the   Seminole   Nation.
                        deceased
                                    Postoffice   Maud, O.T.

AFFIDAVIT OF ATTENDING PHYSICIAN OR MID-WIFE.

~~UNITED STATES OF AMERICA, Indian Territory,~~ }   Territory of Oklahoma } SS
              ~~DISTRICT.~~   Pottawatomie County }

I,   Liza Larney   , a mid-wife   , on oath state that I attended on Mrs.
Hulleah   , wife of   Billy Chupcogee   on the   7th   day of November , 1902;
that there was born to her on said date a   boy   child; that said child is now living and
is said to have been named Oscar Chupcogee   her
                                                  Liza x Larney
Witnesses To Mark: mark
    { Thos. H. Tribbey
    { EH Bond

Subscribed and sworn to before me this 27th   day of   June   , 1905.

                            EH Bond
                                  Notary Public.

Sem NB 142
BIRTH AFFIDAVIT.

DEPARTMENT OF THE INTERIOR.
COMMISSION TO THE FIVE CIVILIZED TRIBES.

IN RE APPLICATION FOR ENROLLMENT, as a citizen of the   Seminole   Nation, of
Oscar Chupcogee   , born on the   7th   day of   November   , 1902

Name of Father: Billy Chupcogee   (279)   a citizen of the   Seminole   Nation.
Name of Mother: Hulleah, deceased,   (1386)   a citizen of the   Seminole   Nation.

                        Postoffice   Maud, OT

Applications for Enrollment of Seminole Newborn
Act of 1905   Volume II

Child at Mission

AFFIDAVIT OF ~~MOTHER~~.

Father

Mother dead

UNITED STATES OF AMERICA, Indian Territory, ⎱
  Western   DISTRICT. ⎰

I,   Billy Chupcogee   , on oath state that I am   30   years of age and a citizen by   blood   , of the   Seminole   Nation; that I am the lawful ~~wife of~~ husband of Hulleah, deceased   , who ~~is~~ was a citizen, by   blood   of the   Seminole Nation; that a   male   child was born to ~~me~~ her on   7th   day of   November   , 1902; that said child has been named   Oscar Chupcogee   , and was living March 4, 1905.

his
Billy x Chupcogee
mark

Witnesses To Mark:
⎰ Frank C. Sabourin
⎱ Chas E Webster

Subscribed and sworn to before me this 11th   day of   May   , 1905.

Chas E Webster
Notary Public.

Wewoka, Indian Territory, May 19, 1905.

Billy Chupcogee,
    Maud, Oklahoma.

Dear Sir:

On May 11, 1905, you appeared before this office and made application for the enrollment of Oscar Chupcogee, minor son of yourself and Hulleah, deceased, as a citizen of the Seminole Nation, but no affidavit was made by the attending physician or midwife.

It will be necessary, therefore, to furnish this office with such affidavit, said person either to appear before the Seminole Enrollment Office, at Wewoka, Indian Territory, prior to June 1, 1905, or to have the inclosed blank affidavit filled out and properly executed before a Notary Public, returning same to this office in the inclosed envelope, which requires no postage.

Respectfully,

Enc.

Clerk in Charge.

Father appeared at Wewoka, May 31 and states
midwife is still sick and unable to either appear
or have affidavit made

May 31/05

Seminole-NB-148.

Muskogee, Indian Territory, June 29, 1905.

Billy Chupcogee,
Maud, Oklahoma Territory.

Dear Sir:

Receipt is hereby acknowledged of the affidavits of Eliza Larney as to the birth of your son, Oscar Chupcogee, and the same is returned to you herewith for the reason that a discrepancy appears as to the birth of said child, it being stated in the affidavit of the said Eliza Larney that said child was born November 7, 1905, while from your affidavit now on file it appears that said child was born November 7, 1902.

The statement in the affidavit of Eliza Larney that Oscar Chupcogee was born November 7, 1905, is apparently an error, and it would, therefore, be advisable for you to take the same to E. H. Bond, the Notary Public before whom the affidavit was sworn to, for correction. When the same is corrected return it to the Commission in the inclosed envelope.

Respectfully,

VR.29-1.   Chairman.
Env.

Sem Nb-142

Muskogee, Indian Territory, August 15, 1905.

Billy Chupcogee,
Maud, Oklahoma Territory.

Dear Sir:

Receipt is hereby acknowledged of your letter (without date), enclosing the affidavit of Liza Larney, midwife, as to the birth of your minor son, Oscar Chupcogee, on November 7, 1902.

The same has been filed with the records of this Office in the matter of the enrollment of said child as a citizen by blood of the Seminole Nation.

Applications for Enrollment of Seminole Newborn
Act of 1905 Volume II

Respectfully,

Acting Commissioner.

Sem NB 143
BIRTH AFFIDAVIT.

DEPARTMENT OF THE INTERIOR.
COMMISSION TO THE FIVE CIVILIZED TRIBES.

IN RE APPLICATION FOR ENROLLMENT, as a citizen of the   Seminole   Nation, of
Charles Larney   , born on the 19" day of August   , 1901

Name of Father: Robert Larney (In Penitentiary) a citizen of the   Seminole   Nation.
Name of Mother: Julia Larney (nee Bemo)   a citizen of the   Seminole   Nation.

Postoffice   Wewoka Ind. Ter.

AFFIDAVIT OF ~~MOTHER~~.   Uncle

UNITED STATES OF AMERICA, Indian Territory,
     Western   DISTRICT.

I,   George Scott   , on oath state that I am   38   years of age and a citizen by
blood   , of the   Seminole   Nation; that I am the ~~lawful wife of~~ Uncle of Charles
Larney, an infant , who is a citizen, by blood   of the   Seminole   Nation; ~~that a~~
and who ~~child~~ was born to me on   19th   day of   August   , 1901; that said child has
been named   Charles Larney   , and was living March 4, 1905.

his
George x Scott
mark

Witnesses To Mark:
  ⎰ JB Campbell
  ⎱ Edward Merrick

Subscribed and sworn to before me this   15" day of   April   , 1905.

Edward Merrick
Notary Public.

90

Applications for Enrollment of Seminole Newborn
Act of 1905 Volume II

AFFIDAVIT OF ATTENDING PHYSICIAN OR MID-WIFE.

UNITED STATES OF AMERICA, Indian Territory, ⎱
.... **DISTRICT.** ⎰

I, ..., a ...., on oath state that I attended on Mrs. ....,
wife of .... on the .... day of ...., 1 ....; that there was born to her on
said date a .... child; that said child is now living and is said to have been named
....

Witnesses To Mark:
⎰ ....
⎱ ....

Subscribed and sworn to before me this .... day of ...., 1 ....

....
Notary Public.

#17 Cancelled

See attached ~~application~~ affidavit name should be C̲h̲a̲r̲l̲e̲y̲ as
father has since appeared at this office and made such
request

Sem NB 143
BIRTH AFFIDAVIT.   Father's Roll No 13.
DEPARTMENT OF THE INTERIOR.
COMMISSION TO THE FIVE CIVILIZED TRIBES.

IN RE APPLICATION FOR ENROLLMENT, as a citizen of the   Seminole   Nation, of
Charley Larney   , born on the 15   day of   August   , 1901

Name of Father: Robert Larney   a citizen of the   Seminole   Nation.
Name of Mother: Julia Larney   a citizen of the   Seminole   Nation.

Postoffice   Wewoka

(Child present)

AFFIDAVIT OF MOTHER.

UNITED STATES OF AMERICA, Indian Territory, ⎱
    Western   **DISTRICT.** ⎰

I,   Julia Larney   , on oath state that I am   20   years of age and a citizen by
Blood   , of the   Seminole   Nation; that I am the lawful wife of   Robert Larney   ,
who is a citizen, by blood   of the   Seminole   Nation; that a   Male   child

91

was born to me on 15th   day of   August   , 1901; that said child has been named Charley Larney   , and was living March 4, 1905.

her
Julia x Larney
mark

Witnesses To Mark:

    { John R. McBeth
    { J C Johnson

    Subscribed and sworn to before me this 1st day of   May   , 1905.

J C Johnson
Notary Public.

AFFIDAVIT OF ATTENDING PHYSICIAN OR MID-WIFE.

UNITED STATES OF AMERICA, Indian Territory,
     Western   **DISTRICT.**

    I,   Lydia Bemo   , a midwife   , on oath state that I attended on Mrs. Julia Larney   , wife of Robert Larney   on the 15 day of   August   , 1901; that there was born to her on said date a   child; that said child was living March 4, 1905, and is said to have been named Charley Larney

her
Lydia x Bemo
mark

Witnesses To Mark:

    { John R. McBeth
    { J C Johnson

    Subscribed and sworn to before me this 1st day of   May   , 1905.

J C Johnson
Notary Public.

Parties identified and appeared at this office May 12 over being duplicate enrollment.

(The above Birth Affidavit given again.)

Sem NB 143
BIRTH AFFIDAVIT.

DEPARTMENT OF THE INTERIOR.
COMMISSION TO THE FIVE CIVILIZED TRIBES.

IN RE APPLICATION FOR ENROLLMENT, as a citizen of the   Seminole   Nation, of
James Larney   , born on the 12" day of February , 1903

Name of Father: Robert Larney (In Penitentiary) a citizen of the Seminole   Nation.
Name of Mother: Julia Larney (nee Bemo)   a citizen of the Seminole   Nation.

Postoffice   Wewoka Ind. Ter.

AFFIDAVIT OF ~~MOTHER~~. Uncle

UNITED STATES OF AMERICA, Indian Territory,
    Western   DISTRICT.

I, George Scott   , on oath state that I am   38   years of age and a citizen by
blood   , of the   Seminole   Nation; that I am the ~~lawful wife of~~ brother-in-law of
Julia Larney , who is a citizen, by blood   of the   Seminole   Nation; that a
male child was born to ~~me~~ said Julia Larney on 12th day of February   , 1903;
that said child has been named   James Larney   , and was living March 4, 1905.

                                        his
                            George x Scott
Witnesses To Mark: mark
    { JB Campbell
    { Edward Merrick
    Subscribed and sworn to before me this 15" day of   April   , 1905.

Edward Merrick
Notary Public.

AFFIDAVIT OF ATTENDING PHYSICIAN OR MID-WIFE.

UNITED STATES OF AMERICA, Indian Territory,   See attached affidavit
.... DISTRICT.

I, ..., a ...., on oath state that I attended on Mrs. ....,
wife of .... on the .... day of ...., 1......; that there was born to her on
said date a .... child; that said child is now living and is said to have been named
....

....

93

Applications for Enrollment of Seminole Newborn
Act of 1905   Volume II

Witnesses To Mark:

....

....

Subscribed and sworn to before me this ....day of ...., 1........ .

....

Notary Public.

Sem NB 143

BIRTH AFFIDAVIT.   Father's Roll No 13.

DEPARTMENT OF THE INTERIOR.
COMMISSION TO THE FIVE CIVILIZED TRIBES.

IN RE APPLICATION FOR ENROLLMENT, as a citizen of the   Seminole   Nation, of
Jimmie Larney   , born on the   11   day of   February   , 1903

Name of Father: Robert Larney   a citizen of the   Seminole   Nation.
Name of Mother: Julia Larney   a citizen of the   Seminole   Nation.

Postoffice   Wewoka

(Child present)

AFFIDAVIT OF MOTHER.

UNITED STATES OF AMERICA, Indian Territory,
     Western   **DISTRICT.**

     I,   Julia Larney   , on oath state that I am   20   years of age and a citizen by
Blood   , of the   Seminole   Nation; that I am the lawful wife of   Robert Larney   ,
who is a citizen, by   Blood   of the   Seminole   Nation; that a   male   child
was born to me on   11   day of   February   , 1903; that said child has been named
Jimmie Larney   , and was living March 4, 1905.

                                        her
                                        Julia x Larney
Witnesses To Mark: mark
     John R. McBeth
     J C Johnson

Subscribed and sworn to before me this 1st day of   May   , 1905.

                         J C Johnson
                              Notary Public.

Applications for Enrollment of Seminole Newborn
Act of 1905 Volume II

UNITED STATES OF AMERICA, Indian Territory, ⎱
     Western   DISTRICT. ⎰

    I, Maolie   , a Midwife   , on oath state that I attended on Mrs. Julia
Larney   , wife of Robert Larney   on the 11 day of February   , 1903; that
there was born to her on said date a   child; that said child was living March 4, 1905,
and is said to have been named   Jimmie Larney   her
                                Maolie x
Witnesses To Mark: mark
  ⎰ John R. McBeth
  ⎱ J C Johnson

    Subscribed and sworn to before me this 1ˢᵗ day of   May   , 1905.

                        J C Johnson
                          Notary Public.

Duplicate enrollment see application #4

Sem NB 144
BIRTH AFFIDAVIT.
DEPARTMENT OF THE INTERIOR.
COMMISSION TO THE FIVE CIVILIZED TRIBES.

    IN RE APPLICATION FOR ENROLLMENT, as a citizen of the   Seminole   Nation, of
Jimmy Walker   , born on the 25 day of Sept , 1900

Name of Father: Aleck Walker   (1576)   a citizen of the Seminole   Nation.
Name of Mother: Louina Walker   (1577)   a citizen of the Seminole   Nation.

                    Postoffice   Mekusuky IT

Applications for Enrollment of Seminole Newborn
Act of 1905   Volume II

(Child present)

AFFIDAVIT OF MOTHER.

UNITED STATES OF AMERICA, Indian Territory,
    Western   DISTRICT.

      I,   Louina Walker   , on oath state that I am 25   years of age and a citizen by   blood   , of the   Seminole   Nation; that I am the lawful wife of Aleck Walker   , who is a citizen, by blood   of the   Seminole   Nation; that a male   child was born to me on 25 day of Sept   , 1900; that said child has been named   Jimmy Walker   , and was living March 4, 1905.

her
Louina x Walker
mark

Witnesses To Mark:
  { Chas E Webster
  { Frank C. Sabourin

     Subscribed and sworn to before me this 2 day of   May   , 1905.

Chas E Webster
Notary Public.

AFFIDAVIT OF ATTENDING PHYSICIAN OR MID-WIFE.

UNITED STATES OF AMERICA, Indian Territory,
    Western   DISTRICT.

      I,   Sallie Bowlegs   , a midwife   , on oath state that I attended on Mrs. Louina Walker   , wife of Aleck Walker   on the 25 day of Sept   , 1900; that there was born to her on said date a   male   child; that said child was living March 4, 1905, and is said to have been named Jimmy Walker

her
Sallie x Bowlegs
mark

Witnesses To Mark:
  { Chas E Webster
  { Frank C. Sabourin

     Subscribed and sworn to before me 2 day of   May   , 1905.

Chas E Webster
Notary Public.

NB Card #145

DEPARTMENT OF THE INTERIOR.
COMMISSION TO THE FIVE CIVILIZED TRIBES.

———

In the matter of the death of   Kissie Walker   (NB 221)   a citizen of the Seminole   Nation, who formerly resided at or near   Wewoka   , Ind. Ter., and died on the 4   day of   Sept   , 1905

———

AFFIDAVIT OF RELATIVE.

UNITED STATES OF AMERICA, Indian Territory, ⎫
      Western   **DISTRICT.** ⎭

I,   Ben Walker   , on oath state that I am   35   years of age and a citizen by blood , of the Seminole   Nation; that my postoffice address is   Wewoka   , Ind. Ter.; that I am   the father   of   Kissie Walker   who was a citizen, by   blood   , of the Seminole   Nation and that said   Kissie Walker   died on the   4   day of Sept   , 1905

                        Ben Walker
Witnesses To Mark:
⎧
⎨
⎩

Subscribed and sworn to before me this 6th day of   Sept   , 1905.

                        Chas E Webster
                                Notary Public.

———

Sem NB 145
BIRTH AFFIDAVIT.

DEPARTMENT OF THE INTERIOR.
COMMISSION TO THE FIVE CIVILIZED TRIBES.

———

IN RE APPLICATION FOR ENROLLMENT, as a citizen of the   Seminole   Nation, of Kissie Walker   , born on the   17 day of   April , 1904

Name of Father: Ben Walker   (1579)   a citizen of the Seminole   Nation.
Name of Mother: Lizzie Walker   (1580)   a citizen of the   Seminole   Nation.

            Postoffice   Wewoka

———

97

(Child present)

AFFIDAVIT OF MOTHER.

UNITED STATES OF AMERICA, Indian Territory, ⎱
   Western   DISTRICT. ⎰

    I,   Lizzie Walker   , on oath state that I am 35   years of age and a citizen by   blood   , of the   Seminole   Nation; that I am the lawful wife of   Ben Walker   , who is a citizen, by blood   of the   Seminole   Nation; that a Female   child was born to me on 17   day of   April   , 1904; that said child has been named   Kissie Walker   , and was living March 4, 1905.

her
Lizzie x Walker
mark

Witnesses To Mark:
  ⎰ Chas E Webster
  ⎱ Frank C. Sabourin

    Subscribed and sworn to before me this 3 day of   May   , 1905.

Chas E Webster
Notary Public.

AFFIDAVIT OF ATTENDING PHYSICIAN OR MID-WIFE.

UNITED STATES OF AMERICA, Indian Territory, ⎱
   Western   DISTRICT. ⎰

    I, Lucy Wildcat   , a   midwife   , on oath state that I attended on Mrs. Lizzie Walker   , wife of Ben Walker   on the 17 day of April   , 1904; that there was born to her on said date a   Female   child; that said child was living March 4, 1905, and is said to have been named Kissie Walker

her
Lucy x Wildcat
mark

Witnesses To Mark:
  ⎰ Chas E Webster
  ⎱ Frank C. Sabourin

    Subscribed and sworn to before me this 3 day of   May   , 1905.

Chas E Webster
Notary Public.

Sem NB 145
BIRTH AFFIDAVIT.

DEPARTMENT OF THE INTERIOR.
COMMISSION TO THE FIVE CIVILIZED TRIBES.

IN RE APPLICATION FOR ENROLLMENT, as a citizen of the   Seminole   Nation, of
Stella Walker   , born on the   7   day of   Sept   , 1903

Name of Father: Ben Walker   (1579)   a citizen of the   Seminole   Nation.
Name of Mother: Lizzie Walker   (1580)   a citizen of the   Seminole   Nation.

Postoffice   Wewoka I.T

(Child present)

AFFIDAVIT OF MOTHER.

UNITED STATES OF AMERICA, Indian Territory,
     Western   **DISTRICT.**

   I,   Lizzie Walker   , on oath state that I am   35   years of age and a citizen
by   blood   , of the   Seminole   Nation; that I am the lawful wife of   Ben
Walker   , who is a citizen, by blood   of the   Seminole   Nation; that a
Female   child was born to me on 7   day of   Sept   , 1903; that said child has
been named   Stella Walker   , and was living March 4, 1905.

her
Lizzie x Walker
mark

Witnesses To Mark:
   Chas E Webster
   Frank C. Sabourin

   Subscribed and sworn to before me this 3 day of   May   , 1905.

Chas E Webster
Notary Public.

AFFIDAVIT OF ATTENDING PHYSICIAN OR MID-WIFE.

UNITED STATES OF AMERICA, Indian Territory,
     Western   **DISTRICT.**

   I,   Lucy Wildcat   , a   midwife   , on oath state that I attended on Mrs.
Lizzie Walker   , wife of   Ben Walker   on the 7 day of Sept   , 1903; that
there was born to her on said date a   Female   child; that said child was living March
4, 1905, and is said to have been named Stella Walker

Witnesses To Mark:
{ Chas E Webster
{ Frank C. Sabourin

her
Lucy x Wildcat
mark

Subscribed and sworn to before me this 3 day of   May   , 1905.

Chas E Webster
Notary Public.

Sem NB 146

Muskogee, Indian Territory, June 27, 1906.

Wilmott[sic] & Wilhoit,
Attorneys at Law,
Wewoka, Indian Territory.

Gentlemen:

Receipt is hereby acknowledged of your letter of May 15, 1906, asking the status of the application of Simmer Mico, child of Talehasse and Mulleana Mico a new born citizen of the Seminole Nation.

In reply to your letter you are advised that affidavits to the birth of Simma Mico, child of Talehasse and Mulleana Mico, have been filed as an application for the enrollment of said child as a new born citizen of the Seminole Nation under the act of Congress approved March 3, 1905, and in the event further evidence is necessary to enable this office to pass upon the application for the enrollment of said child you and her parents will be duly notified.

Respectfully,

Commissioner.

Seminole-NB-146.

Muskogee, Indian Territory, June 29, 1905.

Tallahassee Micco,
  Keokuk Falls, Oklahoma Territory.

Dear Sir:

On May 1, 1905, you and your wife, Mulleana Micco, appeared before the Commission and made application for the enrollment of your son, Simma Micco, born September 4, 1902, as a citizen by blood of the Seminole Nation and at that time the affidavit of yourself and wife, as to the birth of said child, was taken.

There being no attending physician or midwife at the birth of said child it will be necessary, before his rights as a citizen by blood of the Seminole Nation, can be finally determined for you to file with the Commission the affidavits of two disinterested persons who know the circumstances attending the birth of the said child, when he was born and whether or not he was living on March 4, 1905.

Please give this matter your immediate attention.

Respectfully,

Chairman.

———————

NBS 146

Muskogee, Indian Territory, November 7, 1905.

Tallahassee Micco,
  Keokuk Falls, Oklahoma.

Dear Sir:

On June 29, 1905, you were requested to furnish this office with affidavits of two disinterested parties who know of the circumstances attending the birth of your minor child, Simma Micco, and for whose enrollment, as a citizen of the Seminole Nation, you made application on May 1, 1905.

You are now advised that it is very urgent that you furnish these affidavits inasmuch as it will be impossible for this office to determine without such affidavits the rights to enrollment of the said minor child.

This matter should receive your very earliest attention.

Respectfully,

Commissioner.

101

Sem NB 146   Father Roll 1598
BIRTH AFFIDAVIT.   Mother " 1599
DEPARTMENT OF THE INTERIOR.
COMMISSION TO THE FIVE CIVILIZED TRIBES.

IN RE APPLICATION FOR ENROLLMENT, as a citizen of the   Seminole   Nation, of
Simma Micco   , born on the 4   day of Sept   , 1902

Name of Father: Tallahasee Micco   a citizen of the   Seminole   Nation.
Name of Mother: Mulleana Micco   a citizen of the   Seminole   Nation.

Postoffice   Keokuk Falls, Okla Ter

AFFIDAVIT OF MOTHER.

UNITED STATES OF AMERICA, Indian Territory,
      Western   **DISTRICT.**

        I, Mulleana Micco   , on oath state that I am 30 years of age and a citizen by
blood   , of the   Seminole   Nation; that I am the lawful wife of   Tallahasee
Micco   , who is a citizen, by   blood   of the   Seminole   Nation; that a
male   child was born to me on 4th day of September   , 1902, that said child
has been named   Simma Micco   , and is now living.

                                her
                        Mulleana x Micco
Witnesses To Mark: mark
      Frank C. Sabourin
      Ed. Merrick

      Subscribed and sworn to before me this 1" day of   May   , 1905.
                                ~~her~~
                        ~~Mulleana x Micco~~
                                ~~mark~~   Notary Public.
                        Edward Merrick N.P.

                Husband
AFFIDAVIT OF ~~ATTENDING PHYSICIAN OR MID-WIFE.~~

UNITED STATES OF AMERICA, Indian Territory,
      Western   **DISTRICT.**

        I,   Tallahasee Micco   , ~~a~~——, on oath state that I attended on Mrs. Mulleana
Micco   my , wife ~~of~~——on the 4   day of   Sept , 1902; that there was born to

Applications for Enrollment of Seminole Newborn
Act of 1905   Volume II

her on said date a   male   child; that said child is now living and is said to have been
named Simma Micco   his
                                         Tallahassee x Micco
Witnesses To Mark: mark
   ⌠ Frank C. Sabourin
   ⌡ Ed. Merrick

   Subscribed and sworn to before me this 1" day of   May   , 1905.

                                    Ed. Merrick
                                       Notary Public.

Sem NB 146
BIRTH AFFIDAVIT.
DEPARTMENT OF THE INTERIOR.
COMMISSION TO THE FIVE CIVILIZED TRIBES.

IN RE APPLICATION FOR ENROLLMENT, as a citizen of the   Seminole   Nation, of
Simma Micco   , born on the 4   day of September , 1902

Name of Father: Tallahassee Micco   a citizen of the   Seminole   Nation.
Name of Mother: Mulleana Micco   a citizen of the   Seminole   Nation.

                    Postoffice   Keokuk Falls Okla

AFFIDAVIT OF MOTHER.

UNITED STATES OF AMERICA, Indian Territory, ⎫
      Western   DISTRICT.   ⎭

   I, Mulleana Micco   , on oath state that I am   years of age and a citizen by
blood   , of the   Seminole   Nation; that I am the lawful wife of   Tallahassee
Micco   , who is a citizen, by blood   of the   Seminole   Nation; that a
male   child was born to me on   fourth   day of   September   , 1902; that said
child has been named   Simma Micco   , and was living March 4, 1905.
                                         her
                                 Mulleana x Micco
Witnesses To Mark: mark
   ⌠ A S McKennon
   ⌡ Alice B. Davis
   Subscribed and sworn to before me this 10ᵗʰ day of   January   , 1906.

                                    B Guy Cutlip
                                       Notary Public.

103

AFFIDAVIT OF ATTENDING PHYSICIAN OR MID-WIFE.

UNITED STATES OF AMERICA, Indian Territory,
    Western   **DISTRICT.**

    I,   Martha Micco   , a midwife   , on oath state that I attended on Mrs. Mulleana Micco   , wife of Tallahassee Micco   on the 4th   day of   September , 1902; that there was born to her on said date a   male   child; that said child was living March 4, 1905, and is said to have been named Simma Micco

her

Martha x Micco

mark

Witnesses To Mark:
  { A S McKennon
  { Alice B. Davis

    Subscribed and sworn to before me this 10th   day of   January   , 1906.

B Guy Cutlip
Notary Public.

Sem NB 146

Sem NB 147
BIRTH AFFIDAVIT.

DEPARTMENT OF THE INTERIOR.
COMMISSION TO THE FIVE CIVILIZED TRIBES.

    IN RE APPLICATION FOR ENROLLMENT, as a citizen of the   Seminole   Nation, of Lizzie Renton   , born on the 1st   day of March , 1902

Name of Father: W[m] Renton   a citizen of the   U.S.   Nation.
Name of Mother: Nelly Renton   (1604)   a citizen of the   Seminole   Nation.

               Postoffice   Keokuk Falls O.T.

AFFIDAVIT OF ATTENDING PHYSICIAN OR MID-WIFE.

Okla

UNITED STATES OF AMERICA, ~~Indian~~ Territory, ⎱
Pottawatomie County   ~~DISTRICT.~~ ⎰

I,   W͟m Renton   , a   , on oath state that I attended on Mrs.   Nelly
Renton, wife of   W͟m Renton   on the   1ˢᵗ day of   March , 1902; that there was
born to her on said date a   Female   child; that said child is now living and is said to
have been named Lizzie Renton

Wm Renton

Witnesses To Mark:

⎰

Subscribed and sworn to before me this 22   day of   May   , 1905.

J E Thompson
Notary Public.

Com Ex Mar 13.07.

Sem NB 147

BIRTH AFFIDAVIT.

DEPARTMENT OF THE INTERIOR.
COMMISSION TO THE FIVE CIVILIZED TRIBES.

IN RE APPLICATION FOR ENROLLMENT, as a citizen of the   Seminole   Nation, of
Robert Renton   , born on the 29   day of May , 1904

Name of Father: W͟m Renton   a citizen of the   U.S.   Nation.
Name of Mother: Nelly Renton   a citizen of the   Seminole   Nation.

Postoffice   Keokuk Falls O.T.

AFFIDAVIT OF ATTENDING PHYSICIAN OR MID-WIFE.

Okla

UNITED STATES OF AMERICA, ~~Indian~~ Territory, ⎱
Pottawatomie County   ~~DISTRICT.~~ ⎰

I,   W͟m Renton   , a   , on oath state that I attended on Mrs.   Nelly
Renton, wife of   W͟m Renton   on the   29   day of   May , 1904; that there was born
to her on said date a   Boy   child; that said child is now living and is said to have
been named Robt. Renton

Wm Renton

Witnesses To Mark:

⎰

105

Subscribed and sworn to before me this 22   day of   May   , 1905.

J E Thompson
Notary Public.

Com Ex Mar 13.07.

———————

Sem NB 147
BIRTH AFFIDAVIT.

DEPARTMENT OF THE INTERIOR.
COMMISSION TO THE FIVE CIVILIZED TRIBES.

———————

IN RE APPLICATION FOR ENROLLMENT, as a citizen of the   Seminole   Nation, of
Minnie Renton   , born on the 29   day of October , 1900

Name of Father: Wm Renton	a citizen of the U.S.	Nation.
Name of Mother: Nelly Renton (1604)	a citizen of the Seminole	Nation.

Postoffice   Keokuk Falls O.T.

———————

Child at home

AFFIDAVIT OF MOTHER.

UNITED STATES OF AMERICA, Indian Territory,
   Western   **DISTRICT.**

   I,   Nellie Renton   , on oath state that I am 31   years of age and a citizen by
blood   , of the   Seminole   Nation; that I am the lawful wife of   Wm Renton   ,
who is a citizen, by ——— of the   U.S.   ~~Nation~~; that a   female   child was born
to me on   29   day of   October   , 1900, that said child has been named   Minnie
Renton   , and is now living.

Nellie Renton

Witnesses To Mark:

   Subscribed and sworn to before me this 18   day of   May   , 1905.

Chas E Webster
Notary Public.

———————

106

Applications for Enrollment of Seminole Newborn
Act of 1905   Volume II

AFFIDAVIT OF ATTENDING PHYSICIAN OR MID-WIFE.

UNITED STATES OF AMERICA, Indian Territory, ⎱
    Western   DISTRICT. ⎰

                                                  saw

I, Mollie Yaeger[sic]   , a midwife   , on oath state that I ~~attended on~~ Mrs. Nellie Renton   , wife of W͟m͟ Renton about two weeks after ~~on~~ the   29   day of October , 1900; that there was born to her on said date a   female   child; that said child is now living and is said to have been named Minnie Renton

                                 Mollie Yeager

Witnesses To Mark:

        {

    Subscribed and sworn to before me this 18   day of   May   , 1905.

                      Chas E Webster
                          Notary Public.

Sem NB 147
BIRTH AFFIDAVIT.
DEPARTMENT OF THE INTERIOR.
COMMISSION TO THE FIVE CIVILIZED TRIBES.

IN RE APPLICATION FOR ENROLLMENT, as a citizen of the   Seminole   Nation, of Minnie Renton   , born on the   29   day of October   , 1900

Name of Father: W͟m Renton   a citizen of the   U.S.   Nation.
Name of Mother: Nelly Renton   a citizen of the   Seminole   Nation.

                 Postoffice   Keokuk Falls O.T.

AFFIDAVIT OF ATTENDING PHYSICIAN OR MID-WIFE.
          Okla
UNITED STATES OF AMERICA, ~~Indian~~ Territory, ⎱
Pottawatomie County   ~~DISTRICT.~~ ⎰

I,   W͟m Renton   , a   , on oath state that I attended on Mrs. Nelly Renton, wife of W͟m Renton   on the   29 day of   October , 1900; that there was born to her on said date a   Female   child; that said child is now living and is said to have been named Minnie Renton

                      Wm Renton

Witnesses To Mark:

        {

Subscribed and sworn to before me this 22   day of   May   , 1905.

J E Thompson
Notary Public.

Com Ex Mar 13.07.

Sem NB 147
BIRTH AFFIDAVIT.

DEPARTMENT OF THE INTERIOR.
COMMISSION TO THE FIVE CIVILIZED TRIBES.

        IN RE APPLICATION FOR ENROLLMENT, as a citizen of the   Seminole   Nation, of
Robert Renton   , born on the   29   day of   May   , 1904

Name of Father: Wm Renton   a citizen of the   U.S.   Nation.
Name of Mother: Nelly Renton   (1604)   a citizen of the   Seminole   Nation.

Postoffice   Keokuk Falls O.T.

Child Present

AFFIDAVIT OF MOTHER.

UNITED STATES OF AMERICA, Indian Territory,
    Western   **DISTRICT.**

        I,   Nellie Renton   , on oath state that I am   31   years of age and a citizen by
blood   , of the   Seminole   Nation; that I am the lawful wife of   Wm Renton   ,
who is a citizen, by ~~blood~~ of the   U.S.   ~~Nation~~; that a   male   child was born
to me on   29   day of   May   , 1904, that said child has been named   Robert Renton ,
and is now living.

Nellie Renton

Witnesses To Mark:

    Subscribed and sworn to before me this   18   day of   May   , 1905.

Chas E Webster
Notary Public.

AFFIDAVIT OF ATTENDING PHYSICIAN OR MID-WIFE.

UNITED STATES OF AMERICA, Indian Territory,
    Western   **DISTRICT.**

                                                        saw
    I,   Mollie Menter   , a   midwife   , on oath state that I ~~attended on~~ Mrs.
Nellie Renton   , wife of   Wm Renton   four days after ~~on~~ the   29   day of   May ,

108

1904; that there was born to her on said date a   male   child; that said child is now living and is said to have been named Robert Renton

her
Molly x Minter
mark

Witnesses To Mark:
- Frank C. Sabourin
- Chas E Webster

Subscribed and sworn to before me this 18   day of   May   , 1905.

Chas E Webster
Notary Public.

Sem NB 147
BIRTH AFFIDAVIT.

DEPARTMENT OF THE INTERIOR.
COMMISSION TO THE FIVE CIVILIZED TRIBES.

IN RE APPLICATION FOR ENROLLMENT, as a citizen of the   Seminole   Nation, of Lizzie Renton   , born on the 1   day of March   , 1902

Name of Father: Wm Renton   a citizen of the   U.S.   Nation.
Name of Mother: Nelly Renton   (1604)   a citizen of the   Seminole   Nation.

Postoffice   Keokuk Falls O.T.

Child at home

AFFIDAVIT OF MOTHER.

UNITED STATES OF AMERICA, Indian Territory, ⎱
     Western   **DISTRICT.** ⎰

     I,   Nellie Renton   , on oath state that I am 31   years of age and a citizen by blood   , of the   Seminole   Nation; that I am the lawful wife of Wm Renton   , who is a citizen, by ——of the   U.S.   Nation; that a   female   child was born to me on 1st day of March   , 1902, that said child has been named   Lizzie Renton , and is now living.

Nellie Renton

Witnesses To Mark:

     Subscribed and sworn to before me this 18   day of   May   , 1905,

Chas E Webster
Notary Public.

109

Applications for Enrollment of Seminole Newborn
Act of 1905   Volume II

AFFIDAVIT OF ATTENDING PHYSICIAN OR MID-WIFE.

UNITED STATES OF AMERICA, Indian Territory,
    Western   **DISTRICT.**

                                                    saw

I,   Mollie Menter   , a   midwife   , on oath state that I ~~attended on~~ Mrs.
Nellie Renton   , wife of W$^{\underline{m}}$ Renton about two weeks after ~~on~~ the 1st day of
March , 1902; that there was born to her on said date a   female   child; that said child
is now living and is said to have been named Lizzie Renton

                                      her
                              Molly x Minter

Witnesses To Mark: mark
    { Frank C. Sabourin
    { Chas E Webster

Subscribed and sworn to before me this 18   day of   May   , 1905.

                                  Chas E Webster
                                      Notary Public.

DEPARTMENT OF THE INTERIOR.

COMMISSION TO THE FIVE CIVILIZED TRIBES.

Wewoka, Indian Territory, May 3, 1905.

In the matter of the application for the enrollment of Eddie Haney as a citizen by blood of the Seminole Nation.

Ahale Marthla, being duly sworn, testified as follows through Mrs. A. B. Davis, official interpreter:

Q. What is your name? A. Ahale Marthla.
Q. What is your age? A. 54.
Q. What is your post office? A. Keokuk Falls.
Q. Do you desire to make application for the enrollment of Eddie Haney as a citizen of the Seminole Nation? A. Yes sir.

Applications for Enrollment of Seminole Newborn
Act of 1905   Volume II

Q. What relation are you to Eddie Haney? A. I am his grandfather.
Q. Who is the father of Eddie Haney? A. Willy Haney.
Q. Is he a citizen of the Seminole Nation? A. Yes sir.

The father of the applicant is identified as Willy Haney, Seminole Card No. 485, Approved Roll No. 1618.

Q. Who is the mother of Eddie Haney? A. Polly Marthla Haney.
Q. Is Polly Haney living? A. No sir.
Q. When did she die? A. About four years ago.
Q. What relation was Polly to you? A. She was my daughter.

The mother of this child is identified on the records of the commission as Polly Marthla, Seminole Card No. 428, Approved Roll No. 1429.

Q. When was Eddie Haney born? A. About six years ago.

The records of the Commission examined, and it does not appear that Eddie Haney has ever been listed as an applicant for enrollment as a citizen of the Seminole Nation.

Q. Do you know why Eddie Haney has never been enrolled as a Seminole citizen? A. I went to the Dawes Commission and talked to them about it, but I don't understand why it was he was not enrolled. The father, Willy Haney, has never taken any interest in the child or looked after him, and never contributes anything to his support.
Q. Who has charge of Eddie Haney now? A. I have.
Q. Where is Willy Haney now? A. He lives near Keokuk Falls.
Q. Is Eddie Haney a full blood Seminole Indian? A. Yes sir.
Q. To what band does he belong? A. Thomas McGeisey.

Eddie Haney -2-

DEPARTMENT OF THE INTERIOR

COMMISSION TO THE FIVE CIVILIZED TRIBES.

In the matter of the application for the enrollment of Eddie Haney as a citizen by blood of the Seminole Nation.

Supplemental testimony taken at Wewoka, Indian Territory, May 4, 1905.

Thomas McGeisey, being duly sworn, testified as follows:

Q. What is your name? A. Thomas McGeisey.
Q. How old are you? A. 48.
Q. What is your post office? A. Wewoka, I. T.
Q. Are you acquainted with Ahale Marthla? A. Yes sir, he belongs to my band.

111

Q. Has he in his charge a child by the name of Eddie Haney? A. Yes sir.
Q. What relation is Eddie Haney to Ahale Marthla? A. He is his grandson.
Q. How old is Eddie Haney? A. I think he might be about six years old.
Q. Was he ever placed on the approved Seminole roll of 1901? A. No sir.
Q. Was he entitled to be placed on that roll? A. Yes sir.
Q. Do you know why the name of Eddie Haney was not placed on the Seminole roll?
A. I do not.
Q. Did you know the mother of Eddie Haney? A. Yes sir.
Q. Was she a Seminole citizen? A. Yes sir.
Q. Is she now living? A. No sir.
Q. Do you know the father of Eddie Haney? A. Yes sir.
Q. What is his name? A. Willy Haney.
Q. Is he a Seminole citizen? A. Yes sir.
Q. Was it by reason of neglect on the part of his father that the name of this child was not placed on the roll? A. Yes sir.
Q. This child, Eddie Haney, is now living? A. Yes sir.
Q. Living with his grandfather? A. Yes sir.
Q. Do you know where Willy Haney is at the present time? A. Yes sir, in the Seminole country.
Q. Was he ever sent to the penitentiary? A. Yes sir, I think he was.
Q. Has he given this child any attention since its birth? A. No sir.
Q. And you think that on account of the neglect of his parents, this child was omitted from the Seminole roll? A. Yes sir.
Q. What was the name of his mother? A. Pollu[sic] Marthla.
Q. Eddie Haney belongs to your band? A. Yes sir.
Q. And in your opinion he is entitled to enrollment as a Seminole citizen? A. Yes sir.
Q. What official position do you hold with the Seminoles? A. I am what they call the band chief.
Q. Of what band? A. Thomas McGeisey Band.

Frank C. Sabourin, being duly sworn, states that the foregoing two pages contain a full and complete transcript of his stenographic notes taken in said case on May 3rd and 4th, 1905.

Subscribed and sworn to before me this 5th day of May, 1905.

Notary Public.

Eddie Haney -3-

Okusky Miller, being duly sworn, testified as follows, through Mrs. A.B. Davis, official interpreter:

Q. What is your name? A. Okusky Miller.
Q. How old are you? A. 56.
Q. What is your post office? A. Keokuk Falls.

Q. Are you acquainted with a child named Eddie Haney? A. Yes sir.
Q. Who has that child in charge? A. Ahale Marthla.
Q. What relation is he to Eddie Haney? A. Grandfather.
Q. What is the name of the mother of Eddie Haney? A. Polly Marthla.
Q. is she living or dead? A. She is dead.
Q. Is she a citizen of the Seminole Nation? A. Yes sir.
Q. Who is the father of Eddie Haney? A. Willy Haney.
Q. Is he living? A. Yes sir.
Q. Is he a citizen of the Seminole Nation? A. Yes sir.
Q. How old is Eddie Haney? A. About six years old.
Q. Do you know whether his name appears on the approved roll of citizens by blood of the Seminole Nation? A. It is on the roll where he draws his headright, but no on the approved roll.
Q. Is Eddie Haney a citizen of the Seminole Nation? A. Yes sir.
Q. Is he entitled to be enrolled as a citizen of the Seminole Nation? A. Yes sir.
Q. he is living now? A. Yes sir.

Frank C. Sabourin, being duly sworn, states that he is a stenographer for the Commission to the Five Civilized Tribes, and that the foregoing three pages contain a full and complete transcript of his stenographic notes taken in said case on May 3rd and 4th, 1905.

Frank C. Sabourin

Subscribed and sworn to before me this 5th day of May, 1905.

⬡ Seal ⬡   Edward Merrick
                                            Notary Public.

Sem NB 148   Mother #1429; ~~Mother~~ #1618 Father
BIRTH AFFIDAVIT.
DEPARTMENT OF THE INTERIOR.
COMMISSION TO THE FIVE CIVILIZED TRIBES.

IN RE APPLICATION FOR ENROLLMENT, as a citizen of the   Seminole   Nation, of
Eddie Haney   , born ~~on the   day of   , 1~~ about 6 years ago

Name of Father: Willie Haney   a citizen of the   Seminole   Nation.
Name of Mother: Polly Marthla Haney   a citizen of the   Seminole   Nation.

                        Postoffice   Keokuk Falls Okla

Applications for Enrollment of Seminole Newborn
Act of 1905   Volume II

UNITED STATES OF AMERICA, Indian Territory, ⎫
    Western   **DISTRICT.** ⎭

    I,   Ahale Marthla ([#]1426)   , on oath state that I am   54   years of age and a citizen by   blood   , of the   Seminole   Nation; that I am the ~~lawful wife of~~   the father of Polly Marthla Haney deceased, who ~~is~~ was a citizen, by   blood   of the Seminole   Nation; that a   male   child was born to ~~me on~~ her about   ~~day of~~ 6 years ago ──,1─; that said child has been named   Eddie Haney   , and was living March 4, 1905.

                                          his

                                Ahale x Marthla

Witnesses To Mark: mark
    ⎰ Ed. Merrick
    ⎱ F.C. Sabourin

    Subscribed and sworn to before me this 3" day of   May   , 1905.

⟨Seal⟩   Edward Merrick
                                    Notary Public.

(The letter below does not belong to this applicant.)

                                                 <u>SNB-148</u>

                  Muskogee, Indian Territory, November 25, 1905.

The Honorable,
    The Secretary of the Interior.

Sir:
    Receipt is hereby acknowledged of Departmental letter of October 23, 1905 (ITD 15272-1905) in which it is requested that the Department be advised whether the records of this office show the enrollment on any tribal roll of Betsie Barnett, as a Seminole citizen.

    In reply I have the honor to report that this office is unable to identify the name of the said Betsie Barnett upon any of the tribal rolls of the Seminole Nation.

                      Respectfully,

                                  Acting Commissioner.

                  Testimony taken 5/3/03

<u>Eddie Haney</u>, aged 6 yrs. (about), son of Polly Marthla [#]1429, was omitted from former roll. He is Grandson of Ahale Marthar[sic] & Okkoseke[sic] Miller knows all about him.

114

Applications for Enrollment of Seminole Newborn
Act of 1905   Volume II

He is a full blood Seminole - Polly, the mother is dead & child lives with grandfather, Ahale Marthar.

Thos McGeisey
Band Chief

Seminole-NB-149.

Muskogee, Indian Territory, June 29, 1905.

Mollie Yeager,
    Keokuk Falls, Oklahoma Territory.

Dear Madam:

    On May 18, 1905, you appeared before the Commission and made application for the enrollment of your son, Thomas Little, Jr., born December 31, 1901, as a citizen by blood of the Seminole Nation and at that time submitted your affidavit only as to the birth of said child stating that no one attended you when he was born of said child.

    You are advised that before the rights of said child, as a citizen by blood of the Seminole Nation, can be finally determined it will be necessary for you to file with the Commission the affidavit of the attending midwife at the birth of said child and a blank for that purpose is inclosed herewith, which you are requested to have filled out, executed and returned to this office.

Respectfully,

B-C.

Chairman.

Env.

Sem NB 149
BIRTH AFFIDAVIT.

DEPARTMENT OF THE INTERIOR.
COMMISSION TO THE FIVE CIVILIZED TRIBES.

    IN RE APPLICATION FOR ENROLLMENT, as a citizen of the   Seminole   Nation, of David Little   , born on the 8 day of March , 1904

Name of Father: Thomas Little, dec'd   (1619)   a citizen of the Seminole Nation.

(1620)

Name of Mother: Mollie Yeager, formerly Little   a citizen of the Seminole Nation.

Postoffice   Keokuk Falls, O.T.

115

Child Present

AFFIDAVIT OF MOTHER.

UNITED STATES OF AMERICA, Indian Territory, ⎱
   Western   **DISTRICT.** ⎰

I, Mollie Yeager, formerly Little   , on oath state that I am 24 years of age and a citizen by   blood   , of the   Seminole   Nation; that I ~~am~~ was the lawful wife of Thomas Little, deceased , who is a citizen, by   blood   of the   Seminole Nation; that a   male   child was born to me on 8   day of   March   , 1904, that said child has been named   David Little   , and is now living.

                                        Mollie Yeager

Witnesses To Mark:
   {

Subscribed and sworn to before me this 18   day of   May   , 1905.

                              Chas E Webster
                                    Notary Public.

AFFIDAVIT OF ATTENDING PHYSICIAN OR MID-WIFE.

UNITED STATES OF AMERICA, Indian Territory, ⎱   No midwife
   Western   **DISTRICT.** ⎰   Father dead
                                                          saw
I,   Nellie Renton   , a ——————, on oath state that I ~~attended on~~ Mrs.   Molly Yeager   then , wife of Thomas Little   about two weeks after ~~on~~ the 8   day of March , 1904; that there was born to her on said date a   male   child; that said child is now living and is said to have been named David Little

                                        Nellie Renton

Witnesses To Mark:
   {

Subscribed and sworn to before me this 18   day of   May   , 1905.

                              Chas E Webster
                                    Notary Public.

Sem NB 149
BIRTH AFFIDAVIT.

DEPARTMENT OF THE INTERIOR.
COMMISSION TO THE FIVE CIVILIZED TRIBES.

IN RE APPLICATION FOR ENROLLMENT, as a citizen of the   Seminole   Nation, of
Thomas Little, Jr   , born on the   31   day of   December   , 1901

Name of Father: Thomas Little, dec'd   (1619)   a citizen of the   Seminole   Nation.
(1620)
Name of Mother: Mollie Yeager, formerly Little   a citizen of the   Seminole   Nation.

Postoffice   Keokuk Falls, O.T.

Child Present

AFFIDAVIT OF MOTHER.

UNITED STATES OF AMERICA, Indian Territory,
　　Western　　　　DISTRICT.

I, Mollie Yeager, formerly Little   , on oath state that I am 24 years of age and
a citizen by   blood   , of the   Seminole   Nation; that I ~~am~~ was the lawful wife
of   Thomas Little, deceased , who is a citizen, by   blood   of the   Seminole
Nation; that a   male   child was born to me on 31   day of   December   , 1901,
that said child has been named   Thomas Little, Jr   , and is now living.

Mollie Yeager

Witnesses To Mark:

Subscribed and sworn to before me this 18 day of   May   , 1905.

Chas E Webster
Notary Public.

Sem NB 149
BIRTH AFFIDAVIT.

DEPARTMENT OF THE INTERIOR.
COMMISSION TO THE FIVE CIVILIZED TRIBES.

IN RE APPLICATION FOR ENROLLMENT, as a citizen of the   Seminole   Nation, of
Thomas Little Jr   , born on the   31   day of   Dec   , 1901

Name of Father: Thomas Little   1619   a citizen of the   Seminole   Nation.
Name of Mother: Mollie Yeager   1620   a citizen of the   Seminole   Nation.

117

Applications for Enrollment of Seminole Newborn
Act of 1905   Volume II

Postoffice   Keokuk Falls, O.T.

_____

Okla

UNITED STATES OF AMERICA, ~~Indian~~ Territory, ⎫
Pottawatomie County   ~~DISTRICT.~~ ⎬

I,   Mehalia Stedham   , a mid wife   , on oath state that I attended on Mrs. Mollie Little (Yeager)   , wife of Thos Little   on the 31 day of Dec , 1901; that there was born to her on said date a   male   child; that said child was living March 4, 1905, and is said to have been named Thomas Little, Jr

her

Mehalia Stedham   x

Witnesses To Mark: mark
  ⎰ Jerome Edward
  ⎱ Grady Reynolds

Subscribed and sworn to before me   10 day of   July   , 1905.

JE Thompson
Notary Public.

Com. Ex. Mar. 13.07.

_____

Sem NB 150
BIRTH AFFIDAVIT.

DEPARTMENT OF THE INTERIOR.
COMMISSION TO THE FIVE CIVILIZED TRIBES.

_____

IN RE APPLICATION FOR ENROLLMENT, as a citizen of the   Seminole   Nation, of Lucinda Mitchell   , born on the 14 day of May , 1902

Name of Father: Legus Mitchell   20   a citizen of the Seminole   Nation.
Name of Mother: Toche   1642   a citizen of the Seminole   Nation.

Postoffice   Wewoka, I.T.

_____

118

(Child present)

AFFIDAVIT OF MOTHER.

UNITED STATES OF AMERICA, Indian Territory, ⎫
    Western   DISTRICT. ⎬
                           ⎭

I, Toche   , on oath state that I am   18   years of age and a citizen by blood   , of the   Seminole   Nation; that I am the lawful wife of   Legus Mitchell   , who is a citizen, by   blood   of the   Seminole   Nation; that a   Female child was born to me on   14   day of   May   , 1902; that said child has been named Lucinda Mitchell   , and was living March 4, 1905.

                                    Toche

Witnesses To Mark:

    Subscribed and sworn to before me this 3 day of   May   , 1905.

                    Chas E Webster
                      Notary Public.

AFFIDAVIT OF ATTENDING PHYSICIAN OR MID-WIFE.

UNITED STATES OF AMERICA, Indian Territory, ⎫   Mother of Toche who
    Western   DISTRICT. ⎬   attended her now dead
                                   know

I, William Mitchell   , a   , on oath state that I ~~attended on~~ Mrs. Toche   , wife of   Legus Mitchell (dead)   on the   14 day of   May   , 1902; that there was born to her on said date a   Female   child; that said child was living March 4, 1905, and is said to have been named   Lucinda Mitchell

                  Wm Mitchell

Witnesses To Mark:

    Subscribed and sworn to before me this 3 day of   May   , 1905.

                    Chas E Webster
                    Notary Public.

Applications for Enrollment of Seminole Newborn
Act of 1905   Volume II

Herman L. McMullin

Mother Liley on Seminole Card #498 Roll# 1651
Two sisters Evelyn May and Minnie Lorine McMullin on Seminole N.B. card 151 Roll Nos 182 and 183 respectively

Herman L. can be enrolled under Act Mar. 3-1905 if living March 4-1905 - *(Illegible)* such proof - Mothers[sic] address Chant, I.T.
  1/17/07   EM

DEPARTMENT OF THE INTERIOR,
COMMISSION TO THE FIVE CIVILIZED TRIBES.
MUSKOGEE LAND OFFICE, Jan. 18, 1900.

In the Matter of the Application of :
Delilah xxxx McMullen, and her   :
child, Herman Lee, as citizens of   :
the Creek Nation.   :
--:

Delilah McMullen being duly sworn, testified as follows.

By Mr. Angell:
Q What is your name? A Delilah McMullen
Q How old are you? A 22
Q What was your name before you were married? A Delilah Carr.
Q How many children have you? A One.
Q What is the name of that child? A Herman Lee McMullen.
Q How old is Herman? A 9 months old.
Q Are you a citizen of the Creek Nation? A Yes
Q Did you ever reside in any other nation? A No.
Q Did you not at one time, live in the Seminole Nation? A No.
Q What was the name of your father? A Washington Carr.
Q Was he a citizen of the Creek Nation? A Yes.
Q Full blood Indian? A Yes.
Q What was the name of your mother? A Tina Carr.
Q Was she a citizen of the Creek Nation? A She was a Seminole and part Creek.
Q Part Creek and part Seminole? A Yes sir.
Q Are you father and mother both living? A No, both dead.
Q How long have they been dead? A I can't tell you; when I was small.
Q A good many years? A Yes.
Q Was your name ever on the Seminole rolls? A Yes, I think it was
Q Do you recollect what Tribe you belonged to? A Thomas Little.
Q Did you ever draw any money in the Seminole Nation? A Not that I know of.
Q Is your name on the Creek roll? A No, couldn't find it on the Creek roll.
Q You mean you don't know? A No, I don't know.

Applications for Enrollment of Seminole Newborn
Act of 1905   Volume II

Q What Creek town do you belong to? A Hitchetee.
Q Do you know whether or not you drew the $29 in 1890? A No, I don't know.
Q Know whether anyone drew it for you? A No.
Q Did you draw the $14.40 in '95? A Yes.
Q What town? A Hitchetee; Mr. Gentry drew the money for me.
Q Did he give you the money? A Yes.
Q Do you know whether or not you were ever transferred from the Seminole rolls to the Creek rolls? A No.
Q What is the name of your husband? A Will McMullen.
Q Is he a citizen of the Creek Nation? A No.
Q Did you ever have any other name besides Delilah McMullen and Delilah Carr?
A No.
Q Did you have an Indian name? A No.
Q Nor no busk name? A No.
Q Have you got any brothers and sisters? A None that I know of; Albert Carr is the only one I ever knew of; I didn't know him.
Q Do you know whether or not he is living? A He is dead.
Q Was he a citizen of the Creek or Seminole Nation? A Seminole.
Q Was he a Seminole? A I don't know whether he was a Creek or Seminole.
Q Where have you been living during the last 8 or 10 years? A At Chekotah.
Q Have you lived there all your life? A Yes.
Q Do you know Mr. Wm. Gentry? A Yes.
Q Has he been acting as your guardian? A Yes.
Q For how long? A About 16 years.
Q Havn't[sic] you lived at one time in the orphan asylum at Okmulgee? A Yes sir.
Q How long did you live there? A I just went to school there.
Q Your home has always been near Chekotah with Wm. Gentry? A Yes.
Q How old are you now? A 22.

William E. Gentry, being duly sworn, testified as follows:

Q What is your name? A Wm. E. Gentry.
Q How old are you? A 57.
Q Are you a citizen of the Creek Nation? A Yes.
Q How long have you resided here? A Ever since 1865.
Q Do you know the applicant here, Delilah McMullen? A Yes.
Q How long have you known her? A Somewhere about 16 years.
Q Have you been looking after her affairs? A Yes sir.
Q In what capacity? A She was brought to our house when she was 6 or 7 years old; they was living up above us on Deep Fork, and she was brought to our house about that age, and we have been looking after her ever since.
Q She has been living with you all this time? A Most of the time. She went to school at Eufaula a little while, and then went to school at Okmulgee.
Q Have you been acting as her guardian? A Yes sir.
Q Have you ever been appointed her legal guardian? A Yes, by Judge Harjo (Beaver).
Q Did you know the mother and father of Delilah? A I knew the father well, Washington Carr.

Applications for Enrollment of Seminole Newborn
Act of 1905   Volume II

Q Did you know the mother? A No, I didn't know her; only knew of her; just heard what her name was

Q Was her father a full blood Creek? A Yes, he couldn't speak a word of English.

Q Was her mother a full blood Creek? A I think she was full blood Indian but part Seminole and part Creek, half and half; that was my understanding.

Q Do you know how long they have been dead? A No, they was dead, all of them, when she came to my house.

Q Do you know whether or not her name was ever on the Seminole roll? A Yes, her name was on the Seminole roll, and Thomas Little sent some down there to me; I disremember what payment it was.

Q You cannot recall the time that payment was made, nor the amount? A No, it was way back there; I think maybe it was sixty some odd dollars.

Q Has she ever been transferred to the Creek rolls? A Yes, she was transferred I suppose about 10 years ago; I don't remember when she went to school; I tried to get her into the school and they wouldn't let her because she was on the Seminole roll, and I had her transferred; I got Little to agree to the transfer and then they let her go to school; they would not let her get in the schools until after she had been transferred/[sic] I talked to the Trustees of the orphan schools, Gibson and Haynes and Belcher, and they wouldn't let her in until I got her transferred; they let her in both schools then.

Q Did you ever draw any money for Delilah in the Creek Nation? A Yes, I got the $14.40 and gave it to her--the last payment; I got it from her member; her members drew it; I think maybe it was W. P. LaBlanch.

Q What town? A Hitchetee.

Q Did you go and draw the money yourself? A No, I got it from one of the members of the council. I am satisfied it was Will Deblanche.

Q Is he now living? A No he is dead.

Q Do you know if Delilah has ever made any attempt to be enrolled as a citizen of the Seminole Nation? A No not to my knowledge; if she ever did, I know nothing about it.

Q Delilah is then, about three-quarters Creek? A Yes sir.

Q Has Delilah ever resided in the Seminole Nation? A No, not since she has been with me; and I don't have any idea she was ever out of the Creek Nation in her life.

Q Know whether or not she has any brothers or sisters? A She had a brother, but he is dead.

Q Is that all the relatives she had? A Yes, there is none of the family left; all dead except her; she is the only one I know of; mother, father, and brother, and she might have lost a sister sometime ago; but if she has got any other, I don't know it.

Q Did she ever have any Indian or busk name? A I am satisfied that she didn't; they have to be older before they have a busk name; some says Lila and some says Delilah, and we knew her father to be a Carr and we put the Carr to it.

> Delilah Carr McMullen recalled.

[sic] Did you ever try to be enrolled as a member of the Seminole Nation? A Not as I know of.

Q You would know if you did, wouldn't you? A Yes.

Applications for Enrollment of Seminole Newborn
Act of 1905   Volume II

Department of the Interior,
Commission to the Five Civilized Tribes

*I hereby certify, upon my official oath as stenographer
to above named Commission, that this transcript is a true,
full and correct translation of my stenographic notes.*

Francis R. Brown

DEPARTMENT OF THE INTERIOR
COMMISSION TO THE FIVE CIVILIZED TRIBES.
Muskogee, Indian Territory, April 19th, 1901.

In the matter of the application of Delilah McMullin and Herman Lee McMullin for enrollment as citizens of the Creek Nation.

W. E. GENTRY, being duly sworn, testified as follows:

(Examination by the Commission( )[sic].
Q What is your name? A W. E. Gentry.
Q What is your age? A 59.
Q What is your post office address? A Checotah.
Q Are you acquainted with Delilah McMullin? A Yes sir, one Delilah.
Q What was her maiden name? A Delilah Carr.
Q Do you know whether she is a citizen of the Creek Nation? A Thats[sic] my understanding.
Q How did she become a citizen of the Creek Nation, -- if you know? A By being transferred from the Seminole Nation to the Creek.
Q In what year was that? A Its[sic] been some good while ago, I don't remember the date, --- -it was when Alex Posey was superintendant[sic].
Q Of what school? A The Orphan school, and George Stidham of the Eufaula High School.
Q On what roll did you have her name placed on when you had her enrolled? A On the Creek roll.
Q Did she ever draw any money in the Creek Nation? A Yes sir, in the $14.40 payment.
Q Do you know whether or not she drew the $14.40 in the regular payment or in the Omitted payment? A I don't know,---- I don't remember, but I do remember getting the money for her.
Q What was her name then? What did she go by? A Delilah Carr.
Q Do you know what name she was carried on the Seminole roll before she was transferred? A Delilah Carr, I received money for her from the Seminole chief and received it as Delilah Carr from Thomas Little.
Q Who was Thomas Little? A Thomas Little was a Seminole, who was a band chief.
Q Delilah belong to his band in the Seminole Nation? A Yes sir.
Q Was she admitted by an act of Council in the Creek Nation? A I did'nt[sic] understand it that way, --- I don't think she was.

123

Q Who placed her name on the Creek roll? A Lets[sic] see, ------- I think it was Willie Lerblance.

Q What position did he hold at that time, if any? A He was king and belong to the Upper House.

Q In the Creek Nation? A Yes sir.

Q Did Delilah Carr have any brothers and sisters that you know of? A She had a brother who lived up there by me, but I disremember his name, but he is dead.

Q Did he die before or after she was transferred? A I don't know, I don't say about that.

Q Do you remember his name if your memory is refreshed? A I think his name was Albert Carr, -- I think now, as well as I remember, and her father was named Washington Carr, I would'nt[sic] be positive about his name but I would be about her father.

Q Do you think Albert was living about the time Delilah was transferred to the Creek Nation? A I don't remember about that, he may have been, -- I can't remember whether he was living or not, he was living up west, and I had nothing to do with him, -- this girl lived with him when she was about 9 or 10 years old.

(By the Commission).

> See Seminole tribal roll for the year 1895, page 21, on which appears the name of Albert and Liley following the name of Taply[sic], and Seminole tribal roll of 1897, page 190, on which appears the name of Liley following the name of Tapley.

Q Do you know anybody by the name of Tapley? A Yes sir.

Q You will state who he was? A I disremember now, but I think they were brothers and sisters, I had forgotten Tapley I was personally acquainted with Tapley.

Q Do you know Tapley's mother, who she was? A No sir.

Q Was Tapley a citizen of the Creek Nation? A That was my understanding, he's always been here, was raised here. He lived 12 miles from me, and that was my understanding, he never lived in the Seminole Nation and I know that.

Q Do you know a family of whom Betsey Powell was the head? A No sir.

Q Do you know any relatives of Tapley by the name of Perry, John? A No sir.

Q Do you know whether or not it was before or after the Colbert Citizenship Commission was in session that Delilah Carr was supposed to have been ~~admitted~~ transferred to the Creek Nation? A I don't remember, it was a case that did'nt[sic] go before them.

Q Do you know whether or not any money has been drawn in the Seminole Nation for Delilah Carr within the past 3 or 4 years? A Not that I know of, I am satisfied there Has'nt[sic].

(By Mr. Jackson, Attorney for applicant).

Q What did you do to have her transferred to the Creek Nation? A Well, I met Thomas Little in Okmulgee and then I asked him him[sic] to excuse her from that roll, who transferred her from that roll and I had her put on the Creek roll. I could'nt[sic] send her to school here and I wanted to send her to school in the Creek Nation, and asked him if he could'nt[sic] grant me this and he did so, and I put her on the Hitchitee roll and sent her to the Eufaula High School.

Q Was it customary to do this? A That was my understanding.

(By Mr. McKellop, Attorney for the Creek Nation).

Q Did Delilah Carr live with you from the time she was married? A She was the time up to the time, a short while before she was married. She was at Mrs. Coffee's when she was married.

Q How long from the time she lived at your home until she was married? A A very short time, only a few months.

Q How long is it since she was married? A I guess its[sic] about three years.

Q Three years? A About that time, may be four, I can't remember.

Q How many payments did you receive for her from the Seminole Nation? A I disremember that. I received payments until about 7 or 8 years ago, and after she was transferred I did'nt[sic] receive any more, and after I got her in school I never did receive any more.

Q This transfer that you speak of was made by you and Thomas Little of the Seminole Nation? A Yes sir, just an agreement as I understood he was to take her off of his roll and I was to have her put on the Creek roll,-- Hitchite.

Q You did'nt[sic] receive any certificate from the chief of the Seminole Nation stating that the name had been erased from the Seminole roll, and Council did'nt[sic] take any action in the matter? A There was nobody that knew anything about it. Willie Lerblance may have known something about it, he taken[sic] business in the transaction up there and when Thomas Little transferred her from the Seminole Nation he knews[sic] that the Hitchitees received her.

Q This transfer that you speak of was done at Okmulgee? A Yes sir, at Okmulgee.

(By the Commission).

Q Did you receive any money from the Seminole Nation for Delilah Carr after you drew the $14.40 from the Nation? A No sir.

See Seminole Card, Field number 498, and Dawes Commission Seminole roll number 1651.

Lona Cummings having been first duly sworn, upon her oath states that as stenographer to the Commission to the Five Civilized Tribes, she reported in full all proceedings had in the above entitled cause on the 19th day of April, A.D., 1901, and that the above and foregoing is a full, true and correct transcript of her stenographic notes of said proceedings on said date.

Lona Cummings

Subscribed and sworn to before
me at Muskogee, Indian Territory,
this 26 day of April, A.D., 1901.

Tams Bixby
Acting Chairman.

125

Applications for Enrollment of Seminole Newborn
Act of 1905 Volume II

DEPARTMENT OF THE INTERIOR,
COMMISSION TO THE FIVE CIVILIZED TRIBES.
Muskogee, Indian Territory, May 29, 1905.

In the matter of the application of Lila McMullin (nee Liley), Seminole citizen roll No. 1651, to enroll her minor children, Evelyn May and Minnie Lorine McMullin, under the act of March 3, 1905.

Lila McMullin, being duly sworn, testified as follows:

Q. What is your name? A. Lila McMullin.
Q. What is your post office address? A. Chant, Indian Territory
Q. What is your age? A. 27.
Q. Is your object in appearing before this Commission today to enroll your minor children, Evelyn May and Minnie Lorine McMullin A. Yes sir.
Q. When was Evelyn May McMullin born? A. She was born in 1902.
Q. When was Minnie Lorine McMullin born? A. Born in 1905.
Q. Are these children both living? A. Yes sir.
Q. Have you ever, before this time, filed with the Commission affidavits of the birth of these two children? A. Yes sir.
Q. Were they filed at this office, or at the Seminole Enrollment office at Wewoka? A. At this office.
Q. What was your father's name? A. Washington Carr.
Q. What was your mother's name? A. I don't remember. They both died when I was very small.
Q. To what band did you belong? A. To the Thomas Liley band.

(Witness is identified as Liley, Seminole citizen roll No. 1651, Field Card No. 498.)

WITNESS EXCUSED.

Eula Jeanes Branson, being duly sworn, states that as stenographer to the Commission to the Five Civilized Tribes, she reported the above proceedings had in this cause on the 29th. day of May, 1905, and that the above is a full and complete transcript of her stenographic notes taken in said cause on said date.

Eula Jeanes Branson

Subscribed and sworn to before me this the 29th. day of May, 1905.

W. S. Hawkins
Notary Public.

126

Sem. N.B. 151.   EM.

DEPARTMENT OF THE INTERIOR,
COMMISSIONER TO THE FIVE CIVILIZED TRIBES.

In the matter of the application for the enrollment of Herman L. McMullin, as a citizen of the Seminole Nation.

DECISION.

It appears from the record herein, that on September 13, 1899, there was filed with the Commission to the Five Civilized Tribes an application, in affidavit form, for the enrollment of Herman L. McMullin, as a citizen of the Creek Nation; that on January 15, 1900, Delilah McMullin appeared before said Commission and made application for the enrollment of herself and her minor child, the said Herman L. McMullin, as citizens of the Creek Nation, and that additional testimony in the matter of said application was offered on April 19, 1901.

It further appears from the records of this office that on May 11, 1901, the Commission to the Five Civilized Tribes rendered its decision in the matter of said application, denying the enrollment of said Delilah McMullin and Herman L. McMullin, as citizens of the Creek Nation. It further appears from said records that said Delilah McMullin is a duly enrolled citizen of the Seminole Nation, approved by the Secretary of the Interior April 2, 1901, opposite roll number 1651, under the name of "Liley".

It further appears from the record herein and the records of this office, that the applicant herein, Herman L. McMullin was born April 10, 1899, and living March 4, 1905, and is the child of Delilah McMullin, a recognized and enrolled citizen of the Seminole Nation, and William M. McMullin, a non-citizen.

Although the original application in this case was made for applicant as a citizen of the Creek Nation, the Commissioner will hold in this case that same is an application for enrollment as a citizen of the Seminole Nation.

The Act of Congress approved March 3, 1905 (33 Stats., 1048), among other things provides:

"That the Commission to the Five Civilized Tribes is authorized for ninety days after the date of the approval of this act to receive and consider applications for enrollment of infant children born prior to March fourth, nineteen hundred and five, and living on said latter date, to citizens of the Seminole tribe whose enrollment has been approved by the Secretary of the Interior; and to enroll and make allotments to such children, giving to each an equal number of acres of land, and such children shall also share equally with other citizens of the Seminole tribe in the distribution of all other tribal property and funds."

Although the applicant herein, Herman L. McMullin, was born to a Seminole citizen prior to December 31, 1899, and living on said date, the Commissioner is of the opinion that he is not authorized to enroll said applicant under the provisions of the Seminole agreement approved June 2, 1900 (31 Stats. 250), for the reason that the

Department in its letter of February 14, 1902 (I.T.D. 1022-1902) affirming the decision of the Commission to the Five Civilized Tribes of May 11, 1901, herein referred to, held that "While the Department feels authorized to make corrections in the roll approved by it April 2, 1901, ... it does not consider that it is warranted in adding any name to that roll of any person whose claim to citizenship was not presented to your Commission or the Department prior to the approval of the roll". February 26, 1902 (I.T.D. 1022 and 1331-1901), the Department adhered to its former decision of February 14, 1902, above referred to.

It is, therefore, ordered and adjudged that under the provisions of law above quoted said Herman L. McMullin is entitled to be enrolled as a citizen of the Seminole Nation, and the application for his enrollment as such is accordingly granted.

Tams Bixby   COMMISSIONER.

Muskogee, Indian Territory,

FEB 5 1907

Sem NB 151
BIRTH AFFIDAVIT.

DEPARTMENT OF THE INTERIOR.
COMMISSION TO THE FIVE CIVILIZED TRIBES.

IN RE APPLICATION FOR ENROLLMENT, as a citizen of the   Seminole   Nation, of Minnie Lorine McMullin   , born on the 6th   day of January   , 1905

Name of Father: William W McMullin   a citizen of the United States Nation.
Name of Mother: Lila McMullin   a citizen of the Seminole   Nation.
(nee Liley 1651)
Postoffice   Chant I.T.

AFFIDAVIT OF MOTHER.

UNITED STATES OF AMERICA, Indian Territory, ⎫
    Central   DISTRICT. ⎭

I, Lila McMullin   , on oath state that I am   27   years of age and a citizen by   Blood   , of the   Seminole   Nation; that I am the lawful wife of   William W McMullin   , who is a citizen, by   of the   United States   Nation; that a Female   child was born to me on 6th   day of January   , 1905; that said child has been named   Minnie Lorine McMullin   , and was living March 4, 1905.

Lila McMullin

Witnesses To Mark:
{

128

Subscribed and sworn to before me this 12th day of   April   , 1905.

Jas H Deets
Notary Public.

AFFIDAVIT OF ATTENDING PHYSICIAN OR MID-WIFE.

UNITED STATES OF AMERICA, Indian Territory,⎫
DISTRICT.⎰

I, B. J. McClure   , a   Physician   , on oath state that I attended on Mrs. Lila McMullin   , wife of   William W McMullin   on the 6th day of   January , 1905; that there was born to her on said date a   Female   child; that said child was living March 4, 1905, and is said to have been named Minnie Lorine McMullin

B. J. McClure, M.D.

Witnesses To Mark:

⎰

Subscribed and sworn to before me 13th day of   April   , 1905.

Jas H Deets
Notary Public.

Sem NB 151
BIRTH AFFIDAVIT.

DEPARTMENT OF THE INTERIOR.
COMMISSION TO THE FIVE CIVILIZED TRIBES.

IN RE APPLICATION FOR ENROLLMENT, as a citizen of the   Seminole   Nation, of Evelyn May McMullin   , born on the 3rd   day of June   , 1902

Name of Father: William W McMullin   a citizen of the United States Nation.
Name of Mother: Lila McMullin   a citizen of the   Seminole   Nation.
(nee Liley 1651)
Postoffice   Chant I.T.

AFFIDAVIT OF MOTHER.

UNITED STATES OF AMERICA, Indian Territory,⎫
Central   DISTRICT.⎰

I, Lila McMullin   , on oath state that I am   27   years of age and a citizen by   Blood   , of the   Seminole   Nation; that I am the lawful wife of   William W McMullin   , who is a citizen, by   of the   United States   Nation; that a

Girl   child was born to me on 3rd   day of   June   , 1902; that said child has been named   Evelyn May McMullin   , and was living March 4, 1905.

Lila McMullin

Witnesses To Mark:

Subscribed and sworn to before me this 12th day of   April   , 1905.

Jas H Deets
Notary Public.

AFFIDAVIT OF ATTENDING PHYSICIAN OR MID-WIFE.

UNITED STATES OF AMERICA, Indian Territory,
          DISTRICT.

I, J. M^cD. Massie   , a   Physician   , on oath state that I attended on Mrs. Lila McMullin   , wife of   Wm W. McMullin   on the 3rd   day of   June , 1902; that there was born to her on said date a   female   child; that said child was living March 4, 1905, and is said to have been named Evelyn May McMullin

J M^cD Massie

Witnesses To Mark:

Subscribed and sworn to before me 15th   day of   April   , 1905.

Jas H Deets
Notary Public.

Department of the Interior,
COMMISSION TO THE FIVE CIVILIZED TRIBES.

IN RE Application for Enrollment, as a citizen of the   Creek   Nation, of Herman L. McMullin   , born on the   10th   day of April   , 1899

Name of Father: Wm W. McMullin   a citizen of the United States Nation.
Name of Mother: Delilah McMullin   a citizen of the   Creek   Nation.

Post-office: Checotah, Ind. Ter.

Applications for Enrollment of Seminole Newborn
Act of 1905   Volume II

AFFIDAVIT OF MOTHER.

UNITED STATES OF AMERICA, ⎫
   INDIAN TERRITORY.   ⎬
   Northern   District. ⎭

I,   Delilah McMullin   , on oath state that I am   22   years of age and a citizen by   blood , of the   Creek   Nation; that I am the lawful wife of Wm W. McMullin   , who is a citizen, by birth of the   United States ~~Nation~~; that a   male child was born to me on   10th   day of April   , 1899 , that said child has been named Herman L. McMullin   , and is now living.

Delliah[sic] McMullin

Subscribed and sworn to before me this 13th *day of* September , 1899.

Tams Bixby
~~NOTARY PUBLIC.~~
Commissioner

AFFIDAVIT OF ATTENDING PHYSICIAN OR MID-WIFE.

UNITED STATES OF AMERICA, ⎫
   INDIAN TERRITORY.   ⎬
   Northern   District. ⎭

I,   Nancy Wood   , a midwife , on oath state that I attended on Mrs. Delilah McMullin , wife of Wm W. McMullin on the 10th day of April , 1899 ; that there was born to her on said date a   male   child; that said child is now living and is said to have been named Herman L. McMullin

her
Nancy x Wood
mark

Witnesses to mark:
   P B Hopkins
   Tams Bixby
Subscribed and sworn to before me this 13th *day of* September , 1899.

Tams Bixby
~~NOTARY PUBLIC.~~
Commissioner

131

Applications for Enrollment of Seminole Newborn
Act of 1905 Volume II

Wewoka, Indian Territory, May 17, 1905.

Lila McMullin,
    Care William W. McMullin,
        Chant, Indian Territory.

Madam:

On April 21, 1905, there were filed with the Commission applications for the enrollment of Evelyn May McMullin and Minnie Lorine McMullin, minor children of William W. McMullin, a citizen of the United States, and yourself.

The Commission is unable to identify you on the approved Seminole Roll, and it will be necessary for you to appear before the Seminole Enrollment Office, at Wewoka, Indian Territory, prior to June 1, 1905, or before the General Office of the Commission at Muskogee, Indian Territory, in order that such identification may be made.

Respectfully,

Clerk in Charge.

Sem. NB 151

Muskogee, Indian Territory, June 22, 1906.

Liley McMullin,
    Chant, Indian Territory.

Dear Sir[sic]:

Receipt is hereby acknowledged of your letter of June 12, 1906, asking what action to take in the matter of the application for the enrollment of your child Herman Lee McMullin for whom affidavits were forwarded in July 1899.

In reply to your letter you are advised that it appears from the records of this office that Evelyn May McMullin and Minnie Lorine McMullin have been enrolled as new born citizens of the Seminole Nation under the act of Congress approved March 3, 1905, and their enrollment as such approved by the Secretary of the Interior July 22, 1905.

You are advised, however, that this office is unable to identify your child Herman McMullin as an applicant for enrollment as a new born citizen of the Seminole Nation.

Respectfully,

Commissioner.

Applications for Enrollment of Seminole Newborn
Act of 1905   Volume II

Sem. N. B. -151

Muskogee, Indian Territory, January 23, 1907.

Lila McMullin,
%William W. McMullin,
Chant, Indian Territory.

Dear Madam:

In the matter of the application for the enrollment of Herman L. McMullin as a New Born citizen of the Seminole Nation, you are advised that it will be necessary that you forward at once affidavits of yourself and two disinterested witnesses to the effect that said child is now living and if not living, the date of his death. These affidavits should be forwarded so as to reach this office not later than January 29, 1907.

Respectfully,

Commissioner.

_____

Seminole
NB-151

Muskogee, Indian Territory, January 30, 1907.

Lila McMullin,
Chant, Indian Territory.

Dear Madam:

Receipt is hereby acknowledged of your affidavit and the affidavits of J. W. Barnes and T. J. Hammons relative to the birth of your child, Herman L. McMullin, and the same have been filed with the record in the matter of the enrollment of said child as a citizen by blood of the Seminole Nation.

Respectfully,

Commissioner.

_____

Sem. N.B. 151

COPY

Muskogee, Indian Territory, February 5, 1907.

Lila McMullin,
Chant, Indian Territory.

Dear Madam:

Applications for Enrollment of Seminole Newborn
Act of 1905   Volume II

Inclosed herewith you will find a copy of the decision of the Commissioner to the Five Civilized Tribes, rendered February 5, 1907, granting the application for the enrollment of Herman L. McMullin as a citizen of the Seminole Nation.

You are hereby advised that the name of Herman L. McMullin will be placed upon the next schedule of citizens of the Seminole Nation, to be submitted to the Secretary of the Interior for his approval.

Respectfully,

SIGNED *Tams Bixby*

Commissioner.

Incl. Sem. NB. 151.
Registered.

Sem. N.B. 151   **COPY**

Muskogee, Indian Territory, February 5, 1907.

Wilmott[sic] and Wilhoit,
    Attorneys at Law,
        Wewoka, Indian Territory.

Dear Sirs:

Inclosed herewith you will find a copy of the decision of the Commissioner to the Five Civilized Tribes, rendered February 5, 1907, granting the application or the enrollment of Herman L. McMullin as a citizen of the Seminole Nation.

You are hereby advised that the name of Herman L. McMullin will be placed upon the next schedule of citizens of the Seminole Nation, to be submitted to the Secretary of the Interior for his approval.

Respectfully,

SIGNED *Tams Bixby*

Commissioner.

Incl. Sem. N. B. 151.
Registered.

Indian Territory   ⎱
   Central District ⎰

J. W. Barnes after being duly sworn deposes and says My name is J. W. Barnes I am 23 years old. I live in Chant I.T. Choctaw Nation. I am a harness maker by trade. I am well acquainted with Lila McMullin and her husband William W. McMullin. I know they have a boy about seven or eight years old. Said boy is named Herman McMullin. I

134

am not related to Lila McMullin or her husband William W. McMullin neither by blood or marriage

J.W. Barnes

Subscribed & sworn before me this 26 Jan. 1907

My Com expires   Floyd Nevins
     Jan 17-1910

Indian Territory   ⎫
   Central District ⎭

T.J. Hammons after being duly sworn deposes and says My name is T.J. Hammons. I am 50 years old. I am a miner by trade. I live in Chant I.T. Choctaw Nation. I am well acquainted with Lila McMullin and her husband William W. McMullin. I have known Lila McMullin about five years and know she has a boy about 8 years old. Said boy is now living and named Herman McMullin. I am not related by blood or marriage to Lila McMullin or her husband William W. McMullin.

(No signature given.)

Subscribed and sworn before this 26 day of January 1907

Floyd Nevins

My Com expires
   Jan. 17-1910

Indian Territory   ⎫
   Central District ⎭

Lila McMullin after being duly sworn deposes and says My name is Lila McMullin. I am 28 years old. I am the lawful wife of Wm. W. McMullin. I live in Chant, I.T. Choctaw Nation. That on April 10-1899 there was born to me a male child. Said child is now living and named Herman Lee McMullin. My name appears on the Seminole roll number 1651. And allotment certificate 2240.

Lila McMullin

Subscribed & sworn before me this 26 day of Jan. 1907.

Floyd Nevins

My com expires Jan. 17-1910

Seminole-NB-152.

Muskogee, Indian Territory, June 29, 1905.

Commission to the Five Civilized Tribes,
Creek Enrollment Division.

Gentlemen:

On May 19, 1905, there was filed with the Commission application for the enrollment of Ollie Conner born December 5, 1901, as a citizen by blood of the Seminole Nation. It is stated in said application that said child is a daughter of Tom Conner, a citizen by blood of the Creek Nation, and Nelly Conner, formerly Foster, a citizen by blood of the Seminole Nation.

You are requested to inform the Seminole Enrollment Division as to whether or not any application has been made to the Commission for the enrollment of Ollie Conner as a citizen of the Creek Nation and if so, what disposition, if any, has been made of such application.

Respectfully,

Chairman.

HGH

DEPARTMENT OF THE INTERIOR.
COMMISSION TO THE FIVE CIVILIZED TRIBES.

Muskogee, Indian Territory, July 11, 1905.

Seminole Enrollment Division,
General Office.

Gentlemen:

Receipt is acknowledged of your letter of June 29, 1905 (Sem. NB. 152), in which you ask if application for the enrollment as a citizen of the Creek Nation has been made for Ollie Conner, child of Tom Conner, a citizen of the Creek Nation, and Nellie Conner, formerly Foster, a citizen by blood of the Seminole Nation.

In reply you are advised that the records of this office have been examined and it does not appear that application has been made for the enrollment of said Ollie Conner, as a citizen of the Creek Nation.

Respectfully,

Tams Bixby   Commissioner.

Sem NB 152
BIRTH AFFIDAVIT.

DEPARTMENT OF THE INTERIOR.
COMMISSION TO THE FIVE CIVILIZED TRIBES.

IN RE APPLICATION FOR ENROLLMENT, as a citizen of the   Seminole   Nation, of
Ollie Conner   , born on the 5 day of Dec   , 1901

Name of Father: Tom Conner   a citizen of the   Creek   Nation.
Name of Mother: Nelly Conner   1652   a citizen of the   Seminole   Nation.
                        formerly Foster
                              Postoffice   Quick, IT

(Child present)

AFFIDAVIT OF MOTHER.

UNITED STATES OF AMERICA, Indian Territory, ⎫
      Western   DISTRICT. ⎰

        I, Nelly Conner   , on oath state that I am   48   years of age and a citizen by
blood   , of the   Seminole   Nation; that I am the lawful wife of   Tom Conner   ,
who is a citizen, by blood   of the   Creek   Nation; that a   Female   child
was born to me on   5   day of   Dec   , 1901; that said child has been named   Ollie
Conner   , and was living March 4, 1905.

                                              her
                                      Nelly x Conner
Witnesses To Mark: mark
      ⎰ Chas E Webster
      ⎱ Frank C. Sabourin

        Subscribed and sworn to before me this 19 day of   May   , 1905.

                              Chas E Webster
                                    Notary Public.

AFFIDAVIT OF ATTENDING PHYSICIAN OR MID-WIFE.
No midwife

UNITED STATES OF AMERICA, Indian Territory, ⎫
      Western   DISTRICT. ⎰
                                              help to
        I,   Tom Conner   , a   , on oath state that I attended on Mrs.   Nelly
Conner   , wife of   my wife   on the 5 day of   Dec   , 1901; that there was
born to her on said date a   Female   child; that said child was living March 4, 1905,
and is said to have been named Ollie Conner   his
                              Tom x Conner
                                    mark

137

Witnesses To Mark:
{ Chas E Webster
{ Frank C. Sabourin

Subscribed and sworn to before me this   19 day of   May   , 1905.

Chas E Webster
Notary Public.

J. B. WILSON
DEALER IN
GENERAL MERCHANDISE.

Creek, I. T.,   190__

Western District
    Indian Territory

We - Faga Bluford and his wife Winey Bluford (Foster) do solemnly swear that our son Sunday Bluford was born May 29-1901 and that our daughter Wesie[sic] Bluford was born January 16, 1903 and that both are still now living (and Nellie Foster was present at their birth) and they are entitled to be enrolled as Creek citizens by blood.

Subscribed on this the 26th day of May 1905.

Faga Bluford
her
Winey x Bluford
mark

Western District }
Indian Territory }

Personally appeared before me Faga Bluford and his wife Minie Bluford both well known to me and subscribed and swore to above statement. This the 26th day of May, 1905.

JB Wilson
Notary Public

Sem NB 153
BIRTH AFFIDAVIT.

DEPARTMENT OF THE INTERIOR.
COMMISSION TO THE FIVE CIVILIZED TRIBES.

IN RE APPLICATION FOR ENROLLMENT, as a citizen of the   Seminole   Nation, of
Wisey Bluford   , born on the   16   day of   Jan   , 1903

Name of Father: Faga Bluford   a citizen of the   Creek   Nation.
Name of Mother: Winey Bluford   1653   a citizen of the   Seminole   Nation.
                      nee Winey
                          Postoffice   Quick I.T.

AFFIDAVIT OF MOTHER.

Mother will be in
UNITED STATES OF AMERICA, Indian Territory,   next week.
.... DISTRICT.

I, ..., on oath state that I am ....years of age and a citizen by ...., of the
.... Nation; that I am the lawful wife of ...., who is a citizen, by .... of
the .... Nation; that a .... child was born to me on ..... day of..............., 1......,
that said child has been named ...., and was living March 4, 1905.

Witnesses To Mark:

See affidavit of mother attached to
B/A of Sunda[sic] Bluford #330

Subscribed and sworn to before me this .... day of..............., 1905.

Notary Public.

AFFIDAVIT OF ATTENDING PHYSICIAN OR MID-WIFE.

UNITED STATES OF AMERICA, Indian Territory,
      Western   DISTRICT.

I,   Nelly Conner   , a   Mother of Winey Bluford   , on oath state that I
attended on Mrs.   Winey Bluford   , wife of   Faga Bluford   on the   16 day of
Jany   , 1903; that there was born to her on said date a   Female   child; that said
child was living March 4, 1905, and is said to have been named Wisey Bluford

her
Nelly x Conner
mark

Witnesses To Mark:
  ⎰ Chas E Webster
  ⎱ Frank C. Sabourin

Subscribed and sworn to before me 19   day of   May   , 1905.

Chas E Webster
Notary Public.

Sem NB 153
BIRTH AFFIDAVIT.

DEPARTMENT OF THE INTERIOR.
COMMISSION TO THE FIVE CIVILIZED TRIBES.

IN RE APPLICATION FOR ENROLLMENT, as a citizen of the   Seminole   Nation, of
Sunday Bluford   , born on the   29   day of May   , 1901

Name of Father: Faga Bluford   a citizen of the   Creek   Nation.
Name of Mother: Winey Bluford   1653   a citizen of the   Seminole   Nation.
                         nee Winey
                         Postoffice   Quick I.T.

AFFIDAVIT OF MOTHER.

Mother will
be in <u>next</u> week.

UNITED STATES OF AMERICA, Indian Territory, ⎱
.... **DISTRICT.** ⎰

I, ..., on oath state that I am ....years of age and a citizen by ...., of the
.... Nation; that I am the lawful wife of ...., who is a citizen, by .... of
the .... Nation; that a .... child was born to me on ..... day of ...., 1......,
that said child has been named ...., and was living March 4, 1905.

Witnesses To Mark:
  ⎰ ....
  ⎱ ....

Subscribed and sworn to before me this .... day of ...., 1905.

Notary Public.

Applications for Enrollment of Seminole Newborn
Act of 1905   Volume II

AFFIDAVIT OF ATTENDING PHYSICIAN OR MID-WIFE.

UNITED STATES OF AMERICA, Indian Territory, ⎫
   Western   DISTRICT. ⎭

I, Nelly Conner , a Mother , on oath state that I attended on Mrs.
Winey Bluford , wife of Faga Bluford on the 29 day of May , 1901;
that there was born to her on said date a Male child; that said child was living
March 4, 1905, and is said to have been named Sunday Bluford

her

Nelly x Conner

mark

Witnesses To Mark:
  ⎰ Chas E Webster
  ⎱ Frank C. Sabourin

Subscribed and sworn to before me 19 day of May , 1905.

Chas E Webster

Notary Public.

Seminole-NB-153.

Muskogee, Indian Territory, June 29, 1905.

Commission to the Five Civilized Tribes,
    Creek Enrollment Division.

Gentlemen:

On May 19, 1905, there was filed with the Commission application for the
enrollment of Sunday Bluford, born May 29, 1901, and Wisey Bluford, born January 16,
1903, as citizens by blood of the Seminole Nation. It appears that the father of said
children is Faga Bluford, a citizen of the Creek Nation, and that their mother is Winey
Bluford, a citizen of the seminole[sic] Nation.

You are requested to inform the Seminole Enrollment Division as to whether or
not any application has been made to the Commission for the enrollment of said children
as citizens of the Creek Nation and if so what disposition, if any, has been made of said
application.

Respectfully,

Chairman.

141

HGH
DEPARTMENT OF THE INTERIOR.
COMMISSION TO THE FIVE CIVILIZED TRIBES.

Sem. Fr. NB. 153).

Muskogee, Indian Territory, July 11, 1905.

Seminole Enrollment Division,
General Office.

Gentlemen:

Receipt is acknowledged of your communication of June 29, 1905 (Sem. Fr. NB. 153), in which you ask if application for enrollment as citizens of the Creek Nation has been made for Sunday and Wisey Bluford, children of Faga Bluford, a citizen of the Creek Nation, and Winey Bluford, a citizen of the Seminole Nation.

In reply you are advised that the records of this office have been examined and it does not appear that application has been made for the enrollment of said Sunday and Wisey Bluford, or either of them, as citizens of the Creek Nation.

Respectfully,
Tams Bixby   Commissioner.

Sem NB 154
BIRTH AFFIDAVIT.
DEPARTMENT OF THE INTERIOR.
COMMISSION TO THE FIVE CIVILIZED TRIBES.

IN RE APPLICATION FOR ENROLLMENT, as a citizen of the   Seminole   Nation, of
Jacob Harrison   , born on the 20"   day of Oct , 1904

Name of Father: Jefferson Harrison   (#35)   a citizen of the   Seminole   Nation.
Name of Mother: Hilly Harrison   (#1695)   a citizen of the   "   Nation.

Postoffice   Wewoka Ind Ter.

Applications for Enrollment of Seminole Newborn
Act of 1905   Volume II

(Child present)

AFFIDAVIT OF MOTHER.

UNITED STATES OF AMERICA, Indian Territory, ⎱
Western   DISTRICT.   ⎰

I,   Hilly Harrison   , on oath state that I am   23   years of age and a citizen by   blood   , of the   Seminole   Nation; that I am the lawful wife of   Jefferson Harrison   , who is a citizen, by blood   of the   Seminole   Nation; that a male   child was born to me on   20th day of   October   , 1904; that said child has been named   Jacob Harrison   , and was living March 4, 1905.

her
Hilly x Harrison
mark

Witnesses To Mark:
⎰ Ed. Merrick
⎱ F.C. Sabourin

Subscribed and sworn to before me this 3" day of   May   , 1905.

⟨Seal⟩

Edward Merrick
Notary Public.

AFFIDAVIT OF ATTENDING PHYSICIAN OR MID-WIFE.

UNITED STATES OF AMERICA, Indian Territory, ⎱
Western   DISTRICT.   ⎰

I,   Eliza Johnson   , a   midwife   , on oath state that I attended on Mrs. Hilly Harrison   , wife of   Jefferson Harrison   on the   20th day of   Oct   , 1904; that there was born to her on said date a   male   child; that said child was living March 4, 1905, and is said to have been named   Jacob Harrison

her
Eliza x Johnson
mark

Witnesses To Mark:
⎰ Edward Merrick
⎱ F.C. Sabourin

Subscribed and sworn to before me this 3" day of   May   , 1905.

⟨Seal⟩

Edward Merrick
Notary Public.

Sem NB 154
BIRTH AFFIDAVIT.

DEPARTMENT OF THE INTERIOR.
COMMISSION TO THE FIVE CIVILIZED TRIBES.

IN RE APPLICATION FOR ENROLLMENT, as a citizen of the   Seminole   Nation, of
Emma Sewell   , born ~~on the~~ in   ~~day of~~ May   , 1902

Name of Father: Tom Sewell   a citizen of the   Creek   Nation.
Name of Mother: Hilly Harrison   ($^{\#}$1695)   a citizen of the   Seminole   Nation.

Postoffice

Child present

AFFIDAVIT OF MOTHER.

UNITED STATES OF AMERICA, Indian Territory, ⎫
       Western   **DISTRICT.**   ⎰

I,   Hilly Harrison   , on oath state that I am   23   years of age and a citizen
by   blood   , of the   Seminole   Nation; that I ~~am~~ was the lawful wife of   Tom
Sewell (but am now separated)   , who is a citizen, by   blood   of the   Creek
Nation; that a   female   child was born to me ~~on   day of~~ in May   , 1902; that
said child has been named   Emma Sewell   , and was living March 4, 1905.

                                    her
                            Hilly x Harrison
Witnesses To Mark: mark
 ⎰ Ed. Merrick
 ⎱ F.C. Sabourin

Subscribed and sworn to before me this 3" day of   May   , 1905.

⟨ Seal ⟩

                            Edward Merrick
                                Notary Public.

AFFIDAVIT OF ATTENDING PHYSICIAN OR MID-WIFE.

UNITED STATES OF AMERICA, Indian Territory, ⎫
       Western   **DISTRICT.**   ⎰

I,   Eliza Johnson   , a   midwife   , on oath state that I attended on Mrs.
Hilly Harrison   who was the , wife of   Tom Sewell, sometime ~~on the   day of~~   in
May   , 1902; that there was born to her on said date a   female   child; that said
child was living March 4, 1905, and is said to have been named   Emma Sewell

Witnesses To Mark:
{ Ed Merrick
{ F.C. Sabourin

her
Eliza x Johnson
mark

Subscribed and sworn to before me this 3" day of   May   , 1905.

< Seal >

Edward Merrick
Notary Public.

Seminole-NB-154.

Muskogee, Indian Territory, June 29, 1905.

Commission to the Five Civilized Tribes,
    Creek Enrollment Division.

Gentlemen:

On May 3, 1905, there was filed with the Commission application for the enrollment of Emma Sewell, born in May, 1902, as a citizen by blood of the Seminole Nation. It is stated in said application that the father of said child is Tom Sewell, a citizen of the Creek Nation and that her mother is Hilly Harrison, formerly Sewell, a citizen by blood of the Seminole Nation.

You are requested to inform the Seminole Enrollment Division as to whether or not an application has been made to the Commission for the enrollment of said Emma Sewell as a citizen of the Creek Nation and if so what disposition, if any, has been made of said application.

Respectfully,

Chairman.

Applications for Enrollment of Seminole Newborn
Act of 1905   Volume II

DEPARTMENT OF THE INTERIOR.
COMMISSION TO THE FIVE CIVILIZED TRIBES.

Muskogee, Indian Territory, July 13, 1905.

Commissioner to the Five Civilized Tribes,
  Seminole Enrollment Division,
    Muskogee, Indian Territory.

Gentlemen:

Receipt is acknowledged of your communication of June 29, 1905 (Sem. NB.54[sic]), in which you ask if application for the enrollment as a citizen of the Creek Nation has been made for Emma Sewell, child of Tom Sewell, a citizen of the Creek Nation, and Hilly Harrison, formerly Sewell, a citizen of the Seminole Nation.

In reply you are advised that the records of this office have been examined and it does not appear that application has been made for the enrollment of said Emma Sewell, as a citizen of the Creek Nation.

Respectfully,

Tams Bixby
Commissioner.

Sem NB 155
BIRTH AFFIDAVIT.
DEPARTMENT OF THE INTERIOR.
COMMISSION TO THE FIVE CIVILIZED TRIBES.

IN RE APPLICATION FOR ENROLLMENT, as a citizen of the   Seminole   Nation, of
Baby Harjo   , born on the 7   day of   Octo , 1904

Name of Father: Fulkah Harjo   1755   a citizen of the   Seminole   Nation.
Name of Mother: Lucy Harjo   1756   a citizen of the   Seminole   Nation.

Postoffice   Sasakwa I.T.

146

Applications for Enrollment of Seminole Newborn
Act of 1905   Volume II

(Child present)

UNITED STATES OF AMERICA, Indian Territory, ⎱
   Western   DISTRICT. ⎰

I,   Lucy Harjo , on oath state that I am about 32   years of age and a citizen by blood   , of the   Seminole   Nation; that I am the lawful wife of Fulkah Harjo   , who is a citizen, by   blood   of the   Seminole   Nation; that a   Male   child was born to me on   7   day of   Octo   , 1904, that said child has been named   Baby Harjo   , and is now living.

her
Lucy x Harjo
mark

Witnesses To Mark:
  ⎰ Chas E Webster
  ⎱ A. B. Davis

Subscribed and sworn to before me this 26 day of   May   , 1905.

Chas E Webster
Notary Public.

UNITED STATES OF AMERICA, Indian Territory, ⎱
   Western   DISTRICT. ⎰

I,   Hillie Harjo   , a   acting as midwife   , on oath state that I attended on Mrs. Lucy Harjo   , wife of   Fulkah Harjo   on the   7   day of   Octo , 1904; that there was born to her on said date a   male   child; that said child is now living and is said to have been named Baby Harjo

Hillie Harjo

Witnesses To Mark:

Subscribed and sworn to before me this 26 day of   May   , 1905.

Chas E Webster
Notary Public.

Sem NB 155
BIRTH AFFIDAVIT.

DEPARTMENT OF THE INTERIOR.
COMMISSION TO THE FIVE CIVILIZED TRIBES.

IN RE APPLICATION FOR ENROLLMENT, as a citizen of the   Seminole   Nation, of
Zora Harjo   , born on the 10   day of   Feb , 1902

Name of Father: Fulkah Harjo   1755   a citizen of the   Seminole   Nation.
Name of Mother: Lucy Harjo   1756   a citizen of the   Seminole   Nation.

Postoffice   Sasakwa I.T.

Child present

AFFIDAVIT OF MOTHER.

UNITED STATES OF AMERICA, Indian Territory,
    Western   DISTRICT.

I,   Lucy Harjo , on oath state that I am   about 32   years of age and a citizen
by   blood   , of the   Seminole   Nation; that I am the lawful wife of   Fulkah
Harjo   , who is a citizen, by   blood   of the   Seminole   Nation; that a
female   child was born to me on   10   day of   Feb   , 1902, that said child has been
named   Zora Harjo   , and is now living.   her
                                          Lucy x Harjo
Witnesses To Mark: mark
  ⎰ Chas E Webster
  ⎱ A. B. Davis

Subscribed and sworn to before me this   26   day of   May   , 1905.

Chas E Webster
Notary Public.

AFFIDAVIT OF ATTENDING PHYSICIAN OR MID-WIFE.

UNITED STATES OF AMERICA, Indian Territory,
    Western   DISTRICT.

I,   Hillie Harjo   , a   cousin   , on oath state that I attended on Mrs. Lucy
Harjo   , wife of   Fulkah Harjo   on the   10   day of   Feb , 1902; that there was
born to her on said date a   female   child; that said child is now living and is said to
have been named Zora Harjo

Hillie Harjo

Witnesses To Mark:

Subscribed and sworn to before me this 26 day of   May   , 1905.

Chas E Webster
Notary Public.

Sem NB 156
BIRTH AFFIDAVIT.

DEPARTMENT OF THE INTERIOR.
COMMISSION TO THE FIVE CIVILIZED TRIBES.

IN RE APPLICATION FOR ENROLLMENT, as a citizen of the   Seminole   Nation, of
Sallie Deer   , born on the 5   day of April   , 1902

Name of Father: Jimmy McGirt   a citizen of the   Creek   Nation.
Name of Mother: Annie McKellop   1765   a citizen of the   Seminole   Nation.
                    formerly McGirt
                              Postoffice   Fentress I.T.

Child present

AFFIDAVIT OF MOTHER.

UNITED STATES OF AMERICA, Indian Territory,
    Western   DISTRICT.

I, Annie McKellop   , on oath state that I am   23 years of age and a citizen by
blood   , of the   Seminole   Nation; that I ~~am~~ was the lawful wife of   Jimmy
McGirt   , who is a citizen, by   blood   of the   Creek   Nation; that a   Female
child was born to me on   5   day of April   , 1902, that said child has been named
Sallie Deer   , and is now living.

Annie McKellop
Witnesses To Mark:

Subscribed and sworn to before me this 24   day of   May   , 1905.

Chas E Webster
Notary Public.

149

Applications for Enrollment of Seminole Newborn
Act of 1905 Volume II

AFFIDAVIT OF ATTENDING PHYSICIAN OR MID-WIFE.

Father of Annie McKellop

UNITED STATES OF AMERICA, Indian Territory,
    Western   DISTRICT.

helped

I,   Moses Deer   , on oath state that I attended on Mrs. Annie McKellop   former , wife of Jimmy McGirt   on the   5   day of April , 1902; that there was born to her on said date a   Female   child; that said child is now living and is said to have been named Sallie Deer   his

Moses x Deer

Witnesses To Mark: mark
    Chas E Webster
    A. B. Davis

Subscribed and sworn to before me this 24   day of   May   , 1905.

Chas E Webster
Notary Public.

Mother not living with Jimmy McGirt, former husband and wishes child to be named Sallie Deer.

(The above Birth Affidavit given again with note at bottom of application.)

Sem NB 156
BIRTH AFFIDAVIT.

DEPARTMENT OF THE INTERIOR.
COMMISSION TO THE FIVE CIVILIZED TRIBES.

IN RE APPLICATION FOR ENROLLMENT, as a citizen of the   Seminole   Nation, of Sallie Deer   , born on the 5   day of April , 1902

Name of Father: Jimmy McGirt   a citizen of the   Creek   Nation.
Name of Mother: Annie McKellop   1765   a citizen of the   Seminole   Nation.
                  formerly McGirt
                        Postoffice   Fentress I.T.

150

Applications for Enrollment of Seminole Newborn
Act of 1905   Volume II

AFFIDAVIT OF ATTENDING PHYSICIAN OR MID-WIFE.

UNITED STATES OF AMERICA, Indian Territory, ⎫
  Western Judicial   DISTRICT. ⎰

I,   Molley Yarhola   , a Mid Wife   , on oath state that I attended on Mrs.
Annie McKellop   , wife of   Jimmy McGirt   on the   5th   day of   April , 1902;
that there was born to her on said date a   Female   child; that said child is now living
and is said to have been named Sallie Deer   her
                                                    Molley Yarhola x
Witnesses To Mark: mark
  ⎰ Thomas McKellop
  ⎱ Nat Williams

Subscribed and sworn to before me this 29th   day of   May   , 1905.

My Com. Ex. July 1-1906.   Nat Williams
                                                  Notary Public.

Sem NB 156
BIRTH AFFIDAVIT.
DEPARTMENT OF THE INTERIOR.
COMMISSION TO THE FIVE CIVILIZED TRIBES.

IN RE APPLICATION FOR ENROLLMENT, as a citizen of the   Seminole   Nation, of
Sallie Deer McGirt   , born on the 5   day of   April   , 1902

Name of Father: Jimmy McGirt   a citizen of the   Creek   Nation.
Name of Mother: Annie McKellop   a citizen of the   Seminole   Nation.
                    (formerly McGirt)
                          Postoffice   Fentress, I.T.

AFFIDAVIT OF MOTHER.

UNITED STATES OF AMERICA, Indian Territory, ⎫
  Western   DISTRICT. ⎰

I,   Annie McKellop   , on oath state that I am   23   years of age and a citizen
by   blood   , of the   Seminole   Nation; that I ~~am~~ was the lawful wife of
Jimmy McGirt   , who is a citizen, by blood   of the   Creek   Nation; that a
female   child was born to me on 5   day of   April   , 1902; that said child has
been named   Sallie Deer McGirt   , and was living March 4, 1905.

                          Annie McKellop

151

Witnesses To Mark:

{

Subscribed and sworn to before me this 5th   day of   August   , 1905.

Com Ex Aug 2^d 1906   Jeff T. Canard
                                                                  Notary Public.

_____

                              father of Annie McKellop
         AFFIDAVIT OF ~~ATTENDING PHYSICIAN OR MID-WIFE~~.

UNITED STATES OF AMERICA, Indian Territory, ⎫
        Western   **DISTRICT.** ⎭

                                              helped to
        I,   Moses Deer   , a   , on oath state that I attended on Mrs. Annie
McKellop   formerly   , wife of   Jimmy McGirt   on the 5 day of   April   ,
1902; that there was born to her on said date a   female   child; that said child was
living March 4, 1905, and is said to have been named Sallie Deer McGirt
                                              his
                                  Moses x Deer
Witnesses To Mark: mark
  { Joe Yarhola
  { F.J. McKellop

        Subscribed and sworn to before me 5th day of   August   , 1905.

Com Ex Aug 2^d 1906   Jeff T. Canard
                                                                  Notary Public.

_____

BIRTH AFFIDAVIT.
                        DEPARTMENT OF THE INTERIOR.
                COMMISSION TO THE FIVE CIVILIZED TRIBES.

_____

        IN RE APPLICATION FOR ENROLLMENT, as a citizen of the   Seminole   Nation, of
Lena McKellop   , born on the 5   day of Feb , 1905

Name of Father: Thomas McKellop   a citizen of the   Creek   Nation.
Name of Mother: Annie McKellop   1765   a citizen of the   Seminole   Nation.
                        formerly McGirt
                            Postoffice   Fentress, I.T.

_____

Applications for Enrollment of Seminole Newborn
Act of 1905   Volume II

AFFIDAVIT OF ATTENDING PHYSICIAN OR MID-WIFE.

UNITED STATES OF AMERICA, Indian Territory, ⎫
Western Judicial   DISTRICT. ⎰

I,   Lou Watson   , a Mid-Wife   , on oath state that I attended on Mrs. Annie McKellop   , wife of Thomas McKellop   on the 5th day of Feby , 1905; that there was born to her on said date a   Female   child; that said child is now living and is said to have been named Lena McKellop

her
Lou Watson x
mark

Witnesses To Mark:
⎰ Nat Williams
⎱ Thomas McKellop

Subscribed and sworn to before me this 29th day of   May   , 1905.

My Com. Ex. July 1-1906.

Notary Public.

Sem NB
BIRTH AFFIDAVIT.

DEPARTMENT OF THE INTERIOR.
COMMISSION TO THE FIVE CIVILIZED TRIBES.

IN RE APPLICATION FOR ENROLLMENT, as a citizen of the   Seminole   Nation, of Lena McKellop   , born on the 5   day of Feb , 1905

Name of Father: Thomas McKellop   a citizen of the   Creek   Nation.
Name of Mother: Annie McKellop   (1765)   a citizen of the   Seminole   Nation.
                        formerly McGirt
                        Postoffice   Fentress I.T.

(Child present)

AFFIDAVIT OF MOTHER.

UNITED STATES OF AMERICA, Indian Territory, ⎫
Western   DISTRICT. ⎰

I, Annie McKellop   , on oath state that I am 23 years of age and a citizen by blood   , of the   Seminole   Nation; that I am the lawful wife of   Thomas McKellop   , who is a citizen, by   blood   of the   Creek   Nation; that a Female   child was born to me on 5 day of Feb.   , 1905, that said child has been named   Lena McKellop   , and is now living.

Annie McKellop

153

Applications for Enrollment of Seminole Newborn
Act of 1905   Volume II

Witnesses To Mark:

{

Subscribed and sworn to before me this 24 day of   May   , 1905.

Chas E Webster
Notary Public.

AFFIDAVIT OF ATTENDING PHYSICIAN OR MID-WIFE.
Father of Lena McKellop

UNITED STATES OF AMERICA, Indian Territory,
Western   **DISTRICT.**

I,   Thomas McKellop   , ~~a~~   , on oath state that I attended on Mrs.   Annie McKellop , ~~wife of~~   my wife   on the 5   day of Feb , 1905; that there was born to her on said date a   Female   child; that said child is now living and is said to have been named Lena McKellop

Thomas McKellop

Witnesses To Mark:

{

Subscribed and sworn to before me this 24 day of   May   , 1905.

Chas E Webster
Notary Public.

HGH
DEPARTMENT OF THE INTERIOR.
COMMISSION TO THE FIVE CIVILIZED TRIBES.

Muskogee, Indian Territory, July 11, 1905.

Seminole Enrollment Division,
General Office.

Gentlemen:

Receipt is acknowledged of your communication of June 29, 1905 (Sem. NB.156), in which you ask if application for the enrollment as a citizen of the Creek Nation has been made for Sallie Deer, child of Annie McKellop (nee Deer), a citizen by blood of the Seminole Nation, and Jimmie McGirt, a citizen of the Creek Nation, and Lena McKellop, child of said Annie McKellop and Thomas McKellop, a citizen of the Creek Nation.

154

Applications for Enrollment of Seminole Newborn
Act of 1905   Volume II

In reply you are advised that the records of this office have been examined and it does not appear that application has been made for the enrollment of said Sallie Deer and Lena McKellop, or either of them, as citizens of the Creek Nation.

Respectfully,
Tams Bixby   Commissioner.

Seminole
NB-156.

Muskogee, Indian Territory, July 25, 1905.

Annie McKellop,
Fentress, Indian Territory.

Dear Madam:
In the matter of the application for the enrollment of your daughter Sallie it appears from the evidence on file that the father of said child is Jimmy McGirt and that prior to and at the time of the birth of your said daughter you were the lawful wife of said Jimmy McGirt.

It therefore appears that the correct surname of your said daughter is McGirt and it will be necessary, before the rights of said child as a citizen by blood of the Seminole Nation can be finally determined, for you to furnish this office with affidavits showing the correct name of your said daughter.

For that purpose a blank which has been partially filled out is inclosed herewith and you are requested to appear before a notary public, execute the same and return it to this office. Be careful to see that the notary public, before whom the affidavits are sworn to, attaches his name and seal to each affidavit. In case any signature is by mark, it must be attested by two disinterested witnesses.

You should give this matter your prompt attention.

Commissioner.

CTD-3.
Env.

Applications for Enrollment of Seminole Newborn
Act of 1905   Volume II

Seminole
NB-156.

Muskogee, Indian Territory, August 9, 1905.

Annie McKellop,
Fentress, Indian Territory.

Dear Madam:

Receipt is hereby acknowledged of your affidavit and the affidavit of Moses Deer as to the birth of your minor daughter Sallie Deer McGirt, born April 5, 1902, and the same have been filed with the records of this office in the matter of the enrollment of said child as a citizen by blood of the Creek Nation.

Respectfully,

Acting Commissioner.

———————

Seminole-NB-156.

Muskogee, Indian Territory, June 29, 1905.

Commission to the Five Civilized Tribes,
Creek Enrollment Division.

Gentlemen:

On May 24, 1905, there were filed with the Commission applications for the enrollment, as citizens by blood of the Seminole Nation, of Sallie Deer, born April 5, 1902, and Lena McKellop, born February 5, 1905. It is stated in said applications that the mother is Annie McKellop (nee Deer), a citizen by blood of the Seminole Nation; that the father of Sallie Deer is Jimmy McGirt, a citizen by blood of the Creek Nation, and that the father of Lena McKellop is Thomas McKellop, a citizen by blood of the Creek Nation.

You are requested to inform the Seminole Enrollment Division as to whether or not any applications have been made to the Commission for the enrollment of said Sallie Deer and Lena McKellop as citizens of the Creek Nation and if so what disposition, if any, has been made of said applications.

Respectfully,

Chairman.

Sem NB 157
BIRTH AFFIDAVIT.

DEPARTMENT OF THE INTERIOR.
COMMISSION TO THE FIVE CIVILIZED TRIBES.

IN RE APPLICATION FOR ENROLLMENT, as a citizen of the   Seminole   Nation, of
Rutherford D Aldridge   , born on the 6   day of   July , 1902

Name of Father: Eugene C Aldridge   a citizen of the   U.S.   ~~Nation~~.
Name of Mother: Myrtle Aldridge   (1773)   a citizen of the   Seminole   Nation.
                         nee Davis
                              Postoffice   Wewoka, I. T.

(Child present)

AFFIDAVIT OF MOTHER.

UNITED STATES OF AMERICA, Indian Territory, ⎫
      Western   DISTRICT. ⎬
                                      ⎭

        I,   Myrtle Aldridge (nee Davis)   , on oath state that I am   22   years of age
and a citizen by   blood   , of the   Seminole   Nation; that I am the lawful wife of
Eugene C. Aldridge   , who is a citizen, ~~by~~   of the   U.S.   Nation; that
a   male   child was born to me on   6   day of   July   , 1902; that said child has
been named   Rutherford D. Aldridge   , and was living March 4, 1905.

                                        Myrtle Aldridge
Witnesses To Mark:
   ⎧
   ⎨
   ⎩
        Subscribed and sworn to before me this   3ʳᵈ   day of   May   , 1905.

                                        Chas E Webster
                                              Notary Public.

AFFIDAVIT OF ATTENDING PHYSICIAN OR MID-WIFE.
                              Okla.
UNITED STATES OF AMERICA, ~~Indian~~ Territory, ⎫
      Pottawatomie County   DISTRICT. ⎬
                                           ⎭

        I,   H.D. Owen M.D.   , a Physician   , on oath state that I attended on Mrs.
Myrtle Aldridge   , wife of   Eugene Aldridge   on the 6ᵗʰ day of July , 1902;
that there was born to her on said date a   male   child; that said child was living
March 4, 1905, and is said to have been named Rutherford D. Aldridge

                                        H.D. Owen M.D.

157

Witnesses To Mark:
{ *(Illegible)* E. Church
{ WCE, Ige

Subscribed and sworn to before me 2   day of   May   , 1905.

JE Thompson
Notary Public.

Com Ex Mar 13. 19__07__

Sem NB 158
BIRTH AFFIDAVIT.

DEPARTMENT OF THE INTERIOR.
COMMISSION TO THE FIVE CIVILIZED TRIBES.
C O P Y.

IN RE APPLICATION FOR ENROLLMENT, as a citizen of the   Seminole   Nation, of
Gertrude Howell   , born on the 2 day of   March   , 1905

Name of Father: A. J. Howell   a citizen of the   U S   ~~Nation~~.
Name of Mother: Henrietta Howell   1790   a citizen of the   Seminole   Nation.
(nee Barnett)
Postoffice   Kanawa I. T.

Child present)

AFFIDAVIT OF MOTHER.

UNITED STATES OF AMERICA, Indian Territory,
Western   **DISTRICT.**

I, Henrietta Howell   , on oath state that I am 31   years of age and a citizen
by   blood   , of the   Seminole   Nation; that I am the lawful wife of   A. J.
Howell   , who is a citizen, by   of the   U. S.   Nation; that a   child
was born to me on 2   day of   March   , 1905; that said child has been named
Gertrude Howell   , and ~~was living March 4, 1905~~. is now living

Henrietta Howell

Witnesses To Mark:
{

158

Subscribed and sworn to before me this 31 day of   May   , 1905.

Chas E Webster
Notary Public.

—————————

BIRTH AFFIDAVIT.

DEPARTMENT OF THE INTERIOR.
COMMISSION TO THE FIVE CIVILIZED TRIBES.
C O P Y

—————————

IN RE APPLICATION FOR ENROLLMENT, as a citizen of the   Seminole   Nation, of
Gertrude Howell   , born on the 7 day of May , 1905

Name of Father: A. J. Howell   a citizen of the Siminole[sic] Nation.
Name of Mother: Henrietta Howell   a citizen of the Siminole[sic] Nation.

Postoffice   Kanawa I. T.

—————————

Child present)

AFFIDAVIT OF MOTHER.

UNITED STATES OF AMERICA, Indian Territory, ⎫
     Western District   **DISTRICT.** ⎬

  I,   Henrietta Howell   , on oath state that I am   31   years of age and a citizen
by   Birth   , of the   Seminole   Nation; that I am the lawful wife of   A. J.
Howell   , who is a citizen, by   marriage   of the   Seminole   Nation; that a
female   child was born to me on 7   day of   May   , 1905; that said child has been
named   Gertrude, and was living ~~March 4~~, 1905.
     May 7
      Henrietta Howell

Witnesses To Mark:
 ⎧ J. M. Harris
 ⎩ S. P. Maucy

  Subscribed and sworn to before me this 27 day of   July   , 1905.
(SEAL)
     W. M. Davis
      Notary Public.
My Com- expires March 17-09

—————————

AFFIDAVIT OF ATTENDING PHYSICIAN OR MID-WIFE.

UNITED STATES OF AMERICA, Indian Territory, ⎱
    Western   **DISTRICT.** ⎰

I, E. M. Harris   , a   M. D.   , on oath state that I attended on Mrs. Henrietta Howell   , wife of A. J. Howell   on the 7 day of   May   , 1905; that there was born to her on said date a   Female   child; that said child was living ~~March 4~~, 1905, and is said to have been named Gertrude
7th day of May

                              E M Harris M. D.

Witnesses To Mark:
  ⎰ J M Harris
  ⎱ Claude S. Butler

    Subscribed and sworn to before me this 27 day of   July   , 1905.
(SEAL)

                        W. M. Davis
                                Notary Public.
My com expires March 17-09

W.F.
Sem. NB-158.

DEPARTMENT OF THE INTERIOR,
COMMISSIONER TO THE FIVE CIVILIZED TRIBES.

    In the matter of the application for the enrollment of Gertrude Howell as a citizen by blood of the Seminole Nation.

--: D E C I S I O N :--

    It appears from the record herein that on May 31, 1905 there was filed with the Commission to the Five Civilized Tribes an application for the enrollment of Gertrude Howell as a citizen by blood of the Seminole Nation.
    It further appears from the application filed with the Commission to the Five Civilized Tribes on May 31, 1905 that the said Gertrude Howell was born on March 2, 1905 and is the child of Henrietta Howell, who is identified as Henrietta Barnett, number 1790 upon the final roll of citizens by blood of the Seminole Nation, and A. J. Howell, a citizen of the United States.
    On July 10, 1905 the said Henrietta Howell addressed a letter to this office stating that her baby (referring to the applicant herein) was born a few days too late to be enrolled and on July 30, 1905 there was filed with this office corrected affidavits as to the birth of said Gertrude Howell from which it appears that said applicant was born May 7, 1905.
    The Act of Congress approved March 3, 1905 (Public No. 212) among other things provides:

Applications for Enrollment of Seminole Newborn
Act of 1905   Volume II

"That the Commission to the Five Civilized Tribes is authorized for ninety days after the date of the approval of this act to receive and consider applications for enrollment of infant children born prior to March fourth, nineteen hundred and five, and living on said latter date, to citizens of the Seminole tribe whose enrollment has been approved by the Secretary of the Interior; and to enroll and make allotments to such children, giving to each an equal number of acres of land, and such children shall also share equally with other citizens of the Seminole tribe in the distribution of all other tribal property and funds."

I am of the opinion that, inasmuch as the applicant Gertrude Howell was not born prior to March 4, 1905, the Commission to the Five Civilized Tribes was without authority to receive or consider the application for her enrollment as a citizen by blood of the Seminole Nation and that, therefore, I should decline to receive or consider such application, under the provision of law above quoted, and it is so ordered.

Tams Bixby   Commissioner.

Muskogee, Indian Territory Indian Territory,

SEP 28 1905

Sem. NB-158

COPY.

Muskogee, Indian Territory, September 28, 1905.

Henrietta Howell,
Kanawa, Indian Territory

Dear Madam:

Inclosed herewith you will find a copy of the decision of the Commissioner to the Five Civilized Tribes, rendered September 28, 1905, declining to receive or consider the application for the enrollment of your infant child, Gertrude Howell, as a citizen by blood of the Seminole Nation.

The decision, with the record of proceedings in the case, is this day transmitted to the Secretary of the Interior for review. The final decision of the Secretary will be made known to you as soon as this office is informed of the same.

Respectfully,

SIGNED   Tams Bixby
Commissioner.

Registered.
Inc. Sem. NB-158.

Sem. NB-158

COPY.

Muskogee, Indian Territory, September 28, 1905.

McKennon & Willmott,
  Attorneys for Seminole Nation,
    Wewoka, Indian Territory.
Gentlemen:

Inclosed herewith you will find a copy of the decision of the Commissioner to the Five Civilized Tribes, rendered September 28, 1905, declining to receive or consider the application for the enrollment of your infant child, Gertrude Howell, as a citizen by blood of the Seminole Nation.

The decision, with the record of proceedings in the case, is this day transmitted to the Secretary of the Interior for review. The final decision of the Secretary will be made known to you as soon as this office is informed of the same.

Respectfully,

SIGNED *Tams Bixby*
Commissioner.

Inc. Sem. NB-158.

COPY.

Muskogee, Indian Territory, September 28, 1905.

The Honorable,
  The Secretary of the Interior.

Sir:

There is herewith transmitted the record of proceedings in the matter of the application for the enrollment of Gertrude Howell as a citizen by blood of the Seminole Nation, including the decision of the Commissioner to the Five Civilized Tribes, dated September 28, 1905, declining to receive or consider said application.

Respectfully,

SIGNED *Tams Bixby*
Commissioner.

Through the
  Commissioner of Indian Affairs.

2 inc. Sem. NB-158.

Sem NB 158
BIRTH AFFIDAVIT.

DEPARTMENT OF THE INTERIOR.
COMMISSION TO THE FIVE CIVILIZED TRIBES.
C O P Y.

IN RE APPLICATION FOR ENROLLMENT, as a citizen of the   Seminole   Nation, of
Elizabeth Howell   , born on the   30   day of   April   , 1901

Name of Father: A. J. Howell   a citizen of the   U S   ~~Nation~~.
Name of Mother: Henrietta Howell   1790   a citizen of the   Seminole   Nation.
                    (nee Barnett)
                    Postoffice   Konawa, I. T.

Child present

AFFIDAVIT OF MOTHER.

UNITED STATES OF AMERICA, Indian Territory,
    Western   DISTRICT.

I,   Henrietta Howell   , on oath state that I am   31   years of age and a citizen
by   blood   , of the   Seminole   Nation; that I am the lawful wife of   A. J.
Howell   , who is a citizen, by   of the   U. S.   Nation; that a   female
child was born to me on   30   day of   April   , 1901; that said child has been named
Elizabeth Howell   , and is now living.

Henrietta Howell

Witnesses To Mark:

Subscribed and sworn to before me this 31 day of   May   , 1905.

Chas E Webster
Notary Public.

AFFIDAVIT OF ATTENDING PHYSICIAN OR MID-WIFE.

Midwife or mother of Henrietta

UNITED STATES OF AMERICA, Indian Territory,   Howell is now in Texas
    Western   DISTRICT.

I,   A.J. Howell   , ~~a~~   , on oath state that I attended on Mrs.   Henrietta
Howell   , ~~wife of~~   my wife   on the 30 day of   April   , 1901; that there was
born to her on said date a   female   child; that said child was living March 4, 1905,
and is said to have been named Elizabeth Howell

A J Howell

163

Witnesses To Mark:

{

Subscribed and sworn to before me this 31 day of   May   , 1905.

Chas E Webster
Notary Public.

Sem. NB-158.

Muskogee, Indian Territory, August 2, 1905.

Henrietta Howell,
Kanawa, Indian Territory.

Dear Madam:

Receipt is hereby acknowledged of your affidavit and the affidavit of E. M. Harris as to the birth of your daughter Gertrude Howell on May 7, 1905 and the same have been filed with the records of this office.

Respectfully,

Commissioner.

Sem NB 159
BIRTH AFFIDAVIT.

DEPARTMENT OF THE INTERIOR.
COMMISSION TO THE FIVE CIVILIZED TRIBES.

IN RE APPLICATION FOR ENROLLMENT, as a citizen of the   Seminole   Nation, of
Sele Luste   , born on the 19" day of   July   , 1903

Name of Father: Punluste   ($^{\#}$1797)   a citizen of the   Seminole   Nation.
Name of Mother: Mary Condella   ($^{\#}$1798)   a citizen of the   "   Nation.

Postoffice   Sasakwa I.T.

Applications for Enrollment of Seminole Newborn
Act of 1905   Volume II

(Child present)

AFFIDAVIT OF MOTHER.

UNITED STATES OF AMERICA, Indian Territory, ⎰
   Western   DISTRICT. ⎰

I, Mary Condella , on oath state that I am 26 years of age and a citizen by blood , of the Seminole Nation; that I am the lawful wife of Punluste , who is a citizen, by blood of the Seminole Nation; that a female child was born to me on 19ᵗʰ day of July , 1903; that said child has been named Sele Luste , and was living March 4, 1905.

Mary Condella

Witnesses To Mark:

{

Subscribed and sworn to before me this 3" day of May , 1905.

(Seal)

Edward Merrick
Notary Public.

AFFIDAVIT OF ATTENDING PHYSICIAN OR MID-WIFE.

UNITED STATES OF AMERICA, Indian Territory, ⎰
   Western   DISTRICT. ⎰

I, Minnie Porter , a midwife , on oath state that I attended on Mrs. Mary Condella , wife of Punluste on the 19ᵗʰ day of July , 1903; that there was born to her on said date a female child; that said child was living March 4, 1905, and is said to have been named Sele Luste

Minnie Porter

Witnesses To Mark:

{

Subscribed and sworn to before me 3" day of May , 1905.

<Seal>

Edward Merrick
Notary Public.

Sem NB 159
BIRTH AFFIDAVIT.

DEPARTMENT OF THE INTERIOR.
COMMISSION TO THE FIVE CIVILIZED TRIBES.

IN RE APPLICATION FOR ENROLLMENT, as a citizen of the   Seminole   Nation, of
Martha Luste   , born on the 2" day of   Feby   , 1901

Name of Father: Punluste   ($^{\#}$1797)   a citizen of the   Seminole   Nation.
Name of Mother: Mary Condella ($^{\#}$1798)   a citizen of the   "   Nation.

Postoffice   Sasakwa I.T.

(Child present)
AFFIDAVIT OF MOTHER.

UNITED STATES OF AMERICA, Indian Territory,
Western   **DISTRICT.**

I,   Mary Condella   , on oath state that I am   26   years of age and a citizen
by   blood   , of the   Seminole   Nation; that I am the lawful wife of   Punluste   ,
who is a citizen, by blood   of the   Seminole   Nation; that a   female
child was born to me on   2nd day of   February   , 1901; that said child has been
named   Martha Luste   , and was living March 4, 1905.

Mary Condella
Witnesses To Mark:

Subscribed and sworn to before me this 3" day of   May   , 1905.

⬡ Seal ⬡

Edward Merrick
Notary Public.

AFFIDAVIT OF ATTENDING PHYSICIAN OR MID-WIFE.

UNITED STATES OF AMERICA, Indian Territory,
Western   **DISTRICT.**

I,   Minnie Porter   , a   midwife   , on oath state that I attended on Mrs.
Mary Condella   , wife of   Punluste   on the 2" day of   Feby   , 1901; that
there was born to her on said date a   female   child; that said child was living March
4, 1905, and is said to have been named   Martha Luste

Minnie Porter

166

Applications for Enrollment of Seminole Newborn
Act of 1905   Volume II

Witnesses To Mark:

{

    Subscribed and sworn to before me   3" day of   May   , 1905.

⟨ Seal ⟩

                       Edward Merrick
                            Notary Public.

                                       Klamath Agency, Oregon.
                                       February 27, 1931.

Adrian M. Landman, Sup't,
Five Civilized Tribes Agency,
Muskogee, Oklahoma.

Dear Sir:

      Please advise me if there has been any application at your agency for the enrollment of Loyette Lucile Moppin. This child was born July 19, 1930, at Maud, Oklahoma, to Mildred George, a Klamath Indian girl, and Sherman Moppin, who is said to be a fullblood Seminole Indian enrolled at your agency. I am advised that the parents were not married. Application has been made for the enrollment of this child with the Klamath Tribe of Indians, but I should like to know whether there is any likelihood of enrolling her at your agency.

                          Very truly yours,

                          Signed, L. D. Arnold,

                          Superintendent.

                File in jacket of Sherman Moppin,
                Seminole N.B. 191

Sem NB 160
BIRTH AFFIDAVIT.

DEPARTMENT OF THE INTERIOR.
COMMISSION TO THE FIVE CIVILIZED TRIBES.

IN RE APPLICATION FOR ENROLLMENT, as a citizen of the   Seminole   Nation, of
Sherman Moppin   , born on the 15 day of   May , 1900

Name of Father: George Moppin   (1848[sic]) a citizen of the   Seminole   Nation.
Name of Mother: Lucy Moppin   (1964[sic]) a citizen of the   Seminole   Nation.

Postoffice   Kanawah Ind. Ter.

(Child present)

AFFIDAVIT OF MOTHER.

UNITED STATES OF AMERICA, Indian Territory,
    Western   **DISTRICT.**

I, Lucy Moppin   , on oath state that I am 40   years of age and a citizen by
blood   , of the   Seminole   Nation; that I am the lawful wife of George Moppin ,
who is a citizen, by adoption   of the   Seminole   Nation; that a   male
child was born to me on 15   day of   May   , 1900; that said child has been named
Sherman Moppin   , and was living March 4, 1905.

                                                    her
                                            Lucy x Moppin
Witnesses To Mark: mark
   Frank C. Sabourin
   Edward Merrick

Subscribed and sworn to before me this 2nd day of   May   , 1905.

⟨ Seal ⟩   Edward Merrick
                                            Notary Public.

AFFIDAVIT OF ATTENDING PHYSICIAN OR MID-WIFE.

UNITED STATES OF AMERICA, Indian Territory,
    Western   **DISTRICT.**

I,   Lou Smith   , a midwife   , on oath state that I attended on Mrs. Lucy
Moppin   , wife of   George Moppin   on the 15" day of   May   , 1900; that
there was born to her on said date a   male   child; that said child was living March 4,
1905, and is said to have been named Sherman Moppin

Witnesses To Mark:

{ Frank C. Sabourin
{ Edward Merrick

her
Lou x Smith
mark

Subscribed and sworn to before me 2nd day of   May   , 1905.

⬙ Seal ⬙

Edward Merrick
Notary Public.

Sem NB 160
BIRTH AFFIDAVIT.

DEPARTMENT OF THE INTERIOR.
COMMISSION TO THE FIVE CIVILIZED TRIBES.

IN RE APPLICATION FOR ENROLLMENT, as a citizen of the   Seminole   Nation, of
Jimus Moppin   , born on the   11th   day of   Apr , 1902

Name of Father: George Moppin   (1964)   a citizen of the   Seminole   Nation.
Name of Mother: Lucy Moppin   (1848)   a citizen of the   Seminole   Nation.

Postoffice   Kanawah Ind. Ter.

(Child present)

AFFIDAVIT OF MOTHER.

UNITED STATES OF AMERICA, Indian Territory, ⎫
     Western   **DISTRICT.** ⎭

I, Lucy Moppin   , on oath state that I am 40   years of age and a citizen by
Blood   , of the   Seminole   Nation; that I am the lawful wife of George Moppin ,
who is a citizen, by Adoption   of the   Seminole   Nation; that a   male
child was born to me on   11th   day of   April   , 1902; that said child has been
named   Jimus Moppin   , and was living March 4, 1905.

her
Lucy x Moppin
mark

Witnesses To Mark:

{ Frank C. Sabourin
{ Edward Merrick

Subscribed and sworn to before me this 2nd day of   May   , 1905.

⬙ Seal ⬙

Edward Merrick
Notary Public.

AFFIDAVIT OF ATTENDING PHYSICIAN OR MID-WIFE.

UNITED STATES OF AMERICA, Indian Territory, }
     Western   DISTRICT.

I,   Lou Smith   , a midwife   , on oath state that I attended on Mrs.   Lucy
Moppin   , wife of   George Moppin   on the 11th day of   April   , 1902; that
there was born to her on said date a   male   child; that said child was living March 4,
1905, and is said to have been named Jimus Moppin

her
Lou x Smith
mark

Witnesses To Mark:
  { Edward Merrick
  { Frank C. Sabourin

Subscribed and sworn to before me 2nd day of   May   , 1905.

⟨ Seal ⟩

Edward Merrick
Notary Public.

Sem NB 161
BIRTH AFFIDAVIT.

DEPARTMENT OF THE INTERIOR.
COMMISSION TO THE FIVE CIVILIZED TRIBES.

IN RE APPLICATION FOR ENROLLMENT, as a citizen of the   Seminole   Nation, of
Phoenie Cosar   , born on the 20   day of February , 1902

Name of Father: Lofey Cosar   (1852)   a citizen of the   Seminole   Nation.
Name of Mother: Sophrona Cosar   (1853)   a citizen of the   Seminole   Nation.

Postoffice   Maud, O.T.

Applications for Enrollment of Seminole Newborn
Act of 1905 Volume II

Child Present

AFFIDAVIT OF MOTHER.

UNITED STATES OF AMERICA, Indian Territory, ⎫
    Western   DISTRICT. ⎭

      I, Sophrona Cosar   , on oath state that I am 30 years of age and a citizen by blood   , of the   Seminole   Nation; that I am the lawful wife of Lofey Cosar , who is a citizen, by   blood   of the   Seminole   Nation; that a   female child was born to me on 20th   day of   February   , 1902, that said child has been named   Phoenie Cosar   , and is now living.

her
Sophrona x Cosar

Witnesses To Mark: mark
  ⎰ Frank C. Sabourin
  ⎱ Chas E Webster

      Subscribed and sworn to before me this 6th day of   May   , 1905.

Chas E Webster
Notary Public.

AFFIDAVIT OF ATTENDING PHYSICIAN OR MID-WIFE.

UNITED STATES OF AMERICA, Indian Territory, ⎫
    Western   DISTRICT. ⎭

      I,   Lofey Cosar   , ~~a~~   , on oath state that I attended on Mrs. Sophrona Cosar   my , wife ~~of~~   on the   20   day of February , 1902; that there was born to her on said date a   female   child; that said child is now living and is said to have been named Phoenie Cosar   his

Lofey x Cosar

Witnesses To Mark: mark
  ⎰ Frank C. Sabourin
  ⎱ Chas E Webster

      Subscribed and sworn to before me this 6th day of   May   , 1905.

Chas E Webster
Notary Public.

Sem NB 161
BIRTH AFFIDAVIT.

DEPARTMENT OF THE INTERIOR.
COMMISSION TO THE FIVE CIVILIZED TRIBES.

IN RE APPLICATION FOR ENROLLMENT, as a citizen of the   Seminole   Nation, of
Willie Cosar   , born on the 10th   day of December , 1904

Name of Father: Lofey Cosar   (1852)   a citizen of the Seminole   Nation.
Name of Mother: Sophrona Cosar   (1853)   a citizen of the Seminole   Nation.

Postoffice   Maud, O.T.

Child Present

AFFIDAVIT OF MOTHER.

UNITED STATES OF AMERICA, Indian Territory, ⎤
    Western   DISTRICT. ⎦

I, Sophrona Cosar   , on oath state that I am 30 years of age and a citizen by
blood   , of the   Seminole   Nation; that I am the lawful wife of Lofey Cosar   ,
who is a citizen, by   blood   of the   Seminole   Nation; that a   male   child
was born to me on 10th   day of   December   , 1904, that said child has been named
Willie Cosar   , and is now living.

                                          her
                                    Sophrona x Cosar
Witnesses To Mark: mark
   ⎰ Frank C. Sabourin
   ⎱ Chas E Webster

Subscribed and sworn to before me this 6th   day of   May   , 1905.

                              Chas E Webster
                                    Notary Public.

AFFIDAVIT OF ATTENDING PHYSICIAN OR MID-WIFE.

UNITED STATES OF AMERICA, Indian Territory, ⎤
    Western   DISTRICT. ⎦

I,   Lofey Cosar   , a   , on oath state that I attended on Mrs. Sophrona
Cosar   my , wife of ———on the   10th   day of December , 1904; that there was
born to her on said date a   male   child; that said child is now living and is said to
have been named Willie Cosar   his
                                          Lofey x Cosar
                                               mark

172

Applications for Enrollment of Seminole Newborn
Act of 1905   Volume II

Witnesses To Mark:
  { Frank C. Sabourin
  { Chas E Webster

Subscribed and sworn to before me this 6th day of   May   , 1905.

Chas E Webster
Notary Public.

Sem NB 162
BIRTH AFFIDAVIT.

DEPARTMENT OF THE INTERIOR.
COMMISSION TO THE FIVE CIVILIZED TRIBES.

IN RE APPLICATION FOR ENROLLMENT, as a citizen of the   Seminole   Nation, of
Fannie Anderson   , born on the 21   day of   Dec , 1901

Name of Father: Will Anderson   a citizen of the   Creek   Nation.
Name of Mother: Munnah   (1865)   a citizen of the   Seminole   Nation.

Postoffice   Barnard, I.T.

(Child present)

AFFIDAVIT OF MOTHER.

UNITED STATES OF AMERICA, Indian Territory, ⎱
   Western   **DISTRICT.** ⎰

I, Munnah   , on oath state that I am about 40 years of age and a citizen by
blood   , of the   Seminole   Nation; that I am not the lawful wife of   Will
Anderson   , who is a citizen, by   blood   of the   Seminole[sic]   Nation; that
a   Female   child was born to me on 21   day of Dec   , 1901, that said child
has been named   Fannie Anderson   , and is now living.

her
Munnah x
mark

173

Applications for Enrollment of Seminole Newborn
Act of 1905   Volume II

Witnesses To Mark:
⎰ Chas E Webster
⎱ A. B. Davis

Subscribed and sworn to before me this 24 day of   May   , 1905.

Chas E Webster
Notary Public.

_____

(Midwife Sophie Robison Dead)

UNITED STATES OF AMERICA, Indian Territory,
Western   DISTRICT.

saw

I,   Lena Jones   , ~~a~~   , on oath state that I ~~attended on~~ Mrs. Munnah   , ~~wife of~~ My Mother   on the 9th of Jan. 1902 and know that on the   21   day of   Dec., 1901; that there was born to her on said date a   female   child; that said child is now living and is said to have been named Fannie Anderson

Lena Jones

Witnesses To Mark:

⎰
⎱

Subscribed and sworn to before me this 24 day of   May   , 1905.

Chas E Webster
Notary Public.

_____

Seminole-NB-162.

Muskogee, Indian Territory, June 29, 1905.

Commission to the Five Civilized Tribes,
        Creek Enrollment Division.

Gentlemen:

On May 24, 1905, there was filed with the Commission application for the enrollment of Fannie Anderson, born December 21, 1901, as a citizen by blood of the Seminole Nation. It is stated in said application that said child is a daughter of Will Anderson, a citizen by blood of the Creek Nation, and Munnah, a citizen by blood of the Seminole Nation.

You are requested to inform the Seminole Enrollment Division as to whether or not any application has been made to the Commission for the enrollment of said Fannie

Anderson, as a citizen by blood of the Seminole Nation blood of the Creek Nation, and if so what disposition, if any, has been made of said application.

Respectfully,

Tams Bixby

Chairman.

_____

HGH

DEPARTMENT OF THE INTERIOR.
COMMISSION TO THE FIVE CIVILIZED TRIBES.

Muskogee, Indian Territory, July 11, 1905.

Seminole Enrollment Division,
General Office.

Gentlemen:

Receipt is acknowledged of your communication of June 29, 1905 (Sem. NB. 162), in which you ask if application for the enrollment as a citizen of the Creek Nation has been made for Fannie Anderson, child of Will Anderson, a citizen of the Creek Nation, and Munnah, a citizen by blood of the Seminole Nation.

In reply you are advised that the records of this office have been examined and it does not appear that application has been made for the enrollment of said Fannie Anderson, as a citizen of the Creek Nation.

Respectfully,
Tams Bixby   Commissioner.

Sem NB 163
BIRTH AFFIDAVIT.

DEPARTMENT OF THE INTERIOR.
COMMISSION TO THE FIVE CIVILIZED TRIBES.

———

IN RE APPLICATION FOR ENROLLMENT, as a citizen of the   Seminole   Nation, of
Eco-harjoe   , born on the   4   day of   June   , 1903

Name of Father: Keno   (1870)   a citizen of the   Seminole   Nation.
Name of Mother: Salena   (1871)   a citizen of the   Seminole   Nation.

Postoffice   Sasakwa IT

———

AFFIDAVIT OF MOTHER.

UNITED STATES OF AMERICA, Indian Territory,
     Western   DISTRICT.

          I,   Salena   , on oath state that I am   25   years of age and a citizen by
blood   , of the   Seminole   Nation; that I am the lawful wife of   Keno   ,
who is a citizen, by blood   of the   Seminole   Nation; that a   male   child
was born to me on   4   day of   June   , 1903; that said child has been named   Eco-harjoe,
and was living March 4, 1905.   her
                                                   Salena x
Witnesses To Mark: mark
     Chas E Webster
     Frank C. Sabourin

     Subscribed and sworn to before me this   10 day of   May   , 1905.

                              Chas E Webster
                                   Notary Public.

———

AFFIDAVIT OF ATTENDING PHYSICIAN OR MID-WIFE.

UNITED STATES OF AMERICA, Indian Territory,
     Western   DISTRICT.

          I, Katie Palmer   , a   midwife   , on oath state that I attended on Mrs.
Salena   , wife of   Keno   on the   4 day of   June   , 1903; that there was born
to her on said date a   male   child; that said child was living March 4, 1905, and is
said to have been named Eco-harjoe   her
                                            Katie x Palmer
                                                   mark

176

Witnesses To Mark:
{ Chas E Webster
{ Frank C. Sabourin

Subscribed and sworn to before me 10   day of   May   , 1905.

Chas E Webster
Notary Public.

Sem NB 163
BIRTH AFFIDAVIT.

DEPARTMENT OF THE INTERIOR.
COMMISSION TO THE FIVE CIVILIZED TRIBES.

IN RE APPLICATION FOR ENROLLMENT, as a citizen of the   Seminole   Nation, of
Alice   , born on the 8 day of March   , 1901

Name of Father: Keno   1870   a citizen of the Seminole   Nation.
Name of Mother: Salina   1871   a citizen of the Seminole   Nation.

Postoffice   Sasakwa IT

(Child present)

AFFIDAVIT OF MOTHER.

UNITED STATES OF AMERICA, Indian Territory,
　　Western   **DISTRICT.**

I,   Salena   , on oath state that I am   25   years of age and a citizen by
blood   , of the   Seminole   Nation; that I am the lawful wife of   Keno   ,
who is a citizen, by blood   of the   Seminole   Nation; that a   Female
child was born to me on 8   day of   March   , 1901; that said child has been named
Alice   , and was living March 4, 1905.   her
                                              Salena x
Witnesses To Mark: mark
{ Chas E Webster
{ Frank C. Sabourin

Subscribed and sworn to before me this 10 day of   May   , 1905.

Chas E Webster
Notary Public.

177

Applications for Enrollment of Seminole Newborn
Act of 1905   Volume II

AFFIDAVIT OF ATTENDING PHYSICIAN OR MID-WIFE.

UNITED STATES OF AMERICA, Indian Territory, ⎱
    Western   DISTRICT. ⎰

    I, Katie Palmer   , a   midwife   , on oath state that I attended on Mrs. Salena   , wife of   Keno   on the 8 day of   March , 1901; that there was born to her on said date a   Female   child; that said child was living March 4, 1905, and is said to have been named Alice   her

                                Katie x Palmer
                                     mark

Witnesses To Mark:
    ⎰ Chas E Webster
    ⎱ Frank C. Sabourin

    Subscribed and sworn to before me 10   day of   May   , 1905.

                              Chas E Webster
                                 Notary Public.

Sem NB 164
BIRTH AFFIDAVIT.

DEPARTMENT OF THE INTERIOR.
COMMISSION TO THE FIVE CIVILIZED TRIBES.

    IN RE APPLICATION FOR ENROLLMENT, as a citizen of the   Seminole   Nation, of Charley E. Ground   , born on the 29" day of April , 1904

Name of Father: A.M. Ground   a citizen of the U.S.   Nation.
Name of Mother: Janette Ground   #1890   a citizen of the Seminole Nation.

                    Postoffice   Henryetta, Ind. Ter.

Applications for Enrollment of Seminole Newborn
Act of 1905   Volume II

Child present

AFFIDAVIT OF MOTHER.

UNITED STATES OF AMERICA, Indian Territory, ⎤
   Western   DISTRICT. ⎦

I,   A. M. Ground   , on oath state that I am   33   years of age and a citizen by
————, of the   United Stated   Nation; that I am the lawful ~~wife of~~ husband of
Janette Ground   , who is a citizen, by blood   of the   Seminole   Nation;
that a   male   child was born to me on   29th day of   April   , 1904; that said
child has been named   Charley E. Ground   , and was living March 4, 1905.

A M Ground

Witnesses To Mark:

{

Subscribed and sworn to before me this   2nd day of   May   , 1905.

⬡ Seal ⬡

                Edward Merrick
                   Notary Public.

Sem NB 164
BIRTH AFFIDAVIT.

DEPARTMENT OF THE INTERIOR.
COMMISSION TO THE FIVE CIVILIZED TRIBES.

IN RE APPLICATION FOR ENROLLMENT, as a citizen of the   Seminole   Nation, of
Charlie Edward Ground   , born on the 29th day of   April   , 1904

Name of Father: Andrew M. Ground   a citizen of the   ————————Nation.
Name of Mother: Jennette Ground   (1890)   a citizen of the   Seminole   Nation.

            Postoffice   Henryetta, Ind. Ter.

AFFIDAVIT OF MOTHER.

UNITED STATES OF AMERICA, Indian Territory, ⎤
   Western Judicial   DISTRICT. ⎦

I, Jennetta Ground   , on oath state that I am   thirty (30)   years of age and a
citizen by   birth   , of the   Seminole   Nation; that I am the lawful wife of
Andrew M Ground   , who is a citizen, by   ——of the   ———— Nation, that a
male   child was born to me on   29th day of   April   , 1904; that said child has
been named Charlie Edward Ground   , and was living March 4, 1905.

179

Janette Ground

Witnesses To Mark:

{

Subscribed and sworn to before me this 23rd day of   May   , 1905.

M.F. Graham
Notary Public.

Duplicate   See 77

AFFIDAVIT OF ATTENDING PHYSICIAN OR MID-WIFE.

UNITED STATES OF AMERICA, Indian Territory, }
    Western   **DISTRICT.**

I, W.C. Mitchener   , a   M.D.   , on oath state that I attended on Mrs. Jennetta Ground   , wife of   Andrew M Ground   on the 29th day of April   , 1904; that there was born to her on said date a   male   child; that said child was living March 4, 1905, and is said to have been named Charlie Edward Ground

W.C. Mitchener M.D.

Witnesses To Mark:

{

Subscribed and sworn to before me this 23rd day of   May   , 1905.

M.F. Graham
Notary Public.

Commission Expires Oct 9th 1907

Sem NB 164
BIRTH AFFIDAVIT.

DEPARTMENT OF THE INTERIOR.
COMMISSION TO THE FIVE CIVILIZED TRIBES.

IN RE APPLICATION FOR ENROLLMENT, as a citizen of the   Seminole   Nation, of Andrew Mark Ground   , born on the 7th day of Feb   , 1902

Name of Father: Andrew M. Ground   a citizen of the   ————————Nation.
Name of Mother: Jennette Ground   1890   a citizen of the   Seminole   Nation.

Postoffice   Henryetta, Ind. Ter.

Applications for Enrollment of Seminole Newborn
Act of 1905   Volume II

AFFIDAVIT OF MOTHER.

UNITED STATES OF AMERICA, Indian Territory,
Western Judicial   DISTRICT.

I, Jennetta Ground   , on oath state that I am   thirty (30)   years of age and a citizen by   birth   , of the   Seminole   Nation; that I am the lawful wife of Andrew M Ground   , who is a citizen, by ——of the ——— Nation; that a male   child was born to me on 7th   day of   Feb   , 1902; that said child has been named Andrew Mark Ground   , and was living March 4, 1905.

Janette Ground

Witnesses To Mark:

{

Subscribed and sworn to before me this 23rd   day of   May   , 1905.

M.F. Graham
Notary Public.

Duplicate   See <u>78</u>

AFFIDAVIT OF ATTENDING PHYSICIAN OR MID-WIFE.

UNITED STATES OF AMERICA, Indian Territory,
Western Judicial   DISTRICT.

I, W.C. Mitchener   , a   M.D.   , on oath state that I attended on Mrs. Jennetta Ground   , wife of   Andrew M Ground   on the 7th   day of Feb , 1902; that there was born to her on said date a   male   child; that said child was living March 4, 1905, and is said to have been named Andrew Mark Ground

W.C. Mitchener

Witnesses To Mark:

{

Subscribed and sworn to before me this 23rd day of   May   , 1905.

M.F. Graham
Notary Public.

Commission Expires Oct 9th 1907

Applications for Enrollment of Seminole Newborn
Act of 1905 Volume II

Sem NB 164
BIRTH AFFIDAVIT.

DEPARTMENT OF THE INTERIOR.
COMMISSION TO THE FIVE CIVILIZED TRIBES.

IN RE APPLICATION FOR ENROLLMENT, as a citizen of the Seminole Nation, of Andrew M. Ground , born on the 7" day of Feby , 1902

Name of Father: A.M. Ground a citizen of the U.S. Nation.
Name of Mother: Janette Ground ($^\#$1890) a citizen of the Seminole Nation.

Postoffice Henryetta, Ind. Ter.

Father
AFFIDAVIT OF ~~MOTHER~~.

UNITED STATES OF AMERICA, Indian Territory,
Western DISTRICT.

I, A. M. Ground , on oath state that I am 33 years of age and a citizen by
———, of the United Stated Nation; that I am the lawful ~~wife of~~ husband of
Janette Ground , who is a citizen, by blood of the Seminole Nation;
that a male child was born to ~~me~~ her on 7th day of February , 1902; that
said child has been named Andrew M. Ground , and was living March 4, 1905.

A M Ground

Witnesses To Mark:

{

Subscribed and sworn to before me this 2" day of May , 1905.

⟨Seal⟩

Edward Merrick
Notary Public.

D.C.LL.

DEPARTMENT OF THE INTERIOR,
COMMISSIONER TO THE FIVE CIVILIZED TRIBES.

In the matter of the application for the enrollment of Lena Salone as a minor citizen of the Seminole Nation.

Sem. NB 165.

Sem NB 165
BIRTH AFFIDAVIT.

DEPARTMENT OF THE INTERIOR.
COMMISSION TO THE FIVE CIVILIZED TRIBES.

IN RE APPLICATION FOR ENROLLMENT, as a citizen of the   Seminole   Nation, of
Lena Salone   , born on the —— day of May   , 1902

Name of Father: Peter   1830   a citizen of the   Nation.
Name of Mother: Rhoda Salone   129   a citizen of the   Seminole   Nation.
                       nee Marty
                            Postoffice   Henryetta IT

AFFIDAVIT OF ~~MOTHER~~.
Band Chief

UNITED STATES OF AMERICA, Indian Territory,
     Western   **DISTRICT.**

I,   Tom Palmer   , on oath state that I am 46 years of age and a citizen by blood   , of the   Seminole   Nation; that I am the ~~lawful wife~~ band chief of Rhoda Salone   , who is a citizen, by   blood   of the   Seminole   Nation; that a   female   child was born to ~~me~~ her on   day of   May   , 1902, that said child has been named   Lena Salone   , and is now living.

                                      Tom Palmer
Witnesses To Mark:

Subscribed and sworn to before me this 31   day of   May   , 1905.

                              Chas E Webster
                                   Notary Public.

Applications for Enrollment of Seminole Newborn
Act of 1905   Volume II

AFFIDAVIT OF ~~MOTHER~~.

UNITED STATES OF AMERICA, Indian Territory, ⎱
    Western   DISTRICT. ⎰

    I, Washington Riley   , on oath state that I am 66 years of age and a citizen by blood   , of the   Creek   Nation; that I ~~am~~ the ~~lawful wife of~~ know Rhoda Salone , who is a citizen, by   blood   of the   Seminole   Nation; that a   male   child was born to ~~me~~ her on 29th   day of   July   , 1904, that said child has been named Lona[sic] Salone   , and is now living.

Washington x Riley

Witnesses To Mark:
    ⎰ Charley W Powell
    ⎱ J.L. Gary

    Subscribed and sworn to before me this 10th   day of   January   , 1907.

J.L. Gary
Notary Public.

AFFIDAVIT OF ATTENDING PHYSICIAN OR MID-WIFE.

UNITED STATES OF AMERICA, Indian Territory, ⎱
    Western   DISTRICT. ⎰

know

    I, Sarah Riley   , an acquaintance   , on oath state that I ~~attended on~~ Mrs. Rhoda Salone   , wife of Peter Salone   on the 29th   day of July , 1904; that there was born to her on said date a   male   child; that said child is now living and is said to have been named Lona Salone   her

Sarah x Riley
mark

Witnesses To Mark:
    ⎰ Charley W Powell
    ⎱ J.L. Gary

    Subscribed and sworn to before me this 10th   day of   January   , 1907.

J.L. Gary
Notary Public.

Applications for Enrollment of Seminole Newborn
Act of 1905   Volume II

DEPARTMENT OF THE INTERIOR

COMMISSION TO THE FIVE CIVILIZED TRIBES.

In the matter of the application for the enrollment of Pearl Raiford, Lena Raiford, Lena Salone, Lumpsey Scott, Sam Miller, Elizabeth Cully, Maley, and Albert, as citizens by blood of the Seminole Nation.

Thomas Palmer, being duly sworn, testified as follows, through Mrs. A. B. Davis, official interpreter:

Q. What is your name? A. Thomas Palmer.
Q. What is your age? A. Forty-six.
Q. What is your post office address? A. Sasakwa.
Q. Do you desire to make application for enrollment of the above named children as citizens of the Seminole Nation? A. Yes.
Q. Are you related to any of the above named children? A. No.
Q. What position do you hold? A. I am a band chief.
Q. Are you acquainted with the parents of each of the above named children? A. Yes.
Q. They are all upon the approved Seminole roll, are they? Their names appear upon that roll? A. They are on the roll and have taken allotments.
Q. The names of these children appear upon the records of the Seminoles, do they not; that is upon your record? A. Yes, all of them.
Q. And have drawn their annuities or headright? A. Yes, there was one child that was not born in time, that is has not yet drawn any monty.
Q. He is recognized as a Seminole Indian is he not? A. Yes.
Q. Why is it that the parents of these children do not appear before this office to enroll them? A. Their husbands are snakes. They are not in favor of allotment, and don't come forward to allot their wives and children. They were allotted arbitrarily. These people have never appeared before the Commission. The husbands are Creeks.
Q. Has application ever been made, before this time, for any one of these children, as citizens of the Seminole Nation, or any other nation? A. No, they have never been before the Commission. Their parents are snakes, and would not appear before the Commission. The husbands are snakes.

I, William S. Webb, on oath state that as stenographer to the Commission to the Five Civilized Tribes, I took testimony in the above case, and the above and foregoing is a true transcript of my stenographic [sic] taken in said case on the 31st day of May, A. D. 1905.

William S Webb

Subscribed and sworn to before me, on this the 1st day of June, A. D. 1905.

Chas E Webster
Notary Public.

Applications for Enrollment of Seminole Newborn
Act of 1905   Volume II

DEPARTMENT OF THE INTERIOR,
COMMISSIONER TO THE FIVE CIVILIZED TRIBES.
Sonora, I. T., June 16, 1905.

In the matter of the application for the enrollment of Lillie and Loney Sloan as citizens by blood of the Seminole Nation.

LODIE SLOAN, being duly sworn, testified as follows:

Through Alex Posey Official Interpreter:

BY COMMISSION:
Q What is your name? A Lodie Sloan.
Q How old are you? A I do not know.

Witness appears to be about twenty-eight years of age.

Q What is your post office address? A Henrietta.
Q Are you a citizen of the Creek Nation? A Yes, sir.
Q To what town do you belong? A Weogufke.
Q Do you make application for the enrollment of your two children, Lillie and Loney Sloan as citizens by blood of the Creek Nation? A Yes, sir.
Q If it should be found that these two children are entitled to rights in both the Creek and Seminole Nations in which nation do you elect to have them enrolled? A In the Creek Nation.

---oooOOOooo---

I, D. C. Skaggs, on oath state that the above and foregoing is a full and true transcript of my stenographic notes as taken in said cause on said date.

Subscribed and sworn to before me this____day of_____1905.

Notary Public.

Sem. NB-165.

DEPARTMENT OF THE INTERIOR,
COMMISSIONER TO THE FIVE CIVILIZED TRIBES.

In the matter of the application for the enrollment of Lena Salone as a minor citizen of the Seminole Nation.

-: D E C I S I O N :-

It appears from the record herein that on May 31, 1905, written application was made to the Commission to the Five Civilized Tribes for the enrollment of Lena Salone as a minor citizen of the Seminole Nation under the provisions of the Act of Congress approved March 3, 1905 (33 Stats., 1070).

It further appears from the record herein and from the records of this office, that the applicant, Lena Salone, was born July 29, 1904, and is the daughter of Rhoda Salone, whose name appears upon a schedule of citizens by blood of the Creek Nation approved by the Secretary of the Interior February 19, 1907 opposite No. 10108, and Peter Salone, whose name appears as "Peter" upon the approved roll of citizens by blood of the Seminole Nation opposite No. 1830 approved by the Secretary of the Interior April 2, 1901.

It further appears from the record herein and from the records of this office that the parents of said Lena Salone elected on June 16, 1905 to have said child, Lena Salone enrolled as a citizen by blood of the Creek Nation and to take her allotment of land and distribution of moneys in said nation; and that on February 26, 1907, the Commissioner to the Five Civilized Tribes rendered his decision granting the application for the enrollment of said Lena Salone as a citizen by blood of the Creek Nation.

I am, therefore, of the opinion that the application for the enrollment of Lena Salone as a minor citizen of the Seminole Nation should be dismissed, and it is so ordered.

Tams Bixby   Commissioner.

Muskogee, Indian Territory,
FEB 20 1907

Sem. NB-165.

Muskogee, Indian Territory, March 6, 1907.

Peter Salone,
Henryetta, Indian Territory.

Dear Sir:-

You are hereby advised that the Commissioner to the Five Civilized Tribes on February 20, 1907, rendered his decision, dismissing the application for the enrollment of Lena Salone as a citizen of the Seminole Nation.

187

Respectfully,

SIGNED *Tams Bixby*

Registered.   Commissioner.

Sem. NB-165   **COPY**

Muskogee, Indian Territory, March 6, 1907.

Chief Clerk,
      Creek Enrollment Division:

Dear Sir:-

You are hereby advised that the Commissioner to the Five Civilized Tribes on February 20, 1907, rendered his decision, dismissing the application for the enrollment of Lena Salone as a citizen of the Seminole Nation.

Respectfully,

SIGNED *Tams Bixby*

Commissioner.

Affidavits of Mother & Physician or midwife--In the event of failure to secure one of the above-affidavits of two disinterested parties, who know when said child was born and whether or not it was living on March 4, 1905. witnesses--If neither can be procured-affidavits of four disinterested witnesses

(Illegible)

Seminole-NB-165.

Muskogee, Indian Territory, June 29, 1905.

Rhoda Salone,
      Hanryetta[sic], Indian Territory.

Dear Madam:

On May 31, 1905, Tom Palmer, band chief, appeared before the Commission and made application for the enrollment of your daughter, Lena Salona[sic], as a citizen by blood of the Seminole Nation.

You are advised that before the rights of said child, as a citizen by blood of the Seminole Nation, can be finally determined it will be necessary for you to file with the

Applications for Enrollment of Seminole Newborn
Act of 1905 Volume II

Commission proper proof of birth of said child, and a blank for that purpose in[sic] inclosed you herewith.

In having the same executed be careful to see that all blanks spaces are properly filled, all names written in full, and that the notary public before whom the affidavits are executed attaches his name and seal to each affidavit. In case any signature is by mark it must be attested by two disinterested persons, witnesses thereto.

Please give this matter your prompt attention.

Respectfully,

B-c.
Env.   Chairman.

NBS 165.

Muskogee, Indian Territory, November 7, 1905.

Rhoda Salome[sic],
    Henryetta, Indian Territory.

Dear Madam:

Under date of June 25, 1905, you were requested to furnish this office with the affidavits of yourself and the attending physician or midwife, bearing the date of the birth of your minor children, Lena and Albert Saloma[sic], for whose enrollment, as citizens of the Seminole Nation, Tom Palmer a Band Chief, made application on May 31, 1905.

You are advised that it is very necessary that these affidavits be furnished, inasmuch as it will be impossible for this office to determine without them the rights to enrollment of your said minor children.

This matter should receive your very earliest attention.

Respectfully,

Commissioner.

Sem. NB 165

Muskogee, Indian Territory, December 29, 1905.

McKennon & Willmott,
    Attorneys for the Seminoles,
        Wewoka, Indian Territory.

Gentlemen:

On May 31, 1905, application was made to the Commission to the Five Civilized Tribes by Thomas Palmer, of Sasakwa, Indian Territory, for the enrollment of Lena Saloma as a citizen of the Seminole Nation under the act of Congress approved March 3, 1905.

It appears from the testimony of Thoams[sic] Palmer that the applicant, Lena Salome, was born in the month of May, 1902, and is the child of Peter, Seminole Roll Number, 1830, and Rhoda Saloma, who was identified as Rhoda Marty, Seminole Roll Number 129. It is desirable that this office be supplied with the affidavit of the mother, Rhoda Saloma, to the date of her birth and whether said child is now or was living on March 4, 1905, and also the affidavits of two disinterested parties who know of the birth of said child and that she was living March 4, 1905. Please give this matter your prompt attention.

Respectfully,

BC

Commissioner

Sem NB 165
BIRTH AFFIDAVIT.

Department of the Interior,
COMMISSION TO THE FIVE CIVILIZED TRIBES.

IN RE APPLICATION FOR ENROLLMENT, as a citizen of the   Seminole   Nation,
of   Lena Salone , born on the   day of   May , 1902

Name of Father: Peter   1830   a citizen of the   Nation.
Name of Mother: Rhoda Salone   129   a citizen of the   Seminole   Nation.
                  nee Marty

Post-Office: Henryetta, I.T.

AFFIDAVIT OF MOTHER.

UNITED STATES OF AMERICA,⎫
    INDIAN TERRITORY,   ⎬
    Western   District. ⎭   Band Chief

I,   Tom Palmer   , on oath state that I am   46   years of age and a
citizen by   blood , of the   Seminole   Nation; that I am the ~~lawful wife~~ band

190

chief of   Rhoda Salone   , who is a citizen, by   blood   of the   Seminole Nation; that a   female   child was born to ~~me~~ her on   day of   May   , 1902 , that said child has been named   Lena Salone   , and is now living.

Tom Palmer

WITNESSES TO MARK:

{

Subscribed and sworn to before me this 31 *day of*   May   , 1905.

Chas. E. Webster
Notary Public.

D.C.LL.

DEPARTMENT OF THE INTERIOR,
COMMISSIONER TO THE FIVE CIVILIZED TRIBES.

In the matter of the application for the enrollment of Albert as a minor citizen of the Seminole Nation.

Sem- NB-166.

Sem NB 166
BIRTH AFFIDAVIT.

Department of the Interior,
COMMISSION TO THE FIVE CIVILIZED TRIBES.

IN RE APPLICATION FOR ENROLLMENT, as a citizen of the   Seminole   Nation, of   Albert , born on the 5 day of   Jan , 1900

Name of Father: Willie   503   a citizen of the   Seminole Nation.
Name of Mother: Rhoda Salone 129   a citizen of the   Seminole Nation.
                 nee Marty

Post-Office: Henryetta, I.T.

191

Applications for Enrollment of Seminole Newborn
Act of 1905 Volume II

AFFIDAVIT OF MOTHER.

UNITED STATES OF AMERICA,
INDIAN TERRITORY,
Western   District.   Band Chief

I,   Tom Palmer   , on oath state that I am   46   years of age and a citizen by   blood , of the   Seminole   Nation; that I am the ~~lawful wife~~ Band Chief of   Rhoda Salone   , who is a citizen, by blood   of the   Seminole Nation; that a   male   child was born to ~~me~~ her on   5   day of Jan   , 1900 , that said child has been named   Albert   , and is now living.

Tom Palmer

WITNESSES TO MARK:

{

Subscribed and sworn to before me this 31   *day of*   May   , *1905.*

Charles E. Webster
Notary Public.

DEPARTMENT OF THE INTERIOR

COMMISSION TO THE FIVE CIVILIZED TRIBES.

In the matter of the application for the enrollment of Pearl Raiford, Lena Raiford, Lena Salone, Lumpsey Scott, Sam Miller, Elizabeth Cully, Maley, and <u>Albert</u>, as citizens by blood of the Seminole Nation.

Thomas Palmer, being duly sworn, testified as follows, through Mrs. A. B. Davis, official interpreter:

Q. What is your name? A. Thomas Palmer.
Q. What is your age? A. Forty-six.
Q. What is your post office address? A. Sasakwa.
Q. Do you desire to make application for enrollment of the above named children as citizens of the Seminole Nation? A. Yes.
Q. Are you related to any of the above named children? A. No.
Q. What position do you hold? A. I am a band chief.
Q. Are you acquainted with the parents of each of the above named children? A. Yes.
Q. They are all upon the approved Seminole roll, are they? Their names appear upon that roll? A. They are on the roll and have taken allotments.
Q. The names of these children appear upon the records of the Seminoles, do they not; that is upon your record? A. Yes, all of them.
Q. And have drawn their annuities or headright? A. Yes, there was one child that was not born in time, that is has not yet drawn any monty.
Q. He is recognized as a Seminole Indian is he not? A. Yes.

Q. Why is it that the parents of these children do not appear before this office to enroll them? A. Their husbands are snakes. They are not in favor of allotment, and don't come forward to allot their wives and children. They were allotted arbitrarily. These people have never appeared before the Commission. The husbands are Creeks.

Q. Has application ever been made, before this time, for any one of these children, as citizens of the Seminole Nation, or any other nation? A. No, they have never been before the Commission. Their parents are snakes, and would not appear before the Commission. The husbands are snakes.

I, William S. Webb, on oath state that as stenographer to the Commission to the Five Civilized Tribes, I took testimony in the above case, and the above and foregoing is a true transcript of my stenographic [sic] taken in said case on the 31st day of May, A. D. 1905.

William S Webb

Subscribed and sworn to before me, on this the 1st day of June, A. D. 1905.

Chas. E. Webster
Notary Public.

(SEAL)

Copy

I, Rhoda Salone, (formerly enrolled on the approved roll of the Seminole Nation as Rhoda Marty, and now enrolled upon the approved roll of citizens by blood of the Creek Nation as Mariah Harjo), do hereby elect, in the event that it is found that Albert, the son of myself and Willie, a full blood Seminole, is entitled to enrollment either as a Seminole or as a Creek, that he be enrolled as a citizen by blood of the Creek Nation.

Rhoda Slome[sic]

WITNESSES TO MARK:

_____

_____

Filed Feb 23 1907

Sem. NB-166.

DEPARTMENT OF THE INTERIOR,
COMMISSIONER TO THE FIVE CIVILIZED TRIBES.

DCW

In the matter of the application for the enrollment of Albert as a minor citizen of the Seminole Nation.

-: D E C I S I O N :-

It appears from the record herein that on May 31, 1905, written application was made to the Commission to the Five Civilized Tribes for the enrollment of Albert as a minor citizen of the Seminole Nation under the provisions of the Act of Congress approved March 3, 1905 (33 Stats., 1070).

It further appears from the record herein and from the records of this office that the applicant was born January 5, 1900 and is the son of Rhoda Salone, whose name appears upon a schedule of citizens by blood of the Creek Nation approved by the Secretary of the Interior February 19, 1907 opposite No. 10108, and Willie a Seminole Indian, whose name appears opposite No. 503 upon the final roll of Seminole Indians approved by the Secretary of the Interior.

It further appears from the record herein and from the records of this office that Rhoda Salone (Slome) on February 23, 1907 elected in writing to have said child enrolled as a citizen by blood of the Creek Nation and to take his allotment of land and distribution of moneys in said nation, and that on February 26, 1907, the Commissioner to the Five Civilized Tribes rendered his decision granting the application for the enrollment of said Albert as a citizen by blood of the Creek Nation.

I am, therefore, of the opinion that the application for the enrollment of Albert as a minor citizen of the Seminole Nation should be dismissed, and it is so ordered.

Tams Bixby   Commissioner.

Muskogee, Indian Territory,
FEB 20 1907

Sem. NB-166

Muskogee, Indian Territory, March 6, 1907.

Willie Sloan,
Henryetta, Indian Territory.

Dear Sir:-

You are hereby advised that the Commissioner to the Five Civilized Tribes on February 20, 1907, rendered his decision dismissing the application for the enrollment of Albert Sloan as a citizen of the Seminole Nation.

Respectfully,

SIGNED   *Tams Bixby*

Commissioner.

Sem. NB-166   **COPY**

Muskogee, Indian Territory, March 6, 1907.

Chief Clerk,
     Creek Enrollment Division.

Dear Sir:-

You are hereby advised that the Commissioner to the Five Civilized Tribes on February 20, 1907, rendered his decision dismissing the application for the enrollment of Albert Sloan[sic] as a citizen of the Seminole Nation.

Respectfully,

SIGNED   *Tams Bixby*

Commissioner.

Albert is son of Willie [#]503 and is living with him at Sasawka[sic].
Tom Palmer says child has filed.

Gary

Affidavits of mother & physician or midwife--If only one can be secured- then two disinterested witnesses- If neither four disinterested witnesses.

Seminole NB-166

Muskogee, Indian Territory, June 29, 1905.

Rhoda Salone,
     Henryetta, Indian Territory.

Dear Madam:

On May 31, 1905, Tom Palmer, band chief, appeared before the commission and made application for the enrollment of your son, Albert Salone, as a citizen by blood of the Seminole Nation.

You are advised that before the rights of said child, as a citizen by blood of the Seminole Nation, can be finally determined it will be necessary for you to file with the

Commission proper proof of birth of said applicant, and a blank for the purpose is inclosed you herewith.

In having same executed be careful to see that all blank spaces are properly filled, all names written in full, and that the Notary Public before whom the affidavits are executed attaches his name and seal to each affidavit. In case any signature is by mark it must be attested by two disinterested witnesses.

Please give this matter your immediate attention.

Respectfully,

B-C/[sic]   Chairman.
Env.

Sem N B 165, 166

Muskogee, Indian Territory, December 29, 1905.

Rhoda Salone,
        Henryetta, Indian Territory.

Dear Madam:

You are hereby advised that a representative of the Commissioner to the Five Civilized Tribes will be in Wewoka, Indian Territory, Friday and Saturday, January 4 and 5, 1907, for the purpose of hearing testimony in Seminole enrollment cases and you should appear at that place on one of those days, accompanied by the physician or midwife who was in attendance at the birth of your children, Albert and Lena Salone, for the purpose of testifying relative to the right of these children to enrollment.

Respectfully,

Commissioner.

Sem. NB 166.

Muskogee, Indian Territory, December 29, 1905.

McKennon & Willmott,
        Attorneys for the Seminoles,
                Wewoka, Indian Territory.

Gentlemen:

On May 31, 1905, application was made to the Commission to the Five Civilized Tribes by Thomas Palmer, of Sasakwa, Indian Territory, for the enrollment of Albert as a citizen of the Seminole Nation under the act of Congress approved March 3, 1905.

196

Applications for Enrollment of Seminole Newborn
Act of 1905   Volume II

It appears from the testimony of Thomas Palmer that the applicant, Albert, was born January 5, 1900, and is the child of Willie, Seminole Roll Number 503, and Rhoda Salone, who was identified as Rhoda Marty, Seminole Roll, Number 129.   The post office address of Rhoda Salone appears to have been Henryetta, Indian Territory.

It is desirable that this office be supplied with the affidavit of the mother, Rhoda Salone, to the date of his birth and whether said child is now or was living on March 4, 1905, and also the affidavits of two disinterested parties who know of the birth of said child and that she[sic] was living March 4, 1905.   Please give this matter your early attention.

Respectfully,

B C   Commissioner

DEPARTMENT OF THE INTERIOR,

COMMISSION TO THE FIVE CIVILIZED TRIBES.

In the matter of the application of Elisha J. Brown, Jr., for enrollment as a citizen of the Seminole Nation.

Elisha J. Brown, Jr., being duly sworn, testified as follows:

Q. What is your name? A. Elisha J. Brown, Jr.
Q. Your post office? A. Keokuk Falls.
Q.   You now desire to make application for enrollment as a citizen of the Seminole Nation? A. Yes sir.
Q. What is your mother's name? A. Maynee M. Brown.
Q. Is she a citizen of the Seminole Nation? A. No sir.
Q. What is the name of your father? A. Elisha J. Brown.
Q. Is he a citizen of the Seminole Nation? A. Yes sir.
Q. By blood? A. No sir, by adoption.

The father, Elisha J. Brown is identified on the approved Seminole roll, opposite No. 631.

Q. When were you born? A. In '73.
Q. What month and day? A. 28th of June.
Q. You were born the 28th day of June, 1873? A. Yes, sir.
Q. Are you recognized by the Seminole Nation as a citizen? A. No sir.

Q. Have you ever drawn any headright or annuities paid by the Seminole Nation?
A. No sir.
Q. Upon what do you base your claim as a citizen of the Seminole Nation? A. My father's name is on the approved roll. He was a citizen prior to my birth.
Q. Have you ever, before this time, applied to this Commission for enrollment as a citizen of the Seminole Nation, or any other nation? [sic] No sir, that is have made none for myself I never did.

(Witness Excused)

I, William S. Webb, being duly sworn, on oath state that as stenographer to the Commission to the Five Civilized [sic] I took testimony in the above case, and the above and foregoing is a true transcript of my notes taken in the above case on the 1st day of June, 1905.

William S Webb

Subscribed and sworn to before me, this 1st day of June, A. D. 1905.

Chas E Webster
Notary Public.

DEPARTMENT OF THE INTERIOR,

COMMISSION TO THE FIVE CIVILIZED TRIBES.

In the matter of the application of Harry R. Brown, for enrollment as a citizen of the Seminole Nation.

Harry R. Brown, being duly sworn, testified as follows:

Q. What is your name? A. Harry R. Brown.
Q. Your post office? A. Wewoka.
Q. You now desire to make application for enrollment as a citizen of the Seminole Nation? A. Yes sir.
Q. What is your mother's name? A. Maynee M. Brown.
Q. Is she a citizen of the Seminole Nation? A. No sir.
Q. Did she ever draw any money or headright from the Nation? A. Yes she drew money once, but for some reason she was not continued on the roll.
Q. Is she now living? A. No sir.
Q. What is your father's name? A. Elisha J. Brown.
Q. Is he recognized as a citizen of the Seminole Nation? A. Yes sir.
Q. When were you born? [sic] I must have been born 22nd of October 1871.
Q. Have you ever been recognized as a citizen of the Seminole Nation? A. No sir.
Q. You have never drawn any headright or annuities paid by the Nation? A. No sir.

Q. Upon what do you base your claim? [sic] From the fact that my father is a citizen of the Seminole Nation, and has been for a time prior to my birth. Always had been recognized as a citizen of the Seminole, on the approved roll.
Q. A. citizen by blood? A. By adoption.
Q. Have you ever before made application before this Commission for enrollment as a citizen of the Seminole Nation or any other Nation? A. No, never have.
Q. Did your father ever make application for you? A. He may have, I don't know.

(Witness excused)

I, William S. Webb, on oath state that as stenographer to the Commission to the five civilized tribes I took testimony in the above case, and the above and foregoing is a true transcript of my stenographic notes taken in said case on the 1st day of June, A. D. 1905.

William S Webb

Subscribed and sworn to before me, this 1st day of June, A. D. 1905.

Chas E Webster
Notary Public.

SEM NB 167.   EM

COPY
DEPARTMENT OF THE INTERIOR,
COMMISSIONER TO THE FIVE CIVILIZED TRIBES.

In the matter of the application for the enrollment of Elisha J. Brown, Jr. and Harry R. Brown, as citizens of the Seminole Nation.

D E C I S I O N.

It appears from the record herein that on June 1, 1905, the applicants, Elisha J. Brown, Jr. and Harry R. Brown, appeared in person before the Commission to the Five Civilized Tribes and made application for enrollment as citizens of the Seminole Nation.

It further appears from the record herein and the records of the office that the applicants, Elisha J. Brown, Jr. and Harry R. Brown, were born June 28, 1873, and October 22, 1871, respectively, and are children of Elisha J. Brown, a recognized and enrolled citizen of the Seminole Nation, whose name appears upon the final roll of citizens of said Nation, opposite No. 631, and Maynee M. Brown, a non-citizen.

It does not appear from the records of this office that the applicants herein have ever been recognized as citizens of the Seminole Nation by the tribal authorities thereof; and further it does not appear that the names of said applicants are upon any of the tribal rolls of said Nation. It has never been the custom of the Seminole tribe of Indians to recognize as citizens of the Seminole Nation, the children of a non-citizen mother.

The act of Congress approved March 3, 1905 (Public No. 212), among other things provides:

199

"That the Commission to the Five Civilized Tribes is authorized for ninety days after the date of the approval of this act to receive and consider applications for enrollment of <u>infant children</u> born prior to March fourth, nineteen hundred and five, and living on said latter date, to citizens of the Seminole tribe whose enrollment has been approved by the Secretary of the Interior; and to enroll and make allotments to such children, giving to each an equal number of acres of land, and such children shall also share equally with other citizens of the Seminole tribe in the distribution of all other tribal property and funds."

I am of the opinion that, inasmuch as the applicants, Elisha J. Brown, Jr. and Harry R. Brown were never recognized as citizens of the Seminole Nation, and their names not appearing upon any of the tribal rolls of said Nation, and for the further reason that they are not, and were not at the time said application was made, <u>infant children</u> of a citizen of the Seminole tribe, the Commission to the Five Civilized Tribes was without authority to receive or consider the applications for their enrollment as citizens of the Seminole Nation, and that, therefore, I should decline to receive or consider their applications, under the provision of law above quoted, and it is so ordered.

Tams Bixby

Commissioner.

Muskogee, Indian Territory,
SEP 15 1906

COPY

Sem. NB 167

Muskogee, Indian Territory, September 17, 1906.

Elisha J. Brown,
    Keokuk Falls, Oklahoma.

Dear Sir:

Inclosed herewith you will find a copy of the decision of the Commissioner to the Five Civilized Tribes, rendered September 15, 1906, declining to receive the application for the enrollment of Elisha J. Brown, Jr., and Harry R. Brown as new born citizens of the Seminole Nation.

The decision, with the record of proceedings in the case, is this day transmitted to the Secretary of the Interior for review. The final decision of the Secretary will be made known to you as soon as this office is informed of the same.

Respectfully,

SIGNED   *Tams Bixby*

Registered.
Incl. Sem. NB 167.

Commissioner.

200

COPY

Sem. NB-167

Muskogee, Indian Territory, September 17, 1906.

McKennon & Wilmott[sic],
    Attorneys at Law,
        Wewoka, Indian Territory.

Gentlemen:

Inclosed herewith you will find a copy of the decision of the Commissioner to the Five Civilized Tribes, rendered September 15, 1906, declining to receive the application for the enrollment of Elisha J. Brown, Jr., and Harry R. Brown as new born citizens of the Seminole Nation.

The decision, with the record of proceedings in the case is this day transmitted to the Secretary of the Interior for review. The final decision of the Secretary will be made known to you as soon as this office is informed of the same.

Respectfully,

SIGNED   *Tams Bixby*

Incl. Sem. NB-167.   Commissioner.

COPY

Muskogee, Indian Territory, September 17, 1906.

The Honorable,
    The Secretary of the Interior.

Sir:

There is transmitted herewith record of proceedings in the matter of the application for the enrollment of Elisha J. Brown, Jr., and Harry R. Brown as new born citizens of the Seminole Nation, including the decision of the Commissioner to the Five Civilized Tribes, dated September 15, 1906, declining to receive said application.

Respectfully,
SIGNED   *Tams Bixby*

2 Incl. Sem. NB-167.   Commissioner.
Through the Commis-
        sioner of Indian Affairs.

JPJr.

DEPARTMENT OF THE INTERIOR, LLB
WASHINGTON.

I. T. D. 2674-1907.

February 12, 1907.

LRS

Direct.

Commissioner to the Five Civilized Tribes,
Muskogee, Indian Territory.

Sir:

September 17, 1906, you transmitted the record in the matter of the application for the enrollment of application for the enrollment of Elisha J. Brown, Jr., and Harry R. Brown as new-born citizens of the Seminole Nation, including your decision of September 15, 1906, adverse to the applicants.

Reporting February 5, 1907 (Land 81809-1906), the Indian Office recommended that your decision be approved. A copy of its letter is inclosed.

The Department concurs in said recommendation, and your decision is hereby affirmed.

The papers in the case and a carbon copy hereof have been sent to the Indian Office.

Respectfully,
Thos Ryan
First Assistant Secretary.

1 inc. and 3 to Ind. Of.

A F Mc
2-13-07

--Copy--

DEPARTMENT OF THE INTERIOR,
LAND   OFFICE OF INDIAN AFFAIRS
81809-1906   WASHINGTON.

February 5, 1907.

The Honorable,
    The Secretary of the Interior.

Sir:-

    There is forwarded herewith report of Commissioner Bixby, dated September 17, 1906, relative to the application for the enrollment of Elisha J. Brown, Jr. and Harry R. Brown as new born citizens of the Seminole Nation, including the decision of the Commissioner, dated September 15, 1906, declining to receive the application.

    The record herein shows that application was made to the Commission to the Five Civilized Tribes as above on June 1, 1905. It further appears from the record that the applicants, Elisha J. Brown, Jr. and Harry R. Brown, were born June 28, 1873, and on October 22, 1871, respectively, and are children of Elisha J. Brown a recognized and enrolled citizen of the Seminole Nation, and Maynee M. Brown, a non-citizen.

    The Commissioner says that the records of his office do not show that the applicants herein have ever been recognized as citizens of the Seminole Nation by the tribal authorities thereof, nor does it appear that their names are on any of the tribal rolls of the Nation. He also says that it has never been the custom of the Seminole tribe to recognize as citizens of the Nation the children of a non-citizen mother.

    Under the provisions of the Act of March 3, 1905, (33 Stat. L., 1048), the Commission to the Five Civilized Tribes is authorized for ninety days after the approval of the Act to receive and consider applications for enrollment of infant children born prior to March 4, 1905, and living on that date, to citizens of the Seminole Nation whose enrollment has been approved by the Department, and to enroll and make allotments to such children.

    It appearing that the applicants, Elisha J. Brown, Jr. and Harry R. Brown, were never recognized as citizens of the Seminole Nation and that their names are not on any of the tribal rolls thereof, and for the further reason that they are not and were not, at the time of making the application, infant children of a citizen of the Seminole tribe, it is the opinion of the Office that the Commission to the Five Civilized Tribes was without authority to receive or consider their application for enrollment, under the provisions of the law referred to, and it is recommended that the case be dismissed.

Very respectfully,
C.F. Larrabee,
AJW-EH   Acting Commissioner.

Sem. NB-167

Muskogee, Indian Territory, February 27, 1907.

Elisha J. Brown,
    Keokuk Falls, Oklahoma.

Dear Sir:-

You are hereby advised that on February 12, 1907, the Secretary of the Interior the Interior affirmed the order of the Commissioner to the Five Civilized Tribes of September 15, 1906, declining to receive the application for the enrollment of Elisha J. Brown, Jr., and Harry R. Brown as new born citizens of the Seminole Nation.

Respectfully,

Commissioner.

Sem. N. B. -167

Muskogee, Indian Territory, February 28, 1907.

McKennon & Wilmott[sic],
    Attorneys at Law.
        Wewoka, Indian Territory.

Gentlemen:-

You are hereby advised that on February 12, 1907, the Secretary of the Interior the Interior affirmed the order of the Commissioner to the Five Civilized Tribes of September 15, 1906, declining to receive the application for the enrollment of Elisha J. Brown, Jr., and Harry R. Brown as new born citizens of the Seminole Nation.

Respectfully,

Commissioner.

Applications for Enrollment of Seminole Newborn
Act of 1905   Volume II

DEPARTMENT OF THE INTERIOR,
COMMISSIONER TO THE FIVE CIVILIZED TRIBES.

In the matter of the application for the enrollment of Elisha J. Brown, Jr. and Harry R. Brown, as citizens of the Seminole Nation.

DECISION.

The records in this case show that on June 1, 1905, there was filed with the Commission to the Five Civilized Tribes at Wewoka, Indian Territory, the application of Harry R Brown and Elisha J. Brown, Jr., for their enrollment as citizens by blood of the Seminole Nation.

The evidence shows that Harry R. Brown was born October 22, 1871, and Elisha J. Brown Jr., was born June 28, 1873; that they are both children of Maynee N. Brown, a non citizen white woman, and Elisha J. Brown, a white man who was adopted as a citizen of the Seminole Nation, by an act passed by the Seminole Council in the year of 1869, and that his name appears upon the approved roll of the Seminole Nation, opposite number 631.

The evidence further shows that neither Harry R. Brown or Elisha J. Brown Jr., have ever been recognized as citizens of said Nation.

The Act of Congress of March 3, 1905 (33 Stat., 1048) provides:

"That the Commission to the Five Civilized Tribes is authorized for ninety days after the date of the approval of this act to receive and consider applications for enrollment of infant children born prior to March fourth, nineteen hundred and five, and living on said latter date, to citizens of the Seminole tribe whose enrollment has been approved by the Secretary of the Interior; and to enroll and make allotments to such children, giving to each an equal number of acres of land, and such children shall also share equally with other citizens of the Seminole tribe in the distribution of all other tribal property and funds."

It is, therefore, ordered and adjudged that there is no authority of law for the enrollment of said Harry R. Brown and Elisha J. Brown Jr., as citizens by blood of the Seminole Nation, and that the application for their enrollment as such are accordingly denied.

Muskogee, Indian Territory,   Commissioner.
_____

_____

JPJr.

DEPARTMENT OF THE INTERIOR, LLB
WASHINGTON.

I. T. D. 2674-1907.

February 12, 1907.

LRS
    Direct.

Commissioner to the Five Civilized Tribes,
    Muskogee, Indian Territory.

Sir:

September 17, 1906, you transmitted the record in the matter of the application for the enrollment of application for the enrollment of Elisha J. Brown, Jr., and Harry R. Brown as new-born citizens of the Seminole Nation, including your decision of September 15, 1906, adverse to the applicants.

Reporting February 5, 1907 (Land 81809-1906), the Indian Office recommended that your decision be approved. A copy of its letter is inclosed.

The Department concurs in said recommendation, and your decision is hereby affirmed.

The papers in the case and a carbon copy hereof have been sent to the Indian Office.

Respectfully,
Thos Ryan
First Assistant Secretary.

1 inc. and 3 to Ind. Of.

A F Mc
2-13-07

--Copy--

DEPARTMENT OF THE INTERIOR,
LAND   OFFICE OF INDIAN AFFAIRS
81809-1906   WASHINGTON.

February 5, 1907.

The Honorable,
    The Secretary of the Interior.

Sir:-

Applications for Enrollment of Seminole Newborn
Act of 1905   Volume II

There is forwarded herewith report of Commissioner Bixby, dated September 17, 1906, relative to the application for the enrollment of Elisha J. Brown, Jr. and Harry R. Brown as new born citizens of the Seminole Nation, including the decision of the Commissioner, dated September 15, 1906, declining to receive the application.

The record herein shows that application was made to the Commission to the Five Civilized Tribes as above on June 1, 1905. It further appears from the record that the applicants, Elisha J. Brown, Jr. and Harry R. Brown, were born June 28, 1873, and on October 22, 1871, respectively, and are children of Elisha J. Brown a recognized and enrolled citizen of the Seminole Nation, and Maynee M. Brown, a non-citizen.

The Commissioner says that the records of his office do not show that the applicants herein have ever been recognized as citizens of the Seminole Nation by the tribal authorities thereof, nor does it appear that their names are on any of the tribal rolls of the Nation. He also says that it has never been the custom of the Seminole tribe to recognize as citizens of the Nation the children of a non-citizen mother.

Under the provisions of the Act of March 3, 1905, (33 Stat. L., 1048), the Commission to the Five Civilized Tribes is authorized for ninety days after the approval of the Act to receive and consider applications for enrollment of infant children born prior to March 4, 1905, and living on that date, to citizens of the Seminole Nation whose enrollment has been approved by the Department, and to enroll and make allotments to such children.

It appearing that the applicants, Elisha J. Brown, Jr. and Harry R. Brown, were never recognized as citizens of the Seminole Nation and that their names are not on any of the tribal rolls thereof, and for the further reason that they are not and were not, at the time of making the application, infant children of a citizen of the Seminole tribe, it is the opinion of the Office that the Commission to the Five Civilized Tribes was without authority to receive or consider their application for enrollment, under the provisions of the law referred to, and it is recommended that the case be dismissed.

Very respectfully,
C.F. Larrabee,
Acting Commissioner.

AJW-EH

Wewoka, Indian Territory, May 17, 1905.

Anna Spencer,
  Keokuk Falls, Oklahoma.

Madam:

On May 1, 1905, you appeared before the Seminole Enrollment Office, at Wewoka, Indian Territory, and made application for the enrollment of Mary Spencer, the minor child of Yona Spencer and yourself.

The Commission is unable to identify either you or Yona Spencer upon the approved Seminole Roll, and it will be necessary, therefore, for you to appear before this office prior to June 1, 1905, in order that such identification may be made.

Respectfully,
Clerk in Charge.

Sem NB 168   Father's Roll No *(nothing given)*
BIRTH AFFIDAVIT.
DEPARTMENT OF THE INTERIOR.
COMMISSION TO THE FIVE CIVILIZED TRIBES.

IN RE APPLICATION FOR ENROLLMENT, as a citizen of the   Seminole   Nation, of
Mary Spencer   , born on the 11th day of Apr   , 1903

Name of Father: Yona Spencer   a citizen of the Seminole   Nation.
Name of Mother: Anna Spencer   (961)   a citizen of the Seminole   Nation.

Postoffice   Keokuk Falls, Okla

(Child present)
AFFIDAVIT OF MOTHER.

UNITED STATES OF AMERICA, Indian Territory, ⎫
   Western   **DISTRICT.** ⎭

I, Anna Spencer   , on oath state that I am 19   years of age and a citizen by blood   , of the   Seminole   Nation; that I am the lawful wife of Yona Spencer   , who is a citizen, by   blood   of the   Seminole   Nation; that a   female child was born to me on 11th day of April   , 1903, that said child has been named Mary Spencer   , and is now living.

her
Anna x Spencer
mark

208

Applications for Enrollment of Seminole Newborn
Act of 1905   Volume II

Witnesses To Mark:
{ Frank C. Sabourin
{ Edward Merrick

Subscribed and sworn to before me this 1" day of   May   , 1905.

Edward Merrick
Notary Public.

AFFIDAVIT OF ATTENDING PHYSICIAN OR MID-WIFE.

UNITED STATES OF AMERICA, Indian Territory,
    Western   DISTRICT.

I,   Toge Harjo   , a   Midwife   , on oath state that I attended on Mrs.   Anna
Spencer   , wife of   Yona Spencer   on the   11th   day of   April   , 1903; that there
was born to her on said date a   female   child; that said child is now living and is said
to have been named   Mary Spencer   her
                                                      Toge x Harjo
Witnesses To Mark: mark
{ Frank C. Sabourin
{ Ed. Merrick

Subscribed and sworn to before me this 1" day of   May   , 1905.

Edward Merrick

Notary Public.

Sem NB 169
BIRTH AFFIDAVIT.
DEPARTMENT OF THE INTERIOR.
COMMISSION TO THE FIVE CIVILIZED TRIBES.

IN RE APPLICATION FOR ENROLLMENT, as a citizen of the   Seminole   Nation, of
Lydia Porter   , born on the   26   day of   August   , 1903

Name of Father: Alfred Porter   *(156)*   a citizen of the   Seminole   Nation.
Name of Mother: Amy Porter   *(157)*   a citizen of the   Seminole   Nation.

Applications for Enrollment of Seminole Newborn
Act of 1905   Volume II

Postoffice   Sasakwa I.T.

(Child present)

AFFIDAVIT OF MOTHER.

UNITED STATES OF AMERICA, Indian Territory,
　　Western　　　　　　**DISTRICT.**

　　I,　Amy Porter　, on oath state that I am　27　years of age and a citizen by blood　, of the　Seminole　Nation; that I am the lawful wife of　Alfred Porter　, who is a citizen, by blood　of the　　Seminole　　Nation; that a　Female child was born to me on　26　day of　August　, 1903; that said child has been named　Lydia Porter　, and was living March 4, 1905.

　　　　　　　　　　　　　　　Amy Porter

Witnesses To Mark:
　{

　　Subscribed and sworn to before me this　1st　day of　May　, 1905.

　　　　　　　　　　　Chas E Webster
　　　　　　　　　　　　　Notary Public.

AFFIDAVIT OF ATTENDING PHYSICIAN OR MID-WIFE.

UNITED STATES OF AMERICA, Indian Territory,
　　Western　　　　　**DISTRICT.**

　　I,　Annie Church　, a　mid wife　, on oath state that I attended on Mrs. Amy Porter　, wife of　Alfred Porter　on the 26　day of　August　, 1903; that there was born to her on said date a　Female　child; that said child was living March 4, 1905, and is said to have been named　Lydia Porter
　　　　　　　　　　　　　her
　　　　　　　　　　　Annie x Church
Witnesses To Mark:　　　　　　　mark
　{ FC Sabourin
　{ Chas E Webster

　　Subscribed and sworn to before me　1st　day of　May　, 1905.

　　　　　　　　　　　Chas E Webster
　　　　　　　　　　　　　Notary Public.

210

Applications for Enrollment of Seminole Newborn
Act of 1905   Volume II

Sem NB 169
BIRTH AFFIDAVIT.

DEPARTMENT OF THE INTERIOR.
COMMISSION TO THE FIVE CIVILIZED TRIBES.

_____

IN RE APPLICATION FOR ENROLLMENT, as a citizen of the   Seminole   Nation, of
Lydia Harjo   , born on the   26th   day of   August   , 1903

Name of Father: Alfah Harjo   (156)   a citizen of the   Seminole   Nation.
Name of Mother: Amey Harjo   a citizen of the   Seminole   Nation.

Postoffice   Sasakwa I.T.

_____

(Child present)

AFFIDAVIT OF MOTHER.

UNITED STATES OF AMERICA, Indian Territory, ⎫
   Western   DISTRICT. ⎭

   I,   Amey Harjo   , on oath state that I am   27   years of age and a citizen by
blood   , of the   Seminole   Nation; that I am the lawful wife of   Alfah Harjo   ,
who is a citizen, by   blood   of the   Seminole   Nation; that a   female
child was born to me on   26th   day of   August   , 1903; that said child has been
named   Lydia Harjo   , and was living March 4, 1905.

Amy Harjo
Witnesses To Mark:

⎰
⎱

   Subscribed and sworn to before me this 11th   day of   Aug   , 1905.

J H Fleet
Notary Public.

_____

AFFIDAVIT OF ATTENDING PHYSICIAN OR MID-WIFE.

UNITED STATES OF AMERICA, Indian Territory, ⎫
   Western   DISTRICT. ⎭

   I,   Annie Church   , a   mid-wife   , on oath state that I attended on Mrs.
Amey Harjo   , wife of   Alfah Harjo   on the 26th   day of   August   , 1903;
that there was born to her on said date a   female   child; that said child was living
March 4, 1905, and is said to have been named   Lydia Harjo
                                                             her
                                        Annie Church   x
                                                            mark

Witnesses To Mark:
  { AJ Brown
  { Frank Fleet

Subscribed and sworn to before me this 11th day of   Aug   , 1905.

J H Fleet
Notary Public.

Wewoka, Indian Territory, May 17, 1905.

Amy Porter,
Sasakwa, Indian Territory.

Madam:

On May 1, 1905, you appeared before the Seminole Enrollment Office, at Wewoka, Indian Territory, and made application for the enrollment of Lydia Porter, the minor child of yourself and Alfred Porter.

The Commission is unable to identify either you or Alfred Porter upon the approved Seminole Roll, and it will be necessary, therefore, for you to appear before this office prior to June 1, 1905, in order that such identification may be made.

Respectfully,
Clerk in Charge.

Seminole
NB-169.

Muskogee, Indian Territory June 29, 1905.

Amy Cully,
Sasakwa, Indian Territory.

Dear Madam:

Your letter of June 26, 1905 addressed to Mr. Charles Webster, an employee of this Commission, has been by him referred to the Commission for appropriate action. Therein you request to be advised as to what steps it will be necessary for you to take to have your child Lydia Porter finally enrolled as a citizen by blood of the Seminole Nation.

In reply to your letter you are advised that the Commission is still unable to identify either you or Alfred Porter, the father of said child, upon the approved Seminole roll. You are therefore requested to inform the Commission of the names under which you and your husband, Alfred Porter, were enrolled, the names and ages of other members of your family and any other information that will enable the Commission to identify you and your husband upon the approved roll of citizens of the Seminole Nation.

If you have received your certificates of allotment you should give your final roll number as same appears thereon.

Please give this matter your immediate attention.

Respectfully,

Chairman.

———————

COPY.

Sasakwa, I. T.

7 - 2 - 05

Tams Bixby
Chairman Dawes Commission
Muskogee, I. T.

Sir:-

In reply to your letter of the 29th inst will say that my husband's name on the roll is Alfred Harjo and myself as Amy Harjo. There is another Amy Harjo that lives in about 2 miles of my place that gets my mail out of the P. O. so I do not get my mail for a good many days some times. Please address me as below

Yours Respc't

Amy Cully.

INDORSED:
Indexed. Commission to the Five Tribes. No 32402 1905
Received Jul 3 1905. Cully, Amy, Sasakwa, I. T., Seminole Nation, July 2, 1905. States her husband is enrolled as Alfred Harjo, and she as Amy Harjo. In re application for enrollment of her child, Lydia Porter.

———————

Applications for Enrollment of Seminole Newborn
Act of 1905   Volume II

Seminole NB-169.

Muskogee, Indian Territory July 6, 1905.

Amey Cully,
    Sasakwa, Indian Territory.

Dear Madam:

Receipt is hereby acknowledged of your letter of July 2, 1905 stating that your husband was finally enrolled by the Commission to the Five Civilized Tribes as Alfred Harjo and that you were finally enrolled as Amy Harjo.

The information contained in your letter has enabled this office to identify your husband and yourself as Alfah Harjo and Amey Harjo, numbers 156 and 157, respectively, upon the final roll of citizens by blood of the Seminole Nation.

Respectfully,

Commissioner.

Seminole
NB-169.

Muskogee, Indian Territory, July 25, 1905.

Amy Cully,
    Sasakwa, Indian Territory.

Dear Madam:

From your letter of July 2, 1905 you and your husband, Alfred, were identified upon the approved roll of citizens by blood as Amey Harjo and Alfah Harjo, respectively.

It appears from your letter and from your affidavit filed in the matter of the enrollment of your daughter, Lydia, that you and your husband are now known by the surname of Porter and that when you made application for the enrollment of your daid[sic] daughter Lydia before the Commission to the Five Civilized Tribes on May 1, 1905 you said that she had been named Lydia Porter. The name of said child must necessarily follow that of her parents and inasmuch as you and your said husband have been finally enrolled under the name of Harjo it appears that the correct name of said child is Lydia Harjo.

You are advised that it will, therefore, be necessary for you to furnish this office with proof of birth of said child showing her correct name and an affidavit for that purpose properly filled out is inclosed herewith. Be careful to sign your name to the affidavit as "Amey Harjo" as you are finally enrolled, and as your name appears in the body of the affidavit.

214

Applications for Enrollment of Seminole Newborn
Act of 1905   Volume II

In case Annie Church, the midwife who attended you at the birth of said child, is unable to write and her signature is by mark the same must be attested by two disinterested witnesses. Be careful to see that the notary public, before whom the affidavits are sworn to attaches his name and seal to each affidavit.

Please give this matter your prompt attention.

Respectfully,

Commissioner.

CTD-2
Env.

_____

Seminole
NB-169.

Muskogee, Indian Territory, August 15, 1905.

Amy Cully (or Harjo),
    Sasakwa, Indian Territory.

Dear Madam:

Receipt is hereby acknowledged of your affidavit and the affidavit of Annie Church, midwife, relative to the birth of your minor daughter Lydia on August 26, 1903 and the same has been filed with the records of this office in the matter of the application for the enrollment of said child as a citizen by blood of the Seminole Nation.

Respectfully,

Acting Commissioner.

_____

Sasakwa I.T.
June 26th 1905

Mr Chas Webster.
       Sir.
Your letter dated May 17th was to hand yesterday by some other person that had the same name as mine and am sorry to say that I wasnt[sic] at hand by June 1st if I had got that letter I would have had been there by that time. I dont[sic] see why she kept that letter for such a length of time. I would like to know what we shall do about it. Please let me know as Alfred Porter can go and see about it. Address my letters Cully. That is the only way I can get my letters. Name me after my papa. Let me know right away. That is all.

Address Amy Cully
Sasakwa
I.T.

Applications for Enrollment of Seminole Newborn
Act of 1905   Volume II

AFFIDAVIT OF ATTENDING PHYSICIAN OR MID-WIFE.

UNITED STATES OF AMERICA, Indian Territory,
Western   DISTRICT.

I,   Rebecca West   , a   , on oath state that I attended on Mrs.   Lizzie   , wife of   George   on the   12th   day of   July   , 1904; that there was born to her on said date a   female   child; that said child is now living and is said to have been named Amy

Rebecca West

Witnesses To Mark:

Subscribed and sworn to before me this 9th   day of   January   , 1907.

J L Gary
Notary Public.

AFFIDAVIT OF ATTENDING PHYSICIAN OR MID-WIFE.

UNITED STATES OF AMERICA, Indian Territory,
Western   DISTRICT.

I,   Thomas West   , a   band chief   , on oath state that I attended on Mrs.   Lizzie   , wife of   George   on the   12th   day of   July   , 1904; that there was born to her on said date a   female   child; that said child is now living and is said to have been named Amy

Thomas West

Witnesses To Mark:

Subscribed and sworn to before me this 9th   day of   January   , 1907.

J L Gary
Notary Public.

Sem NB 170
BIRTH AFFIDAVIT.

DEPARTMENT OF THE INTERIOR.
COMMISSION TO THE FIVE CIVILIZED TRIBES.

IN RE APPLICATION FOR ENROLLMENT, as a citizen of the   Seminole   Nation, of Amy Barney   , born on the   12   day of   July   , 1904

Name of Father: George Barney   a citizen of the   Seminole   Nation.
Name of Mother: Lizzie Barney   a citizen of the   Seminole   Nation.

216

Applications for Enrollment of Seminole Newborn
Act of 1905   Volume II

Postoffice   Sasakwa, I.T

_____

Child present

AFFIDAVIT OF MOTHER.

UNITED STATES OF AMERICA, Indian Territory, ⎫
     Western   **DISTRICT.** ⎬

I, Lizzie Barney   , on oath state that I am 35   years of age and a citizen by blood   , of the   Seminole   Nation; that I am the lawful wife of   George Barney   , who is a citizen, by blood   of the   Seminole   Nation; that a   Female   child was born to me on 12ᵗʰ   day of   July   , 1904; that said child has been named Amy Barney   , and was living March 4, 1905.

her
Lizzie x Barney
mark

Witnesses To Mark:
⎰ FC Sabourin
⎱ Chas E Webster

Subscribed and sworn to before me this 1ˢᵗ   day of   May   , 1905.

Chas E Webster
Notary Public.

_____

AFFIDAVIT OF ~~ATTENDING PHYSICIAN OR MID-WIFE~~.
grand father

UNITED STATES OF AMERICA, Indian Territory, ⎫
     Western   **DISTRICT.** ⎬

am the father of
I, Passuk Harjo   , ~~a~~   , on oath state that I ~~attended on~~ Mrs.   Lizzie Barney   , wife of   George Barney   on the 12ᵗʰ   day of   July   , 1904; that there was born to her on said date a   Female   child; that said child was living March 4, 1905, and is said to have been named Amy Barney

his
Passuk x Harjo
mark

Witnesses To Mark:
⎰ FC Sabourin
⎱ Chas E Webster

Subscribed and sworn to before me 1ˢᵗ   day of   May   , 1905.

Chas E Webster
Notary Public.

_____

Sem NB 170
BIRTH AFFIDAVIT.

DEPARTMENT OF THE INTERIOR.
COMMISSION TO THE FIVE CIVILIZED TRIBES.

IN RE APPLICATION FOR ENROLLMENT, as a citizen of the   Seminole   Nation, of
Philip Barney   , born on the 27   day of   June   , 1901

Name of Father: George Barney   a citizen of the   Seminole   Nation.
Name of Mother: Lizzie Barney   a citizen of the   Seminole   Nation.

Postoffice   Sasakwa, I.T

(Child present)

AFFIDAVIT OF MOTHER.

UNITED STATES OF AMERICA, Indian Territory,
Western   DISTRICT.

I,   Lizzie Barney   , on oath state that I am 35 years of age and a citizen by
blood   , of the   Seminole   Nation; that I am the lawful wife of George Barney ,
who is a citizen, by   blood   of the   Seminole   Nation; that a   male   child
was born to me on 27   day of   June   , 1901, that said child has been named   Philip
Barney   , and is now living.
                                                                her
                                                    Lizzie X Barney
Witnesses To Mark: mark
    F. C. Sabourin
    Chas E. Webster

Subscribed and sworn to before me this   1st day of   May   , 1905.

                                          Chas. E. Webster
(Seal)   Notary Public.

AFFIDAVIT OF ~~ATTENDING PHYSICIAN OR MID-WIFE~~.
Father

UNITED STATES OF AMERICA, Indian Territory,
    Western   DISTRICT.

                                                      am the father
    I,   George Barney   , ~~a~~   , on oath state that I ~~attended on~~ Mrs. Lizzie
Barney   , ~~wife of~~   on the   27 day of June , 1901; that there was born to her
on said date a   male   child; that said child is now living and is said to have been
named Philip Barney   his
                                              George X Barney
                                                        mark

Applications for Enrollment of Seminole Newborn
Act of 1905   Volume II

Witnesses To Mark:
   { F. C. Sabourin
    Chas. E. Webster

      Subscribed and sworn to before me this   1st day of   May   , 1905.

                               Chas. E. Webster
(Seal)   Notary Public

Sem NB 170
BIRTH AFFIDAVIT.

DEPARTMENT OF THE INTERIOR.
COMMISSION TO THE FIVE CIVILIZED TRIBES.

IN RE APPLICATION FOR ENROLLMENT, as a citizen of the   Seminole   Nation, of
Amy Barney   , born on the 12   day of   July   , 1904

Name of Father: George Barney   a citizen of the   Seminole   Nation.
Name of Mother: Lizzie Barney   a citizen of the   Seminole   Nation.

                  Postoffice   Sasakwa, I. T.

(Child present)
AFFIDAVIT OF MOTHER.

UNITED STATES OF AMERICA, Indian Territory,
Western   **DISTRICT.**

      I,   Lizzie Barney   , on oath state that I am 35 years of age and a citizen by
blood   , of the   Seminole   Nation; that I am the lawful wife of George Barney ,
who is a citizen, by   blood   of the   Seminole   Nation; that a   Female
child was born to me on 12th   day of   July   , 1904, that said child has been named
Amy Barney   , and is now living.   her
                                      Lizzie x Barney
Witnesses To Mark: mark
   { F. C. Sabourin
    Chas. E. Webster

      Subscribed and sworn to before me this   1st day of   May   , 1905.

                              Cas[sic]. E. Webster
(SEAL)   Notary Public.

Applications for Enrollment of Seminole Newborn
Act of 1905   Volume II

Grandfather

UNITED STATES OF AMERICA, Indian Territory, ⎫
    Western   DISTRICT. ⎬
                         ⎭

am the father of

    I, Passuk Harjo   , ~~a~~   , on oath state that I ~~attended on~~ Mrs. Lizzie
Barney   , wife of George Barney   on the   12th day of July , 1904; that there
was born to her on said date a   female   child; that said child is now living and is said
to have been named Amy Barney

his
Passuk X Harjo
mark

Witnesses To Mark:
      ⎰ F. C. Sabourin
      ⎱ Chas. E. Webster

    Subscribed and sworn to before me this 1st day of   May   , 1905.

Chas. E. Webster
(SEAL)   Notary Public

UNITED STATES OF AMERICA, Indian Territory, ⎫
    Western   DISTRICT. ⎬
                         ⎭

    I,   Thomas West   , a band chief   , on oath state that I ~~attended on~~ Mrs.
Lizzie   , wife of   George   on the   27th   day of June   , 1901; that there was
born to her on said date a   child; that said child is now living and is said to have
been named Phillip

Rebecca[sic] West

Witnesses To Mark:
      ⎰

    Subscribed and sworn to before me this 9th day of   January   , 1907.

J L Gary
Notary Public.

220

AFFIDAVIT OF ATTENDING PHYSICIAN OR MID-WIFE.

UNITED STATES OF AMERICA, Indian Territory,
      Western   DISTRICT.

I,   Thomas West   , a band chief   , on oath state that I ~~attended on~~ Mrs.
Lizzie   , wife of   George   on the   27   day of   June   , 1901; that there was born
to her on said date a   male   child; that said child is now living and is said to have
been named Phillip

                              Thomas West

Witnesses To Mark:

{

Subscribed and sworn to before me this 9ᵗʰ   day of   January   , 1907.

                    J L Gary
                              Notary Public.

_____

Sem NB 170
BIRTH AFFIDAVIT.

DEPARTMENT OF THE INTERIOR.
COMMISSION TO THE FIVE CIVILIZED TRIBES.

_____

IN RE APPLICATION FOR ENROLLMENT, as a citizen of the   Seminole   Nation, of
Philip Barney   , born on the   27   day of   June   , 1901

Name of Father: George Barney   a citizen of the   Seminole   Nation.
Name of Mother: Lizzie Barney   a citizen of the   Seminole   Nation.

                    Postoffice   Sasakwa, I.T

_____

(Child present)

AFFIDAVIT OF MOTHER.

UNITED STATES OF AMERICA, Indian Territory,
      Western   DISTRICT.

I,   Lizzie Barney   , on oath state that I am   35   years of age and a citizen by
blood   , of the   Seminole   Nation; that I am the lawful wife of   George Barney ,
who is a citizen, by blood   of the   Seminole   Nation; that a   male   child
was born to me on   27   day of   June   , 1901; that said child has been named
Philip Barney   , and was living March 4, 1905.

                              her
                    Lizzie x Barney
                              mark

221

Applications for Enrollment of Seminole Newborn
Act of 1905   Volume II

Witnesses To Mark:
⎰ FC Sabourin
⎱ Chas E Webster

Subscribed and sworn to before me this 1ˢᵗ   day of   May   , 1905.

Chas E Webster
Notary Public.

AFFIDAVIT OF ~~ATTENDING PHYSICIAN OR MID-WIFE~~.
Father

UNITED STATES OF AMERICA, Indian Territory,
Western   DISTRICT.

am the husband of
I,   George Barney   , ~~a~~   , on oath state that I ~~attended on~~ Mrs.   Lizzie
Barney   , ~~wife of~~   on the 27   day of   June   , 1901; that there was born
to her on said date a   male   child; that said child was living March 4, 1905, and is
said to have been named Philip Barney

his
George x Barney
mark

Witnesses To Mark:
⎰ FC Sabourin
⎱ Chas E Webster

Subscribed and sworn to before me 1ˢᵗ day of   May   , 1905.

Chas E Webster
Notary Public.

COMMISSIONERS:
TAMS BIXBY,
THOMAS B. NEEDLES,
C.R. BRECKINBRIDGE.

WM. O. BEALL
Secretary

DEPARTMENT OF THE INTERIOR,
COMMISSIONER TO THE FIVE CIVILIZED TRIBES.

REFER IN REPLY TO THE FOLLOWING:
_____

ADDRESS ONLY THE
COMMISSION TO THE FIVE CIVILIZED TRIBES.

Wewoka, Indian Territory, May 17, 1905.

Lizzie Barney,
Care George Barney,
Sasakwa, Indian Territory.

Madam:

On May 1, 1905, you appeared before the Seminole Enrollment Office, at
Wewoka, Indian Territory, and made application for the enrollment of Philip Barney and
Amy Barney, minor children of George Barney and yourself.

222

Applications for Enrollment of Seminole Newborn
Act of 1905 Volume II

The Commission is unable to identify either you or George Barney upon the approved Seminole Roll, and it will be necessary, therefore, for you to appear before this office prior to June 1, 1905, in order that such identification may be made.

Respectfully,
Chas. E. Webster
Clerk in Charge.

COMMISSIONERS:
TAMS BIXBY,
THOMAS B. NEEDLES,
C.R. BRECKINBRIDGE.

WM. O. BEALL
Secretary

**DEPARTMENT OF THE INTERIOR,
COMMISSIONER TO THE FIVE CIVILIZED TRIBES.**

REFER IN REPLY TO THE FOLLOWING:

Seminole NB-170.

ADDRESS ONLY THE
COMMISSION TO THE FIVE CIVILIZED TRIBES.

Muskogee, Indian Territory, June 29, 1905.

George Barney,
Sasakwa, Indian Territory.

Dear Sir:

On May 1, 1905, you appeared before the Commission and made applications for the enrollment of your children, Philip Barney, born June 27, 1901, and Amy Barney, born July 12, 1904, as citizens by blood of the Seminole Nation. From the information contained in said applications the Commission is unable to identify either you or your wife, Lizzie Barney, upon the approved Seminole rolls.

You are therefore requested to inform the Commission of the name under which you and your said wife are finally enrolled and if you have received your allotment certificates, state the names and give your final roll numbers as they appear upon said certificates.

You should also state the names and ages of other members of your family who were enrolled at the same time and any other information which will enable the Commission to identify you and your wife as citizens of the Seminole Nation.

Please give this matter your immediate attention.

Respectfully,

Tams Bixby   Chairman.

223

Department of the Interior.
Commissioner to the Five Civilized Tribes,
MUSKOGEE, IND. TER,

Lizzie Barney,
c/o George Barney,
Sasakwa, Indian Territory.

AP

REFER IN REPLY TO THE FOLLOWING:

Sem N B 170

DEPARTMENT OF THE INTERIOR,
COMMISSIONER TO THE FIVE CIVILIZED TRIBES.

Muskogee, Indian Territory, December 29, 1905.

Lizzie Barney,
Care George Barney,
Sasakwa, Indian Territory.

Dear Madam:

You are hereby advised that a representative of the Commissioner to the Five Civilized Tribes will be in Wewoka, Indian Territory, Friday and Saturday, January 4 and 5, 1907, for the purpose of hearing testimony in pending Seminole enrollment cases and you should appear at that place on one of those days, for the purpose of testifying relative to your identification as a Seminole Indian or freedman. You should also secure the attendance of the physician or midwife who acted at the birth of your children, Philip and Amy Barnett[sic], and in event there was no one in attendance, you should present the testimony of two disinterested witnesses who know of the birth of your children, the dates of their birth, the names of their parents and that they were living March 4, 195[sic].

In the event you have witnessess[sic] who can testify to your enrollment on the final roll of Seminoles, you should also have them present at the same time.

Respectfully,
Tams Bixby   Commissioner.

Sem. N B 170

Muskogee, Indian Territory, December 29, 1905.

McKennon & Willmott,
    Attorneys for the Seminoles,
        Wewoka, Indian Territory.

Gentlemen:

    May 1, 1905, Lizzie Barney made application to the Commission to the Five Civilized Tribes for the enrollment of her two minor children, Philip Barney, born June 27, 1901, and Amy Barney, born July 12, 1904, as citizens of the Seminole Nation under the provisions of the act of Congress approved March 3, 1905.

    Lizzie Barney, the mother of these children, stated that she is thirty five years of age, a citizen by blood of the Seminole Nation, that she is the lawful wife of George Barney, who is a citizen by blood of the Seminole Nation and that she and her husband reside at Sasakwa, Indian Territory.

    This office is unable to identify either George Barney or Lizzie Barney, the parents of the two children hereinbefore named, as citizens of the Seminole Nation. It is requested that you advise this office if the said Lizzie or George Barnett[sic] are citizens of the Seminole Nation and if so, whether they have received allotments as such citizens and also their roll numbers as the same appear upon the final roll of the citizens of the Seminole Nation.

    It is desired that this matter receive your early attention in order that disposition may be made of these two pending applications.

                Respectfully,

                      -Commissioner.

D.C-LL.

DEPARTMENT OF THE INTERIOR,
COMMISSIONER TO THE FIVE CIVILIZED TRIBES.

In the matter of the application for the enrollment of Edna Monday and Annie Monday as new born citizens of the Seminole Nation.

Sem. NB-171.

_____

Sem NB 171
BIRTH AFFIDAVIT.

DEPARTMENT OF THE INTERIOR.
COMMISSION TO THE FIVE CIVILIZED TRIBES.

_____

IN RE APPLICATION FOR ENROLLMENT, as a citizen of the   Seminole   Nation, of Edna Monday   , born on the 2nd day of   Sept , 1903

Name of Father: March Monday   a citizen of the   Creek   Nation.
Name of Mother: Lizzie Monday   a citizen of the   Seminole   Nation.

Postoffice   Schulter, Ind. Ter.

_____

AFFIDAVIT OF MOTHER.

UNITED STATES OF AMERICA, Indian Territory,⎤
     Western   **DISTRICT.** ⎦

I, Lizzie Monday   , on oath state that I am   22   years of age and a citizen by   blood   , of the   Seminole   Nation; that I am the lawful wife of   March Monday , who is a citizen, by blood   of the   Creek   Nation; that a   female child was born to me on   2^{d} day of   September   , 1903; that said child has been named   Edna Monday   , and was living March 4, 1905.

Lizzie Monday

Witnesses To Mark:
⎧
⎩

Subscribed and sworn to before me this 24   day of   July   , 1905.

My Commission expires July 12, 1906.   CJ Regnier
                                                   Notary Public.

_____

226

Applications for Enrollment of Seminole Newborn
Act of 1905   Volume II

AFFIDAVIT OF ATTENDING PHYSICIAN OR MID-WIFE.

UNITED STATES OF AMERICA, Indian Territory, ⎰
    Western   DISTRICT. ⎱

I,   Minor Randall   , a   mid wife   , on oath state that I attended on Mrs. Lizzie Monday   , wife of   March Monday   on the 2ⁿᵈ   day of   Sept. , 1903; that there was born to her on said date a   female   child; that said child was living March 4, 1905, and is said to have been named Edna Monday

her
Minor x Randall
mark

Witnesses To Mark:
  ⎰ W.H. Russell
  ⎱ Samuel J Checote

Subscribed and sworn to before me 30   day of   July   , 1905.

Samuel J Checote
Notary Public.

Com. Exp Nov. 6-1906

Sem NB 171
BIRTH AFFIDAVIT.

DEPARTMENT OF THE INTERIOR.
COMMISSION TO THE FIVE CIVILIZED TRIBES.

IN RE APPLICATION FOR ENROLLMENT, as a citizen of the   Seminole   Nation, of Annie Monday   , born on the 13ᵗʰ   day of   December , 1904

Name of Father: March Monday   a citizen of the   Creek   Nation.
Name of Mother: Lizzie Monday   a citizen of the   Seminole   Nation.

Postoffice   Schulter, Ind. Ter.

AFFIDAVIT OF MOTHER.

UNITED STATES OF AMERICA, Indian Territory, ⎰
    Western   DISTRICT. ⎱

I, Lizzie Monday   , on oath state that I am   22   years of age and a citizen by   blood   , of the   Seminole   Nation; that I am the lawful wife of   March Monday , who is a citizen, by blood   of the   Creek   Nation; that a   female child was born to me on   13ᵗʰ   day of   December   , 1904; that said child has been named   Annie Monday   , and was living March 4, 1905.

227

Lizzie Monday

Witnesses To Mark:

{

Subscribed and sworn to before me this 24   day of   July   , 1905.

My Commission expires July 12, 1906.   CJ Regnier
                                                    Notary Public.

AFFIDAVIT OF ATTENDING PHYSICIAN OR MID-WIFE.

UNITED STATES OF AMERICA, Indian Territory, ⎱
        Western   DISTRICT.   ⎰

I,   Minor Randall   , a mid wife   , on oath state that I attended on Mrs.
Lizzie Monday   , wife of   March Monday   on the 13th   day of Dec. , 1904;
that there was born to her on said date a   female   child; that said child was living
March 4, 1905, and is said to have been named Annie Monday

                                                    her
                                          Minor x Randall
Witnesses To Mark: mark
{ W.H. Russell
   Samuel J Checote

Subscribed and sworn to before me 30th day of   July   , 1905.

                                          Samuel J Checote
                                                 Notary Public.
              Com. Exp Nov. 6-1906

DEPARTMENT OF THE INTERIOR.

COMMISSION TO THE FIVE CIVILIZED TRIBES.

In the matter of the application of Edna Monday and Elizabeth Monday, for
enrollment as citizens of the Seminole Nation.

Samuel Haney, Being duly sworn, testified as follows, through Mrs. A. B. Davis, official
interpreter.

Q. What is your name? A. Sam Haney.
Q. What is your age? A. About thirty-six.
Q. What is your post-office address? A. Little.
Q. You desire to make application for enrollment of Edna Monday and Elizabeth
Monday, as citizens of the Seminole Nation? A. Yes.

Applications for Enrollment of Seminole Newborn
Act of 1905   Volume II

Q. What relation are you, if any, to Edna Monday and Elizabeth Monday? A. They are my nieces.
Q. What is the name of the mother of these children? A. Lizzie Monday.
Q. Is she a citizen of the Seminole Nation? A. Yes.
Q. What is her post office? A. I have written to her at Okmulgee.

Upon examination, the name of Lizzie Monday, nee London is identified upon the Approved Seminole roll; opposite No. 1648.

Q. What is the reason the mother does not appear before this Commission? A. He says he could give a number of reasons. They are being detained by high water; and they are not able to pay their fare on the railroad to come down here.

Q. Both of these children are living now, are they not? A. In February saw her with them, living.
Q. You don't know whether they were living in March? A. I have not heard since.
Q. What position do you hold in the Seminole Nation? A. Second, Chief.
Q. The names of these children appear upon your record? A. On his roll the name of Edna appears, but he has not put the name of the other one down?[sic]
Q. When was Elizabeth born? A. In last August, of last year the mother had it, I saw it.
Q. Both of these children have drawn annuities paid by the Seminole Nation? A. Just one. None due since August. The child was born after the payment, and has not yet drawn headright.
Q. You are personally acquainted with the father and mother of these children, are you not? A. Yes.
Q. Is the father a citizen of the Seminole Nation? A. Creek.

(Witness excused)

I, William S. Webb, being duly sworn, states that as stenographer to the Commission to the Five Civilized Tribes I took testimony in the above case. and he above and foregoing is a true transcript of my stenographic notes taken in said case on May 31st, 1905.

William S Webb

Subscribed and sworn to before me, this 1st day of June, 1905.

Chas E Webster
Notary Public.

NG-1093
DEPARTMENT OF THE INTERIOR,
COMMISSIONER TO THE FIVE CIVILIZED TRIBES.

Muskogee, Indian Territory, November 14, 1905.

In the matter of the application for the enrollment of Edna and Annie Monday as citizens of the Creek Nation.

Lizzie Monday, being duly sworn, testified as follows (through Jesse McDermott, Official Interpreter):

EXAMINATION BY THE COMMISSIONER:
Q What is your name? A Lizzie Monday.
Q How old are you? A I don't know.
Q What is your postoffice address? A Schultor.
Q Are you a citizen of any tribe in Indian Territory? A Seminole.
Q Have you some new-born children? if so, name them. A Yes, I have one. The one here and one named Edna.
Q What is the name of this one, here? A Annie.
Q Have you ever called this one by any other name? A No.
Q Was it ever known as "London?" A Yes, that my Indian name. Sam Hayney applied for this child, Annie, and called it Elizabeth.
[sic] Do you know anything about it? A Yes, he told me about it.
Q The child he called Elizabeth he meant the one you named Annie? A Yes, sir. He told me that he did not know her name, and just gave her the mother's name.
Q When was your child, Annie, who was incorrectly called Elizabeth by Hayney, born? A Annie was born December 13, 1904--I am mistaken; it was 1903.
Q How old will it be this December? A 2 years old.
Q Are you sure of that? A Yes sir.
Q Who was the midwife when it was born? A My mother, Mina Randall.
Q And that is the child there? A Yes sir.
Q You made application for this child--you made out an affidavit for the enrollment of this child and so did you mother, Mina Randall; you said that the child was born the 13th of December, 1904. Was it then a mistake, as you now say in your testimony? A Yes sir.
Q This first affidavit you made in April before Mr. McDermott, in the field; That was correct, was it? A Yes sir.
Q Have you another child just older than this one? A Yes sir.
Q What is its name? A Edna.
Q When was Edna born? A September 2.
Q What year? A 1903.
Q It couldn't have been born in 1903, and then this one in December of the same year, only about three months apart. A It was 1902.
Q How old is it now? A Past three.

Q The first affidavit you made about Edna, Indian Territory and Mina made one also, giving the date 1902 iz[sic] correct, and this last one, giving the year 1903 is a mistake, is it? A Yes sir. The last affidavits are written down 1903, and they are errors.

Q Now, Lizzie, if it should be found that Edna and Annie, your two children, are entitled to rights in either the Creek or Seminole Nation, in which Nation do you elect to have them enrolled and take their allotments of land? A In the Creek Nation.

Q You elect to have them enrolled in the Creek Nation, do you? A Yes sir.

Q Is Edna living? A Yes sir.

March Monday, being duly sworn, testified as follows (through Jesse McDermott, Official Interpreter):

EXAMINATION BY THE COMMISSIONER:

Q What is your name? A March Monday.

Q What is the name of your father? A Monday.

Q What is the name of your mother? A Millie Annie.

Q How old are you? A I am not sure, but think I am about 32.

Q What is the name of your Creek Indian Town? A Cussehta.

Q What is you postoffice address? A Schulter.

Q Have you two newborn children by the names of Edna and Annie Monday? A Yes sir.

Q You have one named Elizabeth, have you? A No sir, never did.

Q You never did have a child named Elizabeth? A No sir.

Q If Haney made application for Elizabeth, he meant to refer to Annie, do you think? A Yes sir.

Q How old is Edna? A Three years old, past.

Q How old is this little one, here? A She's going to be two years old.

Q In what month, do you remember? A December.

Q Next month A Yes sir.

Q Is Edna living? A Yes sir.

Q If it should be found that Edna and Annie, these two children, are entitled to rights in either the Creek or Seminole Nation, in which Nation do you elect to have them enrolled and take their allotments of land? A Creek Nation.

Q You elect for them to be enrolled in the Creek Nation, do you? A Yes sir.

Q Are you married to Lizzie, the mother of these children? A Yes sir.

Q Have you ever had any children by her before these two? A No sir. Sam Checotah has my license and I did not bring it with me.

Q How about Jennetta? Is she dead, or are you divorced from her? A We were married according to the Indian custom and separated likewise.

Q You had a child by her, didn't you? A Yes sir.

Q What is its name? A Martin.

Q These two children are your children? A Yes sir.

Q By this woman, Lizzie? A Yes sir.

Applications for Enrollment of Seminole Newborn
Act of 1905   Volume II

INDIAN TERRITORY, Western District

I, J. Y. Miller, a stenographer to the Commissioner to the Five Civilized Tribes, do hereby certify that the above and foregoing is a true and complete translation of my notes as same appear in my stenographic report of this case.

JY Miller

Sworn to and subscribed before me
  this the 15th day of November,
  1905.

J. McDermott
Notary Public.

Indian Territory,   )
                     (SS.
Western District.   )

We, the undersigned, do hereby elect to have our child, Edna Monday, born on the 2 day of Sept. 1902, enrolled as a citizen of the Creek Nation, and to have said child receive her allotment of land and distribution of moneys in said nation.

(Signed) March Monday.

(Signed) Lizzie Monday.

Subscribed and sworn to before me this 26 day of Sept. 1906.

(Signed) H. G. Hains,
Notary Public.

Indian Territory,   )
                     (SS.
Western District.   )

We, the undersigned, do hereby elect to have our child, Annie Monday, born on the 13 day of Dec. 1903, enrolled as a citizen of the Creek Nation, and to have said child receive her allotment of land and distribution of moneys in said nation.

(Signed) March Monday.

(Signed) Lizzie Monday.

Subscribed and sworn to before me this 26 day of Sept. 1906.

(Signed) H. G. Hains,
Notary Public.

Applications for Enrollment of Seminole Newborn
Act of 1905   Volume II

Sem. NB 171.

DEPARTMENT OF THE INTERIOR,
COMMISSIONER TO THE FIVE CIVILIZED TRIBES.

In the matter of the application for the enrollment of Edna Monday and Annie Monday as new born citizens of the Seminole Nation.

-: D E C I S I O N :-

It appears from the record herein that on May 31, 1905, written application was made to the Commission to the Five Civilized Tribes for the enrollment of Edna Monday and Annie Monday as New born citizens of the Seminole Nation.

It further appears from the record herein and from the records of this office that the applicants Edna Monday and Annie Monday were born September 2, 1903 and December 13, 1904, respectively and are the children of Lizzie Monday, whose name appears opposite No. 1648, as Lizzie London upon the final roll of Seminole Indians approved by the Secretary of the Interior April 2, 1902 and March Monday, a citizen of the Creek Nation approved by the Secretary of the Interior.

It further appears from the record herein and from the records of this office that on September 26, 1906, the parents of the applicants herein elected in writing to have the applicants enrolled as citizens of the Creek Nation and to receive their allotments of lands and distribution of moneys in said nation; and that the names of the applicants now appear opposite Nos. 1212 and 1213 upon the final roll of minor citizens of the Creek Nation under the provisions of the Act of Congress approved March 3, 1905 (33 Stats., 1070) and approved by the Secretary of the Interior February 5, 1907.

I am, therefore, of the opinion that the application for the enrollment of Edna Monday and Annie Monday as new born citizens of the Seminole Nation should be dismissed, and it is so ordered.

Tams Bixby   Commissioner.

Muskogee, Indian Territory,
FEB 20 1907

Sem. NB-171

Muskogee, Indian Territory, March 7, 1907.

March Monday,
 Okmulgee, Indian Territory.

Dear Sir:-

You are hereby notified that the Commission to the Five Civilized Tribes on February 20, 1907, rendered his decision dismissing the application for the enrollment of Edna Monday and Annie Monday as citizens of the Seminole Nation.

Respectfully
SIGNED   *Tams Bixby*
Commissioner.

Sem. NB-171   **COPY**

Muskogee, Indian Territory, March 7, 1907.

Chief Clerk,
 Creek Enrollment Division.

Dear Sir:-

You are hereby notified that the Commission to the Five Civilized Tribes on February 20, 1907, rendered his decision dismissing the application for the enrollment of Edna Monday and Annie Monday as citizens of the Seminole Nation.

Respectfully
SIGNED   *Tams Bixby*
Commissioner.

HGH

<table>
<tr><td>REFER IN REPLY TO THE FOLLOWING:
Sem. NB-171.
NBC-1093.</td></tr>
</table>

DEPARTMENT OF THE INTERIOR,
COMMISSIONER TO THE FIVE CIVILIZED TRIBES.

Muskogee, Indian Territory, January 2, 1905.

Chief Clerk of Seminole Enrollment Division,
Muskogee, Indian Territory.

Dear Sir:

Receipt is acknowledged of your letter of December 29, 1905, in which you ask to be informed as to the status of the application for the enrollment of Annie and Edna Monday as citizens of the Creek Nation, together with their Roll numbers if their enrollment has been approved by the Department.

In reply you are advised that the matter of the application for the enrollment of said children, as citizens of the Creek Nation, is pending, and when final action is had in the same you will be duly notified.

Respectfully,

Tams Bixby   Commissioner.

HGH
DEPARTMENT OF THE INTERIOR.
COMMISSION TO THE FIVE CIVILIZED TRIBES.

Muskogee, Indian Territory, July 15, 1905.

Chief Clerk,
Seminole Enrollment Division,
Muskogee, Indian Territory.

Dear Sir:

April 18, 1905, application was made to the Commission to the Five Civilized Tribes for the enrollment of Edna Monday, born September 2, 1902 and Annie Monday, born December 13, 1903, as citizens by blood of the Creek Nation. It is stated in said application that the father of said children is March Monday, a citizen of the Creek Nation, and that the mother is Lizzie Monday, a citizen of the Seminole Nation.

You are requested to inform the Creek Enrollment Division as to whether application has been made for the enrollment of said children as citizens of the Seminole Nation, and if so, what disposition has been made of the same.

Respectfully,

Tams Bixby
Commissioner.

———————

Seminole-NB-171.

Muskogee, Indian Territory, June 29, 1905.

Sam Haney,
    Little, Indian Territory.

Dear Sir:

On May 31, 1905, you appeared before the Commission and made application for the enrollment of your nieces, Edna Monday and Eliza[sic] Monday, as citizens by blood of the Seminole Nation and submitted your testimony only as to the rights of said children to be so enrolled.

You are advised that before the rights of said children, as citizens by blood of the Seminole Nation, can be finally determined further proof of their birth must be filed with the Commission; and blanks for that purpose are inclosed herewith which you are requested to have properly executed and return to this Commission.

This matter should have your immediate attention.

Respectfully,

2 B-C.   Chairman.
Env.

———————

Seminole NB-171.

Muskogee, Indian Territory July 18, 1905.

Lizzie Monday,
    Shulter[sic], Indian Territory.

Dear Madam:

On May 31, 1905 Sam Haney appeared before the Commission to the Five Civilized Tribes and made application for the enrollment of your children Edna Monday and Elizabeth Monday as citizens by blood of the Seminole Nation.

You are advised that before the rights of said children, as citizens by blood of the Seminole Nation, can be finally determined it will be necessary for you to file with this office proper proof of birth of said children and blanks for that purpose are inclosed herewith which you are requested to have properly executed and return with as little delay as possible.

In having said affidavits executed be careful to see that all blanks are properly filled all names written in full and that the notary public before whom the affidavits are acknowledged affixes his name and seal to each separate affidavit. In case any signature is by mark it must be attested by two witnesses.

Respectfully,

2 BC   Commissioner.
Env.

Seminole NB-171.

Muskogee, Indian Territory July 18, 1905.

Chief Clerk,
    Creek Enrollment Division.

Dear Sir:

Receipt is acknowledged of your letter of June 15, 1905 (N??-1093) stating that an application was made to the Commission to the Five Civilized Tribes for the enrollment of Edna Monday, born September 2, 1902, and Annie Monday, born December 13, 1903, children of March Monday, a citizen of the Creek Nation, and Lizzie Monday, a citizen of the Seminole Nation, as citizens by blood of the Creek Nation and requesting to be advised as to whether application has been made for the enrollment of said children as citizens of the Seminole Nation.

In reply to your letter you are advised that on May 31, 1905 Sam Haney appeared before the Commission and made application for the enrollment of his nieces, Edna Monday and Elizabeth Monday, as citizens by blood of the Seminole Nation. He stated in his testimony given at that time that the father of said children was a Creek citizen, that their mother was Lizzie Monday, and that said Elizabeth was born in August, 1904. The name of the father of said children and the date of the birth of Edna Monday are not given. The post office address of said Lizzie Monday is given as Shulter[sic], Indian Territory.

It does not appear from the records of this office that any application has been made for the enrollment of Annie Monday as a citizen of the Seminole Nation.

Respectfully,

Commissioner.

237

Applications for Enrollment of Seminole Newborn
Act of 1905 Volume II

Sem. NB-171.

Muskogee, Indian Territory, August 5, 1905.

Lizzie Monday,
Schulter, Indian Territory.

Dear Madam:

Receipt is hereby acknowledged of your affidavits and the affidavits of Minor Randall, midwife, as to the birth of your minor children Edna Monday, born September 2, 1903, and Annie Monday, born December 13, 1904.

It does not appear from the records of this office that you ever made an application to the Commission to the Five Civilized Tribes for the enrollment of the said Annie Monday as a citizen by blood of the Seminole Nation. However on May 31, 1905, Sam Haney appeared before the Commission to the Five Civilized Tribes and made application for the enrollment of his nieces Edna Monday and Elizabeth Monday as citizens by blood of the Seminole Nation, at that time stating that you were the mother of said children.

You are requested to immediately inform this office as to whether you ever had a child by the name of Elizabeth Monday and if not as to whether Elizabeth Monday, for whom Sam Haney made an application to said Commission on May 31, 1905, and Annie Monday, for whom you now forward proof of birth, are one and the same.

It also appears from the records of this office that on April 18, 1905 you made application to the Commission to the Five Civilized Tribes for the enrollment of Edna Monday and Annie Monday as citizens of the Creek Nation. It appears from the affidavits on file with this office in the matter of the application for the enrollment of said children as citizens of the Creek Nation that the said Edna Monday was born on September 2, 1902 and the said Annie Monday on December 13, 1903.

You are requested to inform this office of the correct dates of the birth of said children and are advised that it will also be necessary for you to file with this office your affidavit and the affidavit of March Monday, the father of said children, electing whether you will have said children finally enrolled as citizens of the Creek Nation or citizens of the Seminole Nation.

Respectfully,

Commissioner.

<table>
<tr><td>

REFER IN REPLY TO THE FOLLOWING:

———————————

NBS-171

</td></tr>
</table>

DEPARTMENT OF THE INTERIOR,
COMMISSIONER TO THE FIVE CIVILIZED TRIBES.

Muskogee, Indian Territory, November 7, 1905.

Lizzie Monday,
    Shulter[sic], Indian Territory.

Dear Madam:

Under date of July 18, 1905, you were requested to furnish this office with affidavits relative to the birth of your minor children, Edward[sic] and Elizabeth Monday, for whose enrollment, as citizens by blood of the Seminole Nation, application was made on May 31, 1905, by Sam Haney, Second Chief of the Seminole Nation.

You are again advised that before the rights of said children, as citizens by blood of the Seminole Nation, can be finally determined, it will be necessary for these affidavits to be furnished.

You are requested to give this matter your very earliest attention.

Respectfully,
Tams Bixby
Commissioner.

———————

Sem. N B 171

Muskogee, Indian Territory, December 29, 1905.

Chief Clerk,
    Creek Enrollment Division.

Dear Sir:

On May 31, 1905, application was made to the Commission to the Five Civilized Tribes, under the provisions of the act of Congress approved March 3, 1905, for the enrollment as citizens of the Seminole Nation of Annie and Edna Monday, children of March Monday a citizen of the Creek Nation, and Lizzie Monday, a citizen of the Seminole Nation.

It appears from the record in this case that application has also been made for the enrollment of these children as new born citizens of the Creek Nation, and you are requested to inform the Seminole Enrollment Division the status of the application for the enrollment of these two children as citizens of the Creek Nation, and if they have been enrolled, that you advise their roll numbers and the date of the approval of their enrollment by the Department.

Respectfully,
Commissioner.

Department of the Interior.
Commissioner to the Five Civilized Tribes,
MUSKOGEE, IND. TER,

March Monday,
Okmulgee, Indian Territory.

AP

REFER IN REPLY TO THE FOLLOWING:

Sem. NB-171

DEPARTMENT OF THE INTERIOR,
COMMISSIONER TO THE FIVE CIVILIZED TRIBES.

Muskogee, Indian Territory, March 7, 1907.

March Monday,
Okmulgee, Indian Territory.

Dear Sir:-

You are hereby notified that the Commissioner to the Five Civilized Tribes on February 20, 1907, rendered his decision dismissing the application for the enrollment of Edna Monday and Annie Monday as citizens of the Seminole Nation.

Respectfully,
Tams Bixby
Commissioner.

Seminole NB-172.

Muskogee, Indian Territory, June 29, 1905.

Chippie Harjoe,
 Sasakwa, Indian Territory.

Dear Sir:

  On May 1, 1905, your wife, Janie Harjoe, appeared before the Commission and made applications for the enrollment of your children, Aaron Harjoe, born March 28, 1902, and Pompey Harjoe, born October 3, 1904, as citizens by blood of the Seminole Nation. From the affidavits on file the Commission is unable to identify either you or your wife upon the approved rolls[sic] Seminole rolls.

  You are, therefore, requested to inform the Commission of the names under which you and your said wife were enrolled, and if you have received your allotment certificates, state your final roll numbers as the same appears upon said certificates. You should also state the names and ages of other members of your family who were enrolled at the same time and any other information which you may have which will enable the Commission to identify you and your said wife upon the final rolls of citizens by blood of the Seminole Nation.

  Please give this matter your immediate attention.

      Respectfully,

          Chairman.

     _____

D C Skaggs 53758-1905

NBS 172

    Muskogee, Indian Territory, November 20, 1905.

Honorable A. S. McKennon,
 Attorney for the Seminoles,
  Wewoka, Indian Territory.

Dear Sir:

  On May 1, 1905, Janie Harjoe, appeared before the Commission to the Five Civilized Tribes at Wewoka, Indian Territory and made application for the enrollment of her minor children, Aaron and Pompey Harjoe, as citizens by blood of the Seminole Nation under the provisions of the Act of Congress, approved March 3, 1905 (Public 212).

This office has been unable to identify the names of Janie Harjoe and her husband, Chippie Harjoe, upon the approved roll of said Nation. Repeated efforts have been made to secure information from them that would enable this office to reach a determination as to the rights to enrollment of the said minor children.

This office will appreciate any information you can furnish as to the identification of the said Janie and Chippie Harjoe.

Respectfully,
Acting Commissioner.

Memo
Jane Church #178
Chippee #160
   M^cK & W

Sem. NB 172

Muskogee, Indian Territory, December 29, 1905.

McKennon & Willmott,
    Attorneys for the Seminoles,
        Wewoka, Indian Territory.

Gentlemen:

May 1, 1905, application was made to the Commission to the Five Civilized Tribes by Janie Harjoe for the enrollment of her two minor children, Aaron Harjoe, born March 28, 1902, and Pompey Harjoe, born October 3, 1904. Janie Harjoe stated at the time of the application that she was a citizen by blood of the Seminole Nation and the lawful wife of Chippie Harjoe, a citizen by blood of the Seminole Nation and that they resided at Sasakwa, Indian Territory. At the time of the submission of the application neither Chippie Harjoe nor Janie Harjoe were identified upon the final roll of the citizens of the Seminole Nation as members of that tribe.

November 20, 1905, your attention was invited to this matter and you were requested, if practicable, to furnish information as to the identification of Chippie Harjoe and Janie Harjoe. You returned the letter of this office of November 20, 1905, with a memorandum that Chippie Harjoe appears upon the roll of Seminole citizens as Chippee opposite Number 160 and that Janie Harjoe appears upon said roll as Jane Church opposite Number 178.

It is requested that you obtain from Chippie Harjoe and Janie Harjoe affidavits that they are the identical persons whose names appear upon the final roll of the citizens of the Seminole Nation opposite Numbers 160 and 178 respectively, as Chippee and Jane Church; that they are the parents of the children, Aaron and Pompey Harjoe, for whom applications were made May 1, 1905, and that said children are now living; it is also desired that in said affidavits an explanation be made as to the change in the names of the parents of these minor applicants.

Respectfully,

Commissioner.

—————————

Muskogee, Indian Territory, April 7, 1906.

Honorable John F. Brown,
Sasakwa, Indian Territory.

Dear Sir:

Receipt is hereby acknowledged of your letter of February 26, 1906, relative to the enrollment of Aaron and Pompey Harjoe, children of Cheppie Harjoe, and asking why he does not receive certificates of allotment for said children.

In reply to your letter you are advised that on December 29, 1905, a letter was address to McKennon & Wilmot[sic], as follows:

"May 1, 1905, application was made to the Commission to the Five Civilized Tribes by Janie Harjoe for the enrollment of her two minor children, Aaron Harjoe, born March 28, 1902, and Pompey Harjoe, born October 3, 1904. Janie Harjoe stated at the time of the application that she was a citizen by blood of the Seminole Nation and the lawful wife of Chippie Harjoe, a citizen by blood of the Seminole Nation and that they resided at Sasakwa, Indian Territory. At the time of the submission of the application neither Chippie Harjoe nor Janie Harjoe were identified upon the final roll of the citizens of the Seminole Nation as members of that tribe.

November 20, 1905, your attention was invited to this matter and you were requested, if practicable, to furnish information as to the identification of Chippie Harjoe and Janie Harjoe. You returned the letter of this office of November 20, 1905, with a memorandum that Chippie Harjoe appears upon the roll of Seminole citizens as Chippee opposite Number 160 and that Janie Harjoe appears upon said roll as Jane Church opposite Number 178.

It is requested that you obtain from Chippie Harjoe and Janie Harjoe affidavits that they are the identical persons whose names appear upon the final roll of the citizens of the Seminole Nation opposite Numbers 160 and 178 respectively, as Chipee[sic] and Jane Church; that they are the parents of the children, Aaron and Pompey Harjoe, for whom applications were made May 1, 1905, and that said children are now living; it is also desired that in said affidavit[sic] an explanation be made as to the change in the names of the parents of these minor applicants."

To this letter no reply has been received and I have therefore to request that if practicable you secure from Chippie Harjoe the affidavits requested in said letter and

243

have the same forwarded to this office as early as practicable in order that disposition may be made of the application for the enrollment of Aaron and Pompey Harjoe as new born citizens of the Seminole Nation.

Respectfully,

Acting Commissioner.

Sem NB 171

Muskogee, Indian Territory, April 14, 1906.

Honorable John F. Brown,
    Sasakwa, Indian Territory.

Dear Sir:

Receipt is hereby acknowledged of your letter of April 10, 1906, stating that if you are furnished blanks for Chippie and Janie Harjoe to sign for the enrollment of their two children you will give the matter prompt attention.

You are advised that this office has no blanks of this description for distribution but if Chippie and Janie Harjoe will each execute affidavits in which are incorporated the statements that they are the identical persons enrolled at Nos. 160 and 178 respectively upon the approved Seminole roll; that they are the parents of Aaron and Pompey Harjoe, the dates of the birth of these children, whether or not they are still living and if not the date of their death, and also explain why their names appear upon the roll as "Chippie" and "Jane Church" and in the affidavits to the birth of these children as Chippie Harjoe and Jane Harjoe it is believed that this will be sufficient evidence in the matter of the enrollment of these children.

Respectfully,

Acting Commissioner.

JOHN F. BROWN
DEALER IN
GENERAL MERCHANDISE

Sasakwa, J. T.   April 18th 1906

To The Hon Commission to the
    Five Civilized Tribes
      Muskogee, I.T.

This is to certify that we Chippie Harjo and Janie Harjo are the identical persons enrolled as Nos 160 & 178 respectively upon the approved Seminole roll. That we are the parents of Aaron Harjo & Pompey Harjo.
Aaron Harjo was born March 28th 1902

244

Pompey Harjo was born Oct 3 1904   And both are living.
The mother of Janie Harjo fears the family name of Church, Chippie & Jane Church were often written instead of Harjo, and in this way came *(illegible)* mentioned instead of Chippie & Janie Harjo as they should have been.   his

Chippie Harjo x
mark

Witness   her
John F. Brown   Janie Harjo x
Frank Fleet   mark
    Above statement sworn to before me this 18th day of Apr. 1906
My Com Exp Apr 1st/07   FH Fleet   Notary Pub.

———————

Sem NB 172
BIRTH AFFIDAVIT.

DEPARTMENT OF THE INTERIOR.
COMMISSION TO THE FIVE CIVILIZED TRIBES.

———————

IN RE APPLICATION FOR ENROLLMENT, as a citizen of the   Seminole   Nation, of
Aaron Harjoe   , born on the 28 day of   March , 1902

Name of Father: Chippie Harjoe   a citizen of the   Seminole   Nation.
Name of Mother: Janie Harjoe   a citizen of the   Seminole   Nation.

Postoffice   Sasakwa I.T.

———————

(Child present)

AFFIDAVIT OF MOTHER.

UNITED STATES OF AMERICA, Indian Territory,
    Western   DISTRICT.

    I,   Janie Harjoe   , on oath state that I am   23   years of age and a citizen by blood   , of the   Seminole   Nation; that I am the lawful wife of   Chippie Harjoe , who is a citizen, by blood   of the   Seminole   Nation; that a   male   child was born to me on 28   day of   March   , 1902; that said child has been named Aaron Harjoe   , and was living March 4, 1905.

Janie Harjoe

Witnesses To Mark:

    Subscribed and sworn to before me this 1st day of   May   , 1905.

Chas E Webster
Notary Public.

245

Applications for Enrollment of Seminole Newborn
Act of 1905   Volume II

UNITED STATES OF AMERICA, Indian Territory, ⎫
      Western   DISTRICT. ⎬
                                  ⎭

I,   Annie Church   , a   midwife   , on oath state that I attended on Mrs. Janie Harjoe   , wife of Chippie Harjoe   on the 28 day of March   , 1902; that there was born to her on said date a   male   child; that said child was living March 4, 1905, and is said to have been named   Aaron Harjoe

her
Annie x Church
mark

Witnesses To Mark:
⎧ Chas E Webster
⎩ FC Sabourin

Subscribed and sworn to before me 1ˢᵗ   day of   May   , 1905.

Chas E Webster
Notary Public.

For identification of parents see affidavits to birth of Aaron Harjo.

Wewoka, Indian Territory, May 17, 1905.

Janie Harjoe,
      Care Chippee Harjoe,
            Sasakwa, Indian Territory.

Madam:

On May 1, 1905, you appeared before the Seminole Enrollment Office and made application for the enrollment of Aaron Harjoe and Pompey Harjoe, minor children of Chippee Harjoe and yourself.

The Commission is unable to identify either you or Chippie Harjoe on the approved Seminole Roll, and it will be necessary, therefore, for you to appear before this office prior to June 1, 1905, in order that such identification may be made.

Respectfully,
Clerk in Charge.

Sem NB 172
BIRTH AFFIDAVIT.

DEPARTMENT OF THE INTERIOR.
COMMISSION TO THE FIVE CIVILIZED TRIBES.

IN RE APPLICATION FOR ENROLLMENT, as a citizen of the   Seminole   Nation, of
Pompey Harjoe   , born on the 3rd day of   Octo , 1904

Name of Father: Chippie Harjoe   a citizen of the   Seminole   Nation.
Name of Mother: Janie Harjoe   a citizen of the   Seminole   Nation.

Postoffice   Sasakwa I.T.

(Child present)

AFFIDAVIT OF MOTHER.

UNITED STATES OF AMERICA, Indian Territory, ⎱
    Western   DISTRICT.   ⎰

I,   Janie Harjoe   , on oath state that I am   23   years of age and a citizen by
blood   , of the   Seminole   Nation; that I am the lawful wife of   Chippie Harjoe ,
who is a citizen, by blood   of the   Seminole   Nation; that a   male   child
was born to me on 3rd day of   Octo   , 1904; that said child has been named
Pompey Harjoe   , and was living March 4, 1905.

Janie Harjoe

Witnesses To Mark:

Subscribed and sworn to before me this 1st day of   May   , 1905.

Chas E Webster
Notary Public.

AFFIDAVIT OF ATTENDING PHYSICIAN OR MID-WIFE.

UNITED STATES OF AMERICA, Indian Territory, ⎱
    Western   DISTRICT.   ⎰

I,   Annie Church   , a   midwife   , on oath state that I attended on Mrs.
Janie Harjoe   , wife of   Chippie Harjoe   on the 3rd day of   Octo   , 1904;
that there was born to her on said date a   male   child; that said child was living
March 4, 1905, and is said to have been named   Pompey Harjoe
her
Annie x Church
mark

247

Witnesses To Mark:
- Chas E Webster
- Frank C Sabourin

Subscribed and sworn to before me 1st day of May , 1905.

Chas E Webster
Notary Public.

Sem NB 172

Muskogee, Indian Territory, April 27, 1906.

Honorable John F. Brown,
Sasakwa, Indian Territory.

Dear Sir:

Receipt is hereby acknowledged of your letter of April 18, 1906, inclosing joint affidavit of Chippie Harjoe and his wife Jane Harjoe in the matter of the application for the enrollment of their children Aaron and Pompey Harjoe and the same has been filed with the record in this case.

Respectfully,

Commissioner.

Department of the Interior.
Commissioner to the Five Civilized Tribes,
MUSKOGEE, IND. TER,

Chippie Harjo,
Sasakwa, Indian Territory.

AP

REFER IN REPLY TO THE FOLLOWING:

Sem NB-172

**DEPARTMENT OF THE INTERIOR,
COMMISSIONER TO THE FIVE CIVILIZED TRIBES.**

Muskogee, Indian Territory, March 2, 1907.

Chippie Harjoe,
    Sasakwa, Indian Territory.

Dear Sir:

    You are hereby advised that on February 12, 1907, the Secretary of the Interior approved the enrollment of your children, Aaron Harjoe and Pompey Harjoe as New Born Citizens of the Seminole Nation, under the Act of Congress approved March 3, 1905, and their names appear upon the roll of such citizens enrolled under said Act, opposite Nos. 236 and 237.

              Respectfully,
                Tams Bixby   Commissioner.

D.C.LL.

**DEPARTMENT OF THE INTERIOR,
COMMISSIONER TO THE FIVE CIVILIZED TRIBES.**

    In the matter of the application for the enrollment of Maley as a citizen of the Seminole Nation.

Sem. NB-173.

Applications for Enrollment of Seminole Newborn
Act of 1905   Volume II

Sem NB 173   Card 578
BIRTH AFFIDAVIT.

DEPARTMENT OF THE INTERIOR.
COMMISSION TO THE FIVE CIVILIZED TRIBES.

IN RE APPLICATION FOR ENROLLMENT, as a citizen of the   Seminole   Nation, of
Maley   , born on the   day of   , 1

Name of Father: a citizen of the   Nation.
Name of Mother: a citizen of the   Nation.

Postoffice   Henryetta IT

AFFIDAVIT OF MOTHER.

Band Chief

UNITED STATES OF AMERICA, Indian Territory, ⎱
    Western   **DISTRICT.** ⎰

I,   Tom Palmer   , on oath state that I am   46   years of age and a citizen by
, of the   Nation; that I am the lawful wife of   , who is a citizen, by
of the   Nation; that a   child was born to me on   day of   , 1, that
said child has been named   Maley   , and is now living.

Tom Palmer

Witnesses To Mark:

  ⎰

Subscribed and sworn to before me this   31   day of   May   , 1905.

Chas E Webster
Notary Public.

DEPARTMENT OF THE INTERIOR,

COMMISSION TO THE FIVE CIVILIZED TRIBES.

In the matter of the application for the enrollment of Pearl Raiford, Lena
Raiford, Lena Salone, Lumpsey Scott, Sam Miller, Elizabeth Cully, Maley and
Albert, as citizens by blood of the Seminole Nation.

Thomas Palmer, being duly sworn, testified as follows, through Mrs. A. B.
Davis, official interpreter.

Q.   What is your name? A. Thomas Palmer.

250

Applications for Enrollment of Seminole Newborn
Act of 1905   Volume II

Q. What is your age? A. Forty-six.

Q. What is your post-office address? A. Sasakwa.

Q. You desire to make application for enrollment of the above named children as citizens of the Seminole Nation? A. Yes.

Q. Are you related to any of the above named children? A. No.

Q. Are you an officer of the Seminole Nation? A. Yes.

Q. What position do you hold? A. I am band chief.

Q. Are you acquainted with the parents of each of the above named children? A. Yes.

Q. They are all upon the approved Seminole roll, are they? Their names appear upon that roll? A. They are on the roll and have taken allotments.

Q. The names of these children appear upon the records of the Seminoles, do they not; that is upon your record? A. Yes, all of them.

Q. And have drawn their annuities or headright? A. Yes, there was one child that was not born in time, that is he has not yet drawn any money.

Q. He is recognized as a Seminole Indian, is he not? A. Yes.

Q. Why is it that the parents of these children do not appear before this Commission to enroll them? A. Their husbands are snakes. They are not in favor of allotment, and don't come forward to allot their wives and children. They were allotted arbitrarily. These people have never appeared before the Commission. The husbands are Creeks.

Q. Has application ever been made, before this time, for any one of these children, as citizens of the Seminole Nation, or any other nation.[sic] A. No, they have never appeared before the Commission. Their parents are snakes, and would not appear before the Commission. The husbands are snakes.

I, William S. Webb, on oath state that as stenographer to the Commission to the Five Civilized Tribes I took testimony in the above case, and that the above and foregoing is a true transcript of my notes taken in said case, on the 31st day of May, A. D. 1905.

William S Webb

Subscribed and sworn to before me, on this the 1st day of June, A. D. 1905.

Chas E Webster
Notary Public.

Seminole NB-173.

Muskogee, Indian Territory, June 29, 1905.

Thomas Palmer,
    Sasakwa, Indian Territory.

Dear Sir:

On May 31, 1905, you appeared before the Commission and made application for the enrollment of Maley as a citizen by blood of the Seminole Nation. Before the rights of said child, as a citizen by blood of the Seminole Nation, can be finally determined it will be necessary that the Commission be furnished with the proper proof of birth of said child, and a blank for that purpose is herewith inclosed.

In having the same executed be careful to see that all blank spaces are properly filled, all names written in full, and that the notary public, before whom the affidavits are executed, attaches his name and seal to each affidavit. In case any signature is by mark it must be attested by two disinterested persons, witnesses thereto.

Please give this matter your immediate attention.

Respectfully,

B-C.
Env.

Chairman.

Sem. N B 173.

Muskogee, Indian Territory, December 29, 1905.

McKennon & Willmott,
    Attorneys for the Seminoles,
        Wewoka, Indian Territory.

Gentlemen:

On May 31, 1905, application was made by Thomas Palmer of Sasakwa, Indian Territory, to the Commission to the Five Civilized Tribes, for the enrollment of Maley as a citizen of the Seminole Nation under the act of Congress approved March 3, 1905.

The testimony of Thomas Palmer does not give the names of the parents of this child nor the date of its birth, but the post office address of the parents is given as Henryetta, Indian Territory.

It is desirable that this office be supplied with affidavits of the mother and that attneding[sic] physician or midwife at the birth of this child, to the date of its birth, the names of its parents, and whether said child is now or was living on March 4, 1905.

Applications for Enrollment of Seminole Newborn
Act of 1905   Volume II

Please give this matter your early attention.

Respectfully,

B C   Commissioner.

Sem NB 173
Sem NB 176

Muskogee, Indian Territory, February ?, 1907.

Thomas Jones,
   Mellette, Indian Territory.

Dear Sir:

Information has been received at this office that Sam Miller and Maley children whose mothers are Seminoles and whose fathers are Creeks, are living with Eliza Tiger in the neighborhood of Yuskeegee[sic] Church in a Seminole settlement.

Application has been made for the enrollment of these two children as Seminoles under the act of Congress approved March 3, 1905, but sufficient evidence has not been furnished in this case to complete the proof of birth.

These are inclosed herewith several blanks for the enrollment of minor children and I have to request that you procure, if possible affidavits to the birth of these children. In the event the affidavits of the mother and physician or midwife cannot be obtained, please procure the affidavits of two disinterested witnesses in lieu of each.

I have also to request that you inquire whether or not application has been made for the enrollment of these children as Creeks and if so the name under which such application was made.

The applications for their enrollment were made by Thomas Palmer and Band Chief and no information could be secured as to the names of their parents.

Respectfully,

4 B.C.   Commissioner.

Applications for Enrollment of Seminole Newborn
Act of 1905   Volume II

DEPARTMENT OF THE INTERIOR,
COMMISSIONER TO THE FIVE CIVILIZED TRIBES.
Muskogee, Ind. Ter., February 28, 1907.

In the matter of the application for the enrollment as citizens of the Seminole Nation of Samuel Miller and Maley; Austin Barnett, having been duly sworn, testified as follows through Jesse McDermott, the official interpreter.

Q What is your name? A Austin Barnett.

Q What is your age? A I am about 25.

Q What is your postoffice address? A Eufaula.

Q Are you married? A Yes Sir.

Q What is your wife's name? A Liza.

Q Do you know anything of two children, Sam Miller and Maley? A I know a person by the name of Maley but I do not know anything about Sam Miller.

Q How old is this Maley that you know? A I do not know how old she is but she is married.

Q On May 31, 1905, Tom Palmer, Band Chief of the Seminole Nation made application for the enrollment as Seminoles of two children, Maley, date of birth not given and Sam Miller, born April 16, 1903 and the names of the parents of these children were not given. Do you know anything of these two children? A I do not know anything about Sam Miller but I do know something about Maley. She is the daughter of my wife, Liza. It is true that Liza's maiden name was Liza Tiger but there is no one living with her by the name of Sam Miller to my knowledge.

Q Has she a child in her family about the age this Sam Miller would be? A She has a child about that age but its name is Edmund Barnett, but he is enrolled in the Creek Nation.

Q You are a citizen of the Creek Nation? A I am.

Q What tribe does your wife, Liza belong to? A Seminole.

Q Do you know Tom Palmer? A I do.

Q Do you think that Tom Palmer could have made application for two of your wife's children under the name of Maley and Sam Miller? A He has the names of my children correct and I do not think that he would have given the Commissions the wrong names. If he had been executing affidavits about the Maley that I have reference to, he would have given the right name, Maley Brown under which name she goes now.

Q One of the men in the field who was sent out to get information about these two children, stated that they were living with Liza Tiger in the neighborhood of Tuskeegee Church. A What is the name of the party who was sent out?

Q His name was Gary. A Was he an Indian or a white man?

Q A white man. A Was he a lawyer?

Q No. A If that is the case I do not know anything about him.

Q The postoffice of the parents of these children was given by Tom Palmer as Henryetta. A I do not know who Tom Palmer could have been referring to in his affidavits. He knows that our postoffice address is Eufaula.

Q Do you know Peter Salone? A No, I do not.

Applications for Enrollment of Seminole Newborn
Act of 1905 Volume II

Q Do you know of anyone by the name of Peter Chupco who lives near Henryetta? A I have seen him several times but am not personally acquainted with him. He lives in the neighborhood of Hickory Ground.

Q It was Peter Salone or Chupco who stated that these two children were living with Liza Tiger or in her neighborhood. A On my part I do not know anything about those parties.

Q Could those two children be living in the neighborhood of Tuskeggee Church and not in your family and you not know anything about it? A I am well acquainted with nearly all the Seminole families in my community but to my knowing I do not know anything of their having those children in their families. Whoever gave the information about Liza Tiger living in the neighborhood of Tuskeegee Church gave the correct information as to where she lived and also her name Liza Tiger but I do not know anything about the children you have questioned me about. Before my wife was married her name was Liza Tiger.

Witness excused.

Elsie Weber, being duly sworn, states that the above and foregoing is a full true and correct transcript of her stenographic notes as taken in said cause on the dates set forth.

Elsie Weber

Subscribed and sworn to before me, this 18 day of February, 1907.

Walter M. Chappell
Notary Public.

Sem. NB-173

DEPARTMENT OF THE INTERIOR,
COMMISSIONER TO THE FIVE CIVILIZED TRIBES.

DCW

In the matter of the application for the enrollment of Maley as a citizen of the Seminole Nation.

-: D E C I S I O N :-

It appears from the record herein that on May 31, 1905, application was made to the Commission to the Five Civilized Tribes for the enrollment of Maley (age not given) as a citizen of the Seminole Nation under the provisions of the Act of Congress approved March 3, 1905 (33 Stats., 1070).

This office through its field parties operating in the Seminole and Creek Nations and its land offices and by interviews at this office of residents of the Seminole and Creek Nations of extensive acquaintance in said nations made every effort to ascertain the whereabouts of the applicant and the names and identification of her parents, but no information has been obtained.

I am, therefore, of the opinion that the application for the enrollment of Maley should be dismissed, and it is so ordered.

Tams Bixby Commissioner.

Muskogee, Indian Territory.
FEB 20 1907

Seminole NB-173.

Muskogee, Indian Territory, June 29, 1905.

Thomas Palmer,
Sasakwa, Indian Territory.

Dear Sir:-

On May 31, 1905, you appeared before the Commission and made application for the enrollment of Maley as a citizen by blood of the Seminole. Before the rights of said child, as a citizen by blood of the Seminole Nation, can be finally determined it will be necessary that the Commission be furnished with the proper proof of birth of said child, and a blank for that purpose is herewith inclosed.

In having the same executed be careful to see that all blank spaces are properly filled, all names written in full, and that the notary public, before whom the affidavits are executed attaches his name and seal to each affidavit. In case any signature is by mark it must be attested by two disinterested persons, witnesses thereto.

Please give this matter your immediate attention.

Respectfully,

Chairman.

B-C
Env.

Sem NB 173, 174
176.

Muskogee, Indian Territory, December 29, 1906.

Thomas Palmer,
Sasakwa, Indian Territory.

Dear Sir:

You, as Band Chief, made application for the enrollment as new born citizens of the Seminole Nation under the act of Congress of March 3, 1905, of Maley, Eliza Cully and Sam Miller. At that time you did not know the names of the parents of these children and no further information than that given by you has been procured by this office.

You are hereby advised that a representative of the Commissioner to the Five Civilized Tribes will be in Wewoka, Indian Territory, Friday and Saturday, January 4 and 5, 1907, for the purpose of hearing testimony in Seminole enrollment cases, and I have to request that you secure the appearance at that place on one of those days, for the purpose of testifying relative to one of these dates of the mothers of these children, accompanied by the physician or midwife who was in attendance at their birth. In the event there was no physician or midwife in attendance, the testimony of two disinterested witnesses who knew of the birth of the children, the names of their parents and that they were living March 4, 1906.

The post office addresses of all these children was given by you, at the time of the application for their enrollment, as Henryetta, Indian Territory.

Your co-operation in securing the attendance of these persons on one of the dates named is greatly desired in order that the necessary evidence to complete the proof of birth of these children may be procured.

Respectfully,
Commissioner.

HGH

REFER IN REPLY TO THE FOLLOWING:

DEPARTMENT OF THE INTERIOR,
COMMISSIONER TO THE FIVE CIVILIZED TRIBES.

Muskogee, Indian Territory, February 8, 1907.

Jesse McDermott,
    c/o Creek Field party,
        Eufaula, Indian Territory.

Dear Sir:

You are hereby directed to secure testimony in the matter of the application for the enrollment of Sam Miller and Maley, Seminole New Born, cards 176 and 173; post office address of the witnesses is at or near Tuskegee church, west of Eufaula.

The records in said cases, together with memoranda as to particular proof required, are herewith enclosed.

Respectfully,
Tams Bixby   Commissioner.

EK-1.

Applications for Enrollment of Seminole Newborn
Act of 1905   Volume II

Sem NB 174
(This folder was marked as empty.)

DEPARTMENT OF THE INTERIOR,
COMMISSIONER TO THE FIVE CIVILIZED TRIBES.

In the matter of the application for the enrollment of Lumpa (Lumber) Scott as a minor citizen of the Seminole Nation.

Sem. -NB-175.

Sem NB 175   See Card 578
BIRTH AFFIDAVIT.

DEPARTMENT OF THE INTERIOR.
COMMISSION TO THE FIVE CIVILIZED TRIBES.

IN RE APPLICATION FOR ENROLLMENT, as a citizen of the   Seminole   Nation, of Lumpa Scott   , born on the   25   day of   Feb   , 1903

Name of Father: a citizen of the   Nation.
Name of Mother: a citizen of the   Nation.

Postoffice   Henryetta, I.T.

AFFIDAVIT OF MOTHER.
                                                  Band Chief

UNITED STATES OF AMERICA, Indian Territory, ⎱
      Western   **DISTRICT.** ⎰

I,   Tom Palmer   , on oath state that I am   46   years of age and a citizen by blood   , of the   Seminole   Nation; that I am the ~~lawful wife~~ band chief of , who is a citizen, by   of the   Nation; that a   male   child was born to

258

~~me~~ her on   25   day of   Feb   , 1903, that said child has been named   Lumpa Scott ,
and is now living.

Tom Palmer

Witnesses To Mark:

$\left\{\vphantom{\begin{array}{c}a\\b\end{array}}\right.$

Subscribed and sworn to before me this   31   day of   May   , 1905.

Chas E Webster
Notary Public.

———————

DEPARTMENT OF THE INTERIOR,

COMMISSION TO THE FIVE CIVILIZED TRIBES.

In the matter of the application for the enrollment of Pearl Raiford, Lena
Raiford, Lena Salone, Lumpsey Scott, Sam Miller, Elizabeth Cully, Maley and
Albert, as citizens by blood of the Seminole Nation.

Thomas Palmer, being duly sworn, testified as follows, through Mrs. A. B.
Davis, official interpreter.

Q. What is your name? A. Thomas Palmer.
Q. What is your age? A. Forty-six.
Q. What is your post-office address? A. Sasakwa.
Q. You desire to make application for enrollment of the above named children as
    citizens of the Seminole Nation? A. Yes.
Q. Are you related to any of the above named children? A. No.
Q. Are you an officer of the Seminole Nation? A. Yes.
Q. What position do you hold? A. I am band chief.
Q. Are you acquainted with the parents of each of the above named children? A. Yes.
Q. They are all upon the approved Seminole roll, are they? Their names appear upon
    that roll? A. They are on the roll and have taken allotments.
Q. The names of these children appear upon the records of the Seminoles, do they not;
    that is upon your record? A. Yes, all of them.
Q. And have drawn their annuities or headright? A. Yes, there was one child that was
    not born in time, that is he has not yet drawn any money.
Q. He is recognized as a Seminole Indian, is he not? A. Yes.
Q. Why is it that the parents of these children do not appear before this Commission to
    enroll them? A. Their husbands are snakes. They are not in favor of allotment, and
    don't come forward to allot their wives and children. They were allotted arbitrarily.
    These people have never appeared before the Commission.   The husbands are
    Creeks.
Q. Has application ever been made, before this time, for any one of these children, as
    citizens of the Seminole Nation, or any other nation.[sic] A. No, they have never

appeared before the Commission. Their parents are snakes, and would not appear before the Commission. The husbands are snakes.

I, William S. Webb, on oath state that as stenographer to the Commission to the Five Civilized Tribes I took testimony in the above case, and that the above and foregoing is a true transcript of my notes taken in said case, on the 31st day of May, A. D. 1905.

William S Webb

Subscribed and sworn to before me, on this the 1st day of June, A. D. 1905.

Chas E Webster
Notary Public.

DEPARTMENT OF THE INTERIOR,
COMMISSION TO THE FIVE CIVILIZED TRIBES.
Sonora, I. T., June 19, 1905.

In the matter of the application for the enrollment of Lumber and Rufus Scott as citizens by blood of the Creek Nation.

POLLIE SCOTT, being duly sworn, testified as follows:

Through Alex Posey Official Interpreter:

BY COMMISSION:
Q What is your name? A Pollie Scott
Q How old are you? A About thirty.
Q What is your post office address? A Sonora.
Q Are you a citizen of the Seminole Nation? A Yes, sir.
Q Do you make application for the enrollment of your minor children, Lumber and Rufus Scott as citizens by bloood[sic] of the Creek Nation? A Yes, sir.
Q If it should be found that these two children are entitled to rights in both the Creek and Seminole Nation in which nation do you elect to have them enrolled? A In the Creek Nation?

---oooOOOooo---

I, D. C. Skaggs, on oath state that the above and foregoing is a full and true transcript of my stenographic notes as taken in said cause on said date.

D. C. Skaggs

Subscribed and sworn to before me this 30 day of Dec 1905.

Edw C Griesel
Notary Public.

Sem. NB-175

DEPARTMENT OF THE INTERIOR,
COMMISSIONER TO THE FIVE CIVILIZED TRIBES.

DCW

In the matter of the application for the enrollment of Lumpa (Lumber) Scott as a minor citizen of the Seminole Nation.

-: D E C I S I O N :-

It appears from the record herein that on May 31, 1905, written application was made to the Commission to the Five Civilized Tribes for the enrollment of Lumpa Scott as a minor citizen of the Seminole Nation under the provisions of the Act of Congress approved March 3, 1905 (33 Stats., 1070).

It further appears from the record herein and from the records of this office, that the applicant, Lumpa (Lumber) Scott was born February 25, 1903 and is the son of Turner Scott, whose name appears upon the final roll of citizens by blood of the Creek Nation approved by the Secretary of the Interior and Polly Scott, whose name appears opposite No. 1668 upon the final roll of Seminole Indians approved by the Secretary of the Interior April 2, 1901.

It further appears from the record herein and from the records of this office that the parents of said Lena Salone elected on June 19, 1905, Polly Scott, the mother of the applicant elected to have the applicant enrolled as a citizen by blood of the Creek Nation and to take his allotment of lands and distribution of moneys in said Nation and that the name of the applicant as Lumber Scott appears opposite No. 1206 upon the final roll of new born citizens of the Creek Nation approved by the Secretary of the Interior February 15, 1907 under the provisions of the Act of Congress approved March 3, 1905, (33 Stats., 1070).

I am therefore of the opinion that the application for the enrollment of Lumpa (Lumber) Scott as a minor citizen of the Seminole Nation should be dismissed and it is so ordered.

Tams Bixby   Commissioner.

Muskogee, Indian Territory,
FEB 20 1907

Sem NB-175   **COPY**
                            Muskogee, Indian Territory, March 6, 190

Turner Scott,
        Henryetta, Indian Territory.

Dear Sir:-

    You are hereby notified that the Commissioner to the Five Civilized Tribes on February 20, 1907, rendered his decision dismissing the application for the enrollment of Lumpa (Lumber) Scott as a citizen of the Seminole Nation.

                            Respectfully,
                                SIGNED *Tams Bixby*
Registered.   Commissioner.

Sem NB-175   **COPY**
                            Muskogee, Indian Territory, March 8, 1907.

Chief Clerk,
        Creek Enrollment Division:

Dear Sir:

    You are hereby notified that the Commissioner to the Five Civilized Tribes, on February 20, 1907, rendered his decision dismissing the application for the enrollment of Lumpa (Lumber) Scott as a citizen of the Seminole Nation.

                            Respectfully,
                                SIGNED *Tams Bixby*
                                    Commissioner.

                                Seminole-NB-175.

                    Muskogee, Indian Territory, June 29, 1905.

Thomas Palmer,
        Sasakwa, Indian Territory.

Dear Sir:

    On May 31, 1905, you appeared before the Commission and made application for the enrollment of Lumpa Scott as a citizen by blood of the Seminole Nation. Before the rights of said child, as a citizen by blood of the Seminole Nation, can be finally

                                    262

determined it will be necessary that the Commission be furnished with the proper proof of birth of said child, and a blank for that purpose is inclosed.

In having the same executed be careful to see that all blank spaces are properly filled, all names written in full and that the notary public, before whom the affidavits are executed, attaches his name and seal to each affidavit. In case any signature is by mark it must be attested by two disinterested persons, witnesses thereto.

Please give this matter your prompt attention.

Respectfully,

B-C.   Chairman.

Env.

_____

HGH

<table>
<tr><td>

REFER IN REPLY TO THE FOLLOWING:

_____

NC-1072.

</td><td>

DEPARTMENT OF THE INTERIOR,
COMMISSIONER TO THE FIVE CIVILIZED TRIBES.

</td></tr>
</table>

Muskogee, Indian Territory, October 23, 1905.

Clerk in Charge,
	Seminole Enrollment Division.

Dear Sir:

Application was made to the Commission to the Five Civilized Tribes for the enrollment of Lumber Scott, born February 25, 1903, and Rufus Scott, born December 17, 1904, children of Turner Scott, a citizen of the Creek Nation, and Polly Scott, a citizen of the Seminole Nation, as citizens by blood of the Creek Nation.

You are requested to inform the Creek Enrollment Division as to whether application has been made for the enrollment of said children as citizens of the Seminole Nation and if so what disposition has been made of same.

Respectfully,
			Tams Bixby Commissioner.

_____

Applications for Enrollment of Seminole Newborn
Act of 1905   Volume II

Muskogee, Indian Territory, October 28, 1905.

Clerk in Charge,
Creek Enrollment Division

Dear Sir:

Receipt is hereby acknowledged of your letter of the 23rd instant, in which you request to be informed whether or not application has been made for the enrollment of Lumber Scott, born February 25, 1903, and Rufus Scott born December 17, 1904, children of Turner Scott, a citizen of the Creek Nation and Polly Scott, a citizen of the Seminole Nation, and as to what disposition has been made of same.

In reply you are advised that no application has been made for the enrollment of Rufus Scott as a citizen of the Seminole Nation, but an application for the enrollment of Lumpa Scott as a citizen of the Seminole Nation was made on May 31, 1905, by Thomas Palmer, a Bank Chief of the Seminole Nation.

Testimony of Thomas Palmer taken on above date, shows that Lumpa Scott was born February 25, 1903, is on the Band Chiefs roll, and that the parents of Lumpa Scott are "snake Indians" and refuse to apply for the enrollment of their child.

The names of Lumpa Scott's parents were not gievn[sic] at the time the application was made but Thomas Palmer said that he would send in these names, which has not been done.

Lumpa Scott has not been finally enrolled as a citizen of the Seminole Nation.

Respectfully,

Commissioner.

————————

HGH

<table>
<tr><td>REFER IN REPLY TO THE FOLLOWING:
————————
N.C. 904</td><td>**DEPARTMENT OF THE INTERIOR,**
COMMISSIONER TO THE FIVE CIVILIZED TRIBES.</td></tr>
</table>

Muskogee, Indian Territory, October 30, 1905.

Chief Clerk,
Seminole Enrollment Division.

Dear Sir:

Receipt is acknowledged of your communication of October 28, 1905, replying to the communication of the Creek Enrollment Division of October 23, 1905, relative to the application for the enrollment of Lumber Scott as a citizen by blood of the Creek Nation.

You state that application has been made for the enrollment of Lumpa Scott, who is now identified as the same person as said Lumber Scott, as a citizen by blood of the Seminole Nation.

There is herewith enclosed copy of testimony taken June 19, 1905 in the matter of the application for the enrollment of application for the enrollment of said Lumber Scott as a citizen by blood of the Creek Nation in which an election is made by the mother of said child for his enrollment in the Creek Nation. Said testimony was taken at Sonora, Indian Territory, by the Creek Enrollment field party and is not yet signed and sworn to. When the same has been properly signed and sworn to, another copy will be sent to your office.

Respectfully,

AG-5c
Tams Bixby   Commissioner.

Sem. N B 175

Muskogee, Indian Territory, December 29, 1905.

Chief Clerk,
    Creek Enrollment Division,

Dear Sir:

On May 31, 1905, application was made for the enrollment of Lumpa Scott, minor child of Pollie Scott, as a citizen of the Seminole Nation. Subsequently on June 19, 1905, Pollie Scott appeared before the enrollment party at Sonora, Indian Territory, and elected for her child, Lumpa (Lumber) Scott to be enrolled as a citizen of the Creek Nation.

You are therefore requested to advise the Seminole Enrollment Division the status of the application for the enrollment of Lumpa (Lumber) Scott as a citizen of the Creek Nation; whether he has been enrolled as a citizen of said nation and if so his roll number and the date of the approval of his enrollment by the Department.

Respectfully,

Commissioner.

265

HGH

| REFER IN REPLY TO THE FOLLOWING: |
| Sem. NB-175. |
| NBC-1072. |

DEPARTMENT OF THE INTERIOR,
COMMISSIONER TO THE FIVE CIVILIZED TRIBES.

Muskogee, Indian Territory, January 2, 1906.

Chief Clerk of Seminole Enrollment Division,
Muskogee, Indian Territory.

Dear Sir:

Receipt is acknowledged of your letter of December 29, 1905 in which you ask to be advised as to the status of the application for the enrollment of Lumpa (Lumber) Scott, minor child of Polly Scott, a citizen of the Seminole Nation, as a citizen of the Creek Nation.

In reply you are advised that the matter of the application for the enrollment of Lumber Scott, child of said Polly Scott, is pending, and that when final action is had in the matter you will be duly notified.

Respectfully,

Tams Bixby
Commissioner.

D.C. LL.

DEPARTMENT OF THE INTERIOR,
COMMISSIONER TO THE FIVE CIVILIZED TRIBES.

In the matter of the application for the enrollment of Sam Miller as a citizen of the Seminole Nation.

Sem. NB-176.

266

Sem NB 176   See Card 578
BIRTH AFFIDAVIT.

DEPARTMENT OF THE INTERIOR.
COMMISSION TO THE FIVE CIVILIZED TRIBES.

IN RE APPLICATION FOR ENROLLMENT, as a citizen of the   Seminole   Nation, of
Sam Miller   , born on the   16   day of   April   , 1903

Name of Father: a citizen of the   Nation.
Name of Mother: a citizen of the   Nation.

Postoffice   Henryetta I.T.

AFFIDAVIT OF MOTHER.
Band Chief

UNITED STATES OF AMERICA, Indian Territory, ⎱
    Western   **DISTRICT.** ⎰

I,   Tom Palmer   , on oath state that I am   46   years of age and a citizen by
blood   , of the   Seminole   Nation; that I am the lawful wife band chief of
, who is a citizen, by   of the   Nation; that a   male   child was born to
me on   16   day of   April   , 1903, that said child has been named   Sam Miller   ,
and is now living.

Tom Palmer

Witnesses To Mark:
⎰
⎱

Subscribed and sworn to before me this 31   day of   May   , 1905.

Chas E Webster
Notary Public.

DEPARTMENT OF THE INTERIOR.
COMMISSION TO THE FIVE CIVILIZED TRIBES.

---

case
In the matter of the ~~death~~ of   Sam Miller   a citizen of the   Seminole
Nation, who formerly resided at or near   Senora I.T.   , Ind. Ter., and ~~died on the
day of   , 190~~

267

Applications for Enrollment of Seminole Newborn
Act of 1905   Volume II

AFFIDAVIT OF RELATIVE.

UNITED STATES OF AMERICA, Indian Territory, ⎫
    Western   DISTRICT. ⎭

      I, Eliza Barnett , on oath state that I am   Thirty five years of age and a citizen by   full blood , of the   Seminole   Nation; that my postoffice address is Eufaula , Ind. Ter.; that I am   Aunt   of Sam Miller   who was a citizen, by blood , of the Seminole   Nation and that said   Sam Miller   died born on the   17th   day of December   , 1905

                                                     her
                                     Eliza x Barnett

Witnesses To Mark: mark
    ⎰ J.M. Price
    ⎱ Toney Bornell

      Subscribed and sworn to before me this   17th   day of   Feby , 1907.

                                   Bunnie McIntosh
My Commission Expires   Notary Public.
          May 16. 1908

AFFIDAVIT OF ACQUAINTANCE.

UNITED STATES OF AMERICA, Indian Territory, ⎫
      Western   DISTRICT. ⎭

      I, Thomas Jones   , on oath state that I am   55 years of age, and a citizen by blood   of the Creek   Nation; that my postoffice address is   Mellette   , Ind. Ter.; that I was personally acquainted with   Sam Miller   who was a citizen, by blood , of the Seminole   Nation; and that said   Sam Miller   died born on the   17 day of   December   , 1905

                                          his
                                    Thomas x Jones

Witnesses To Mark: mark
    ⎰ J. M. Price
    ⎱ Toney Bornell

      Subscribed and sworn to before me this   17th   day of   Feby , 1907.

                                   Bunnie McIntosh
My Commission Expires   Notary Public.
          May 16. 1908

Applications for Enrollment of Seminole Newborn
Act of 1905 Volume II

DEPARTMENT OF THE INTERIOR,

COMMISSION TO THE FIVE CIVILIZED TRIBES.

In the matter of the application for the enrollment of Pearl Raiford, Lena Raiford, Lena Salona[sic], Lumpsey Scott, <u>Sam Miller</u>, Elizabeth Cully, Maley and Albert, as citizens by blood of the Seminole Nation.

Thomas Palmer, being duly sworn, testified as follows, through Mrs. A. B. Davis, official interpreter.

Q What is your name? A Thomas Palmer.
Q What is your age? A Forty-six.
Q What is your post-office address? A Sasakwa.
Q You desire to make application for enrollment of the above named children as citizens of the Seminole Nation? A Yes.
Q Are you related to any of the above named children? A No.
Q Are you an officer of the Seminole Nation? A Yes.
Q What position do you hold? A I am band chief.
Q Are you acquainted with the parents of each of the above named children? A Yes.
Q They are all upon the approved Seminole roll, are they? Their names appear upon that roll? A They are on the roll and have taken allotments.
Q The names of these children appear upon the records of the Seminoles, do they not; that is upon your record? A Yes, all of them.
Q And have drawn their annuities or headright? A Yes, there was one child that was not born in time, that is he has not yet drawn any money.
Q He is recognized as a Seminole Indian, is he not? A Yes.
Q Why is it that the parents of these children do not appear before this Commission to enroll them? A Their husbands are snakes. They are not in favor of allotment, don't come forward to allot their wives and children. They were allotted arbitrarily. These people have never appeared before the Commission. The husbands are Creeks.
Q Has application ever been made, before this time, for any one of these children, as citizens of the Seminole Nation, or any other nation.[sic] A No, they have never appeared before the Commission. Their parents are snakes, and would not appear before the Commission. The husbands are snakes.

I, William S. Webb, on oath state that as stenographer to the Commission to the Five Civilized Tribes I took testimony in the above case, and that the above and foregoing is a true transcript of my notes taken in said case, on the 31st day of May, A. D. 1905.

William S Webb

Subscribed and sworn to before me, on this the 1st day of June, A. D. 1905.

Chas. E. Webster
(SEAL)   Notary Public.

269

Applications for Enrollment of Seminole Newborn
Act of 1905 Volume II

Seminole NB-176.

Muskogee, Indian Territory, June 29, 1905.

Thomas Palmer,
 Sasakwa, Indian Territory.

Dear Sir:

On May 31, 1905, you appeared before the Commission and made application for the enrollment of Sam Miller as a citizen by blood of the Seminole Nation. Before the rights of said child, as a citizen by blood of the Seminole Nation, can be finally determined it will be necessary that the Commission be furnished with the proper proof of birth of said child, and a blank for that purpose is herewith inclosed.

In having the same executed be careful to see that all blank spaces are properly filled, all names written in full, and that the notary public, before whom the affidavits are executed, attaches his name and seal to each separate affidavit. And in the event that the persons signing the affidavits are unable to write, signature by mark must be attested by two witnesses.

Please give this matter your immediate attention.

Respectfully,

B-C.   Chairman.
Env.

Sem. N B 176.

Muskogee, Indian Territory, December 29, 1905.

McKennon & Willmott,
 Attorneys for the Seminoles,
  Wewoka, Indian Territory.

Gentlemen:

On May 31, 1905, application was made to the Commission to the Five Civilized Tribes by Thomas Palmer, of Sasakwa, Indian Territory, for the enrollment of Sam Miller, as a citizen of the Seminole Nation under the act of Congress approved March 3, 1905.

It appears from the testimony of Thomas Palmer that this child was born April 16, 1903, but the names of the parents do not appear, although their address is given as Henryetta, Indian Territory.

It is desirable that this office be supplies with the affidavits of the mother and the attending physician or midwife to the date of its birth, the names of its parents and

270

whether said child is now or was living March 4, 1905. Please give this matter your early attention.

Respectfully,

Commissioner

B C

———————

Sem N B 173, 174
      176

Muskogee, Indian Territory, December 29, 1906.

Thomas Palmer,
    Sasakwa, Indian Territory.

Dear Sir:

You, as Band Chief, made application for the enrollment, as new born citizens of the Seminole Nation under the act of Congress approved March 3, 1905, of Maley, Eliza Cully and Sam Miller. At that time you did not know the names of the parents of these children and no further information than that given by you has been procured by this office.

You are hereby advised that a representative of the Commissioner to the Five Civilized Tribes will be in Wewoka, Indian Territory, Friday and Saturday, January 4 and 5, 1907, for the purpose of hearing testimony in Seminole enrollment cases, and I have to request that you secure the appearance at that place on one of those dates of the mothers of these children, accompanied by the physician or midwife who was in attendance at their birth. In the event there was no physician or midwife in attendance, the testimony of two disinterested witnesses who know of the birth of the children, the names of their parents and that they were living March 4, 1905.

The post office addresses of all these children was given by you, at the time of the application for their enrollment, as Henryetta, Indian Territory.

Your co-operation in securing the attendance of these persons on one of the dates named is greatly desired in order that the necessary evidence to complete the proof of birth of these children may be procured.

Respectfully,

Commissioner.

———————

271

Applications for Enrollment of Seminole Newborn
Act of 1905   Volume II

Sem NB 173
Sem NB 176

Muskogee, Indian Territory, February ?, 1907.

Thomas Jones,
    Melletee[sic], Indian Territory.

Dear Sir:

Information received has been received at this office that Sam Miller and Maley children whose mothers are Seminoles and whose fathers are Creeks, are living with Eliza Tiger in the neighborhood of Yuskeegee Church in a Seminole settlement.

Application has been made for the enrollment of these two children as Seminoles under the act of Congress approved March 3, 1905, but sufficient evidence has not been furnished in this case to complete the proof of birth.

There are inclosed herewith several blanks for the enrollment of minor children and I have to request that you procure, if possible affidavits to the birth of these children. In the event the affidavits of the mother and physician or midwife cannot be obtained, please procure the affidavits of two disinterested witnesses in lieu of each.

I have also to request that you inquire whether or not application has been made for the enrollment of these children as Creeks and if so the name under which such application was made.

The applications for their enrollment were made by Thomas Palmer and Band Chief and no information could be secured as to the names of their parents.

Respectfully,

4 B. C.   Commissioner.

DEPARTMENT OF THE INTERIOR,
COMMISSIONER TO THE FIVE CIVILIZED TRIBES.
Muskogee, Ind. Ter., February 18, 1907.

In the matter of the application for the enrollment as citizens of the Seminole Nation of Samuel Miller and Maley; Austin Barnett, having been duly sworn, testified as follows through Jesse McDermott, the official interpreter.

Q What is your name? A Austin Barnett.
Q What is your age? A I am about 25.
Q What is your postoffice address? A Eufaula.
Q Are you married? A Yes Sir.
Q What is your wife's name? A Liza.

Applications for Enrollment of Seminole Newborn
Act of 1905   Volume II

Q Do you know anything of two children, Sam Miller and Maley? A I know a person by the name of Maley but I do not know anything about Sam Miller.

Q How old is this Maley that you know? A I do not know how old she is but she is married.

Q On May 31, 1905, Tom Palmer, Band Chief of the Seminole Nation made application for the enrollment as Seminoles of two children, Maley, date of birth not given and Sam Miller, born April 16, 1903 and the names of the parents of these children were not given. Do you know anything of these two children? A I do not know anything about Sam Miller but I do know something about Maley. She is the daughter of my wife, Liza. It is true that Liza's maiden name was Liza Tiger but there is no one living with her by the name of Sam Miller to my knowledge.

Q Has she a child in her family about the age this Sam Miller would be? A She has a child about that age but its name is Edmund Barnett, but he is enrolled in the Creek Nation.

Q You are a citizen of the Creek Nation? A I am.

Q What tribe does your wife, Liza belong to? A Seminole.

Q Do you know Tom Palmer? A I do.

Q Do you think that Tom Palmer could have made application for two of your wife's children under the name of Maley and Sam Miller? A He has the names of my children correct and I do not think that he would have given the Commissions the wrong names. If he had been executing affidavits about the Maley that I have reference to, he would have given the right name, Maley Brown under which name she goes now.

Q One of the men in the field who was sent out to get information about these two children, stated that they were living with Liza Tiger in the neighborhood of Tuskeegee Church. A What is the name of the party who was sent out?

Q His name was Gary. A Was he an Indian or a white man?

Q A white man. A Was he a lawyer?

Q No. A If that is the case I do not know anything about him.

Q The postoffice of the parents of these children was given by Tom Palmer as Henryetta. A I do not know who Tom Palmer could have been referring to in his affidavits. He knows that our postoffice address is Eufaula.

Q Do you know Peter Salone? A No, I do not.

Q Do you know of anyone by the name of Peter Chupco who lives near Henryetta? A I have seen him several times but am not personally acquainted with him. He lives in the neighborhood of Hickory Ground.

Q It was Peter Salone or Chupco who stated that these two children were living with Liza Tiger or in her neighborhood. A On my part I do not know anything about those parties.

Q Could those two children be living in the neighborhood of Tuskeggee Church and not in your family and you not know anything about it? A I am well acquainted with nearly all the Seminole families in my community but to my knowing I do not know anything of their having those children in their families. Whoever gave the information about *(no more testimony given.)*

273

Sem. NB-176.

DEPARTMENT OF THE INTERIOR,
COMMISSIONER TO THE FIVE CIVILIZED TRIBES.

DCW

In the matter of the application for the enrollment of Sam Miller as a citizen of the Seminole Nation.

-: D E C I S I O N :-

It appears from the record herein that on May 31, 1905, application was made to the Commission to the Five Civilized Tribes for the enrollment of Sam Miller born April 16, 1903 as a citizen of the Seminole Nation under the provisions of the Act of Congress approved March 3, 1905 (33 Stats., 1070).

This office through its field parties operating in the Seminole and Creek Nations and its land offices and by interviews at this office of residents of the Seminole and Creek Nations of extensive acquaintance in said nations made every effort to ascertain the whereabouts of the applicant and the names and identification of his parents, but no information has been obtained.

I am, therefore, of the opinion that the application for the enrollment of Sam Miller should be dismissed, and it is so ordered.

Tams Bixby Commissioner.

Muskogee, Indian Territory.
FEB 20 1907

Seminole-NB-176.

Muskogee, Indian Territory, June 29, 1905.

Thomas Palmer,
Sasakwa, Indian Territory.

Dear Sir:-

On May 31, 1905, you appeared before the Commission and made application for the enrollment of Sam Miller as a citizen by blood of the Seminole Nation. Before the rights of said child, as a citizen by blood of the Seminole Nation, can be finally determined it will be necessary that the Commission be furnished with the proper proof of birth of said child, and a blank for that purpose is herewith inclosed.

In having the same executed be careful to seee[sic] that all name spaces are properly filled, all names written in full, and that the notary public, before whom the affidavits are executed, attaches his name and seal to each separate affidavit. And in the event that the persons signing the affidavits are unable to write, signatures by mark must be attested by two witnesses.

Please give this matter your immediate attention.

Respectfully,

Chairman.

B-c
Env.

Sem. NB 176

Muskogee, Indian Territory, December 29, 1905.

McKennon & Willmott,
    Attorneys for the Seminoles,
        Wewoka, Indian Territory.

Gentlemen:

On May 31, 1905, application was made to the Commission to the Five Civilized Tribes by Thomas Palmer, of Sasakwa, Indian Territory, for the enrollment of Sam Miller as a citizen of the Seminole Nation under the act of Congress approved March 3, 1905.

It appears from the testimony of Thomas Palmer that this child was born April 16, 1903, but the names of the parents do not appear, although their address is given as Henryetta, Indian Territory.

It is desirable that this office be supplied with the affidavit of the mother and the attending physician or midwife to the date of its birth, the names of its parents and whether said child is now or was living March 4, 1905. Please give this matter your early attention.

Respectfully,

B C   Commissioner

Applications for Enrollment of Seminole Newborn
Act of 1905   Volume II

Sem. N B 173

Muskogee, Indian Territory, December 29, 1905.

McKennon & Willmott,
    Attorneys for the Seminoles,
        Wewoka, Indian Territory.

Gentlemen:

On May 31, 1905, application was made by Thomas Palmer, of Sasakwa, Indian Territory, to the Commission to the Five Civilized Tribes, for the enrollment of Maley as a citizen of the Seminole Nation under the act of Congress approved March 3, 1905.

The testimony of Thomas Palmer does not give the names of the parents of this child nor the date of its birth, but the post office address of the parents is given as Henryetta, Indian Territory.

It is desirable that this office be supplied with the affidavit of the mother and the attending physician or midwife at the birth of this child, to the date of its birth, the names of its parents, and whether said child is now or was living on March 4, 1905. Please give this matter your early attention.

Respectfully,

B C

Commissioner

DEPARTMENT OF THE INTERIOR,
COMMISSIONER TO THE FIVE CIVILIZED TRIBES.

- - - -

In the matter of the application for the enrollment as citizens by blood of the Seminole Nation of . . . .

RICHENDA PRATT HENDRIX.
IVY HENDRIX.

Sem NB 177

276

Applications for Enrollment of Seminole Newborn
Act of 1905 Volume II

Muskogee, Indian Territory, March 31, 1905.

Hon James F. Randlette,
Lt. Col. U.S.A., U.S. Indian Agent,
Anadarko, Oklahoma Territory.

Dear Sir:

It appears from the records of the Commission that Winnie Connor and her children Elly and Lizzie were enrolled as citizens by blood of the Seminole Nation, which enrollment was approved by the Secretary of the Interior, April 21, 1901.

On July 19, 1901 the said Winnie Connor appeared before you under the name of Winnie Hendrix and relinquished all rights, title and interest she may have as a citizen of the Seminole Nation. This was in consideration of the enrollment of herself as a member of the Caddo Tribe of Indians, residing on the Wichita Indian Reservation, Kiowa Agency, Oklahoma Territory.

There is no record of the said Winnie Connor, or Hendrix, having at any time relinquished for her minor children, Elly and Lizzie Connor. However, it is thought she probably at the time relinquished for her entire family, which was inadvertently omitted in her affidavit subscribed and sworn to before you.

The Commission will appreciate any information you can furnish them relative to this matter at your earliest convenience.

Respectfully,

Chairman.

—————————

(COPY)

DC 22522- 1905.

DEPARTMENT OF THE INTERIOR.
UNITED STATES INDIAN SERVICE.
Kiowa Indian Agency.
Anadarko, Oklahoma, May 1, 1905.

Commission to the Five Civilized Tribes,
Muskogee, I. T.

Sirs:

I have the honor to forward herewith for consideration application of Winnie Connor Hendrix for enrollment with the Seminole Tribe of Indians of her two infant children born to her since the lands of the Wichita and affiliated Indians were allotted in

277

severalty. The Agency records show that on March 4, 1905, these children were alive; therefore the application herewith is submitted with recommendation for favorable consideration, by virtue of authority contained in Act of Congress approved March 3, 1905.

Very respectfully,

James F. Randlett,

Col. U.S.A.U.S. Indian Agent

JPB

JPB(B)

Enc.

Card 61

(COPY)   Wynie Connor (223)

Application for the enrollment with the Seminole tribe two infant children by virtue of authority contained in an act of Congress approved March 3, 1905 (H.R. 17474).

194

195

The Honorable,
    The Commission to the
        Five Civilized Tribes,
           Muskogee, Indian Territory.

Sirs:

I respectfully represent that I am a Seminole Indian; that I was duly and regularly enrolled as such under the name of Winnie Connor and that on April 21, 1901 my enrollment was approved by the Secretary of the Interior.

I represent further that on March 6, 1902 there was born to me a girl child; that said child was named Richenda Pratt Hendrix and that she is now and was on the fourth day of March, 1905 alive;

Also, that on August 27, 1904 there was born to your applicant a girl child; that this child was named Ivy Hendrix; that she was alive and in being on March 4, 1905, and that she died on April 29, 1905.

I further represent that neither Richenda Pratt Hendrix nor Ivy Hendrix ever received any allotment of land with the Wichita and Affiliated Indians of Kiowa Agency, Oklahoma Territory.

Wherefore, by reason of the foregoing and by virtue of the authority contained in the Act of Congress approved March 3, 1905, your applicant prays that her two infant children described in this, her application, may be enrolled as members of the Seminole tribe and share equally in the distribution of the Seminole tribal lands and funds.

278

Very respectfully submitted,
Winnie Connor Hendrix,

Frank Everett, being first duly sworn deposes and says that he is familiar with the family of Winnie Connor Hendrix, and knows of his personal knowledge that the statements in the foregoing application are true.

Frank Everett.

Subscribed and sworn to before me this 1st day of May, 1905.
(SEAL)

J. R. Blackmon.
Notary Public.

My commission expires April 7, 1908.

(Endorsed)

194   195
Mothers roll 223   177   NEW BORN   23

Richenda Pratt Hendrix   Ivy Hendrix.

ACT OF CONGRESS APPROVED MARCH 3d, 1905.
DEPARTMENT OF THE INTERIOR.
COMMISSION TO THE FIVE CIVILIZED TRIBES
   F I L E D
            MAY 8 1905.
                Tams Bixby, Chairman.

Seminoles 177   RECEIVED
                                  May 8, 1905)

DEPARTMENT OF THE INTERIOR.
COMMISSION TO THE FIVE CIVILIZED TRIBES.
   F I L E D
            MAY 8-1905
                Tams Bixby, Chairman.

279

Applications for Enrollment of Seminole Newborn
Act of 1905   Volume II

Mrs. Winnie Hendrix, of lawful age, does hereby, for herself, relinquish all rights, title and interest of whatever character which she may now have or might hereafter become entitled to as a Seminole Indian of the Union Agency, Muskogee, Indian Territory; this is consideration of the enrollment of herself as a member of the Caddo tribe of Indians residing on the Wichita Indian Reservation, Kiowa Agency, Oklahoma Territory.

Signature

Witnesses

Chas L. Ellis.   Mrs. Winnie Hendrix.

Jno. P. Blackman.

Subscribed and sworn to before me at Anadarko, O. T., the this 19th day of July, A. D. 1901.

James R. Randlett,
Lt. Col. U.S.A., U.S. Indian Agent.

(Endorsed)

No. 61

12380
14042

Relinquishment of Mrs. Winnie Hendrix to rights as a Seminole Indian, of Union Agency, I. T., in consideration of her enrollment as a member of the Caddo tribe of Indians of Kiowa Agency, Okla.

DEPARTMENT OF THE INTERIOR.
COMMISSIONER TO THE FIVE CIVILIZED TRIBES.

- - - - - - - - -

In the matter of the application for the enrollment of Richenda Pratt Hendrix and Ivy Hendrix as citizens of the Seminole Nation.

-DECISION:-

It appears from the record herein that on May 8, 1905, application was made to the Commission to the Five Civilized Tribes for the enrollment of Richenda Pratt Hendrix and Ivy Hendrix as citizens by blood of the Seminole Nation under the provisions of the Act of Congress approved March 3, 1905 (33 Stats., 1048).

It further appears from the record herein that these applicants were born March 6, 1902, and August 22, 1904, respectively, and are the children of Winnie Connor Hendrix, whose name, as Wynie Connor, appears at number 223 upon the approved roll of Seminole Indians, and a non citizen white man.

It further appears that on July 19, 1901, the said Wynie Connor relinquished all her right, title and interest in and to the lands and tribal property of the Seminole Nation, and accepted her allotment as a citizen of the Caddo tribe of Indians.

I am, therefore, of the opinion that inasmuch as Wynie Connor had, prior to the birth of Richenda Pratt Hendrix and Ivy Hendrix, relinquished her right, title and interest in and to the tribal property of the Seminole Nation, that she could confer no rights in said nation upon said children, and that the application for the enrollment of Richenda Pratt Hendrix and Ivy Hendrix as citizens by blood of the Seminole Nation under the provisions of the Act of Congress approved March 3, 1905, should be denied, and it is so ordered.

Tams Bixby Commissioner.

Muskogee, Indian Territory.
FEB 18 1907

Muskogee, Indian Territory, February 19, 1907.

The Honorable,
The Secretary of the Interior.

Sir:

I have the honor to invite Departmental attention to the names of Wynie Conner, Elly Conner and Lizzie Conner, which appear at numbers 223, 224 and 225, respectively, upon the approved roll of Seminole Indians. On July 19, 1901, Wynie Conner relinquished her right, title and interest in and to the tribal property of the Seminole tribe of Indians, and accepted an allotment as a Caddo Indian; on May 1, 1905, she relinquished for her children, Elly and Lizzie Conner, whose names appear at numbers 224 and 225, respectively, upon the approved Seminole roll, all their right, title and interest in and to the lands and tribal property of the Seminoles, and accepted allotments for said children as citizens of the Wichita tribe of Indians.

I have, therefore, to recommend that the names of Wynie Conner, Elly Conner and Lizzie Conner be cancelled upon the approved roll of the Seminole Indians in the Department and the Indian Office, at numbers 223, 224 and 225 upon said roll, and that this office be authorized to make like cancellation upon the copies of the Seminole roll in its possession.

It appears from the records of this office that on May 8, 1905, applications were received for the enrollment as Seminole Indians under the Act of Congress approved March 3, 1905, of Richenda Pratt Hendrix and Ivy Hendrix, children of Wynie Conner Hendrix, and a non-citizen white man.

Inasmuch as Wynie Conner had relinquished all her right, title and interest in and to the lands of the Seminole tribe of Indians prior to the birth of these children, it would appear that they could acquire no right to enrollment as Seminole Indians through her. A decision has, therefore, been rendered denying the applications for their enrollment as

Applications for Enrollment of Seminole Newborn
Act of 1905   Volume II

Seminole Indians under the Act of Congress approved March 3, 1905, and the same is transmitted herewith.

Respectfully,

Commissioner.

Through the Commissioner,
    of Indian Affairs.

Relinquishment of Indian rights.

For and in consideration of the fact that my minor children Carrie Hendrix and Norman Hendrix, have received allotments of land as members of the Wichita tribe of Indians of Kiowa Agency, Oklahoma;

THEREFORE: We, as the father and mother and natural guardians of said minor children (who were enrolled with the Seminole tribe of Indians as Elly and Lizzie Connor) hereby relinquish for them all their rights, title and interest in and to the property of the Seminole tribe of Indians in Indian Territory.

Witness our hands at Kiowa Agency, Anadarko, Oklahoma Territory, this the first day of May, A. D. nineteen hundred and five.

(Signed) Philip Hendrix
Winnie Connor Hendrix.

Subscribed and sworn to before me at Kiowa Agency, Anadarko, Territory, this the first day of May, A. D. nineteen hundred and five.

(Signed) James F. Randlett,
Col. U.S.A., U.S. Indian Agent.

Kiowa Indian Agency,
Anadarko, Oklahoma, May 2, 1905.

Commission to the Five Civilized Tribes,
    Muskogee, I. T.

Sirs:

There is enclosed herewith relinquishment by Winnie Hendrix of all rights, title and interest her two children Elly and Lizzie Connor (Carrie and Norman Hendrix) may have as members of the Seminole Tribe of Indians of the Seminole Nation.

The delay in complying with request contained in your letter of March 31st, was occasioned by the fact that it was impossible to obtain the presence of Winnie Hendrix at the Agency Office on account of the sicness[sic] and death of her infant child, Ivy Hendrix. The child died April 29th ultimo.

Very respectfully,
(Signed) James F. Randlett,
Col. U.S.A., U.S. Indian Agent.

JPB (B)

_____

Sem NB 177

D. C. 12682.   S. P. Jf. Jr.
I. T. D. 6544-1907.
LRS.   DEPARTMENT OF THE INTERIOR,
DIRECT.   WASHINGTON.   March 2, 1907.

Commissioner to the Five Civilized Tribes,
      Muskogee, Indian Territory.

Sir:

On February 28, 1907 (Land 18552-07), the Indian Office transmitted your report dated February 18, 1907, in the matter of the application for the enrollment of cancelation of the names of Wynie Connor, Elly Connor and Lizzie Connor, which appear opposite Nos. 223, 224 and 225, respectively, upon the approved roll of the Seminole Nation.

You transmit your decision denying the application of these persons for enrolment as Seminole Indians under the act of Congress approved March 3, 1905.

The Indian Office concurs in your recommendation.

For the reasons stated in your decision and report, the application for the enrolment of Wynie, Elly and Lizzie Connor as Seminole Indians is hereby denied.

Authority is also granted for the cancelation of the names of Wynie, Elly and Lizzie Conner, which appear opposite Nos. 223, 224 and 225, respectively, upon the approved roll of the Seminole Indians.

The Department has made said cancelation upon the rolls in its possession and the Indian Office is requested to take similar action upon the copy of the roll in its office.

The papers in the case, together with a carbon copy hereof, have been sent to the Indian Office for its files.

A copy of Indian Office letter is inclosed.

283

Respectfully,
Jesse E. Wilson,
Assistant Secretary.

1 inc. and
2 to Ind. Of.

WCF. 3/3/07.

D. C. 12682   --COPY--
Land.   DEPARTMENT OF THE INTERIOR,
18552-1907.   OFFICE OF INDIAN AFFAIRS,
                         WASHINGTON.   February 28, 1907.

The Honorable,
      The Secretary of the Interior.

Sir:

There is forwarded herewith report dated February 18, 1907, from Commissioner Bixby, relative to the cancellation from the approved roll of Seminole Indians, of the names of Wynie, Elly, and Lizzie Connor, which appear at Nos. 223, 224, and 225, respectively.

Reporting thereon the Commissioner recommends that the names of the persons be cancelled from the approved roll of Seminole Indians.

The Office has examined the record and report of the Commissioner and concurs in his recommendation.

Very respectfully,
C. F. Larrabee,
Acting Commissioner.

AJW:LM

Applications for Enrollment of Seminole Newborn
Act of 1905   Volume II

Sem NB 178
BIRTH AFFIDAVIT.

DEPARTMENT OF THE INTERIOR.
COMMISSION TO THE FIVE CIVILIZED TRIBES.
C O P Y

IN RE APPLICATION FOR ENROLLMENT, as a citizen of the   Seminole   Nation, of
Evaline Barnett   , born on the 18th   day of Jan.   , 1900

Name of Father: Samuel Barnett   a citizen of the   Creek   Nation.
Name of Mother: Betsie Barnett   a citizen of the   Seminole   Nation.

Postoffice   Paro, I.T.

AFFIDAVIT OF MOTHER.

UNITED STATES OF AMERICA, Indian Territory, ⎱
     Western   **DISTRICT.** ⎰

I,   Betsie Barnett   , on oath state that I am   23   years of age and a citizen
by   birth   , of the   Seminole   Nation; that I am the lawful wife of Samuel
Barnett   , who is a citizen, by birth   of the   Creek   Nation; that a
female   child was born to me on   18th   day of   January   , 1900; that said child
has been named   Evaline Barnett   , and was living March 4, 1905.

                                        her
                                  Betsie X Barnett
Witnesses To Mark: mark
⎰ V. W. Snider
⎱ R B. Webster

Subscribed and sworn to before me this   13th   day of   June   , 1905.
(SEAL)
                              V. W. Snider
My Commission Expires Aug 17-1908   Notary Public.

AFFIDAVIT OF ATTENDING PHYSICIAN OR MID-WIFE.

UNITED STATES OF AMERICA, Indian Territory, ⎱
     Western   **DISTRICT.** ⎰

I,   Dina Barnett   , a   midwife   , on oath state that I attended on Mrs.
Samuel Barnett   , wife of   Samuel Barnett   on the 18th   day of   January ,
1900; that there was born to her on said date a   female   child; that said child was
living March 4, 1905, and is said to have been named Evaline Barnett

285

her
Dina X Barnett
mark

Witnesses To Mark:
{ V. W. Snider
{ R. B. Webster

Subscribed and sworn to before me this   13th   day of   June   , 1905.
(SEAL)

V. W. Snider

My Commission Expires Aug 17th 1908   Notary Public.

Sem NB 178
BIRTH AFFIDAVIT.

DEPARTMENT OF THE INTERIOR.
COMMISSION TO THE FIVE CIVILIZED TRIBES.
C O P Y

IN RE APPLICATION FOR ENROLLMENT, as a citizen of the   Seminole   Nation, of
Felix Barnett   , born on the 14th   day of Jan.   , 1902

Name of Father: Samuel Barnett   a citizen of the   Creek   Nation.
Name of Mother: Betsie Barnett   a citizen of the   Seminole   Nation.

Postoffice   Paro, Ind.Ter

AFFIDAVIT OF MOTHER.

UNITED STATES OF AMERICA, Indian Territory,
    Western   **DISTRICT.**

I,   Betsie Barnett   , on oath state that I am   23   years of age and a citizen
by   birth   , of the   Seminole   Nation; that I am the lawful wife of Samuel
Barnett   , who is a citizen, by birth   of the   Creek   Nation; that a
male   child was born to me on   14th day of   January   , 1902; that said child has
been named   Felix Barnett   , and was living March 4, 1905.

her
Betsie X Barnett
mark

Witnesses To Mark:
{ V. W. Snider
{ R. B. Webster

Subscribed and sworn to before me this   13th   day of   June   , 1905.
(SEAL)

286

V. W. Snider

My Commission Expires Aug 17th 1908   Notary Public.

AFFIDAVIT OF ATTENDING PHYSICIAN OR MID-WIFE.

UNITED STATES OF AMERICA, Indian Territory, ⎱
    Western   DISTRICT. ⎰

I,   Dina Barnett   , a   midwife , on oath state that I attended on Mrs. Samuel Barnett   , wife of   Samuel Barnett   on the 14th day of   January , 1902; that there was born to her on said date a   male   child; that said child was living March 4, 1905, and is said to have been named Felix Barnett

her
Dina X Barnett
mark

Witnesses To Mark:
  ⎰ V. W. Snider
  ⎱ R. B. Webster

Subscribed and sworn to before me this 13th   day of   June   , 1905.
(SEAL)

V. W. Snider

My Commission Expires Aug 17th 1908   Notary Public.

Sem NB 178
BIRTH AFFIDAVIT.

DEPARTMENT OF THE INTERIOR.
COMMISSION TO THE FIVE CIVILIZED TRIBES.
C O P Y

IN RE APPLICATION FOR ENROLLMENT, as a citizen of the   Seminole   Nation, of Lewis Barnett   , born on the 16th day of   July , 1903

Name of Father: Samuel Barnett   a citizen of the   Creek   Nation.
Name of Mother: Betsie Barnett   a citizen of the   Seminole   Nation.

Postoffice   Paro, Ind. Ter

AFFIDAVIT OF MOTHER.

UNITED STATES OF AMERICA, Indian Territory, ⎱
    Western   DISTRICT. ⎰

I,   Betsie Barnett   , on oath state that I am   23   years of age and a citizen by   birth   , of the   Seminole   Nation; that I am the lawful wife of Samuel

Barnett   , who is a citizen, by birth   of the   Creek   Nation; that a
male   child was born to me on   16th   day of   July   , 1903; that said child has
been named   Lewis Barnett   , and was living March 4, 1905.

her

Betsie   Barnett

mark

Witnesses To Mark:

⎧ V. W. Snider
⎩ R. B. Webster

    Subscribed and sworn to before me this   13th   day of   June   , 1905.
(SEAL)

V. W. Snider

My Commission Expires Aug 17th 1908   Notary Public.

AFFIDAVIT OF ATTENDING PHYSICIAN OR MID-WIFE.

UNITED STATES OF AMERICA, Indian Territory, ⎤
      Western   **DISTRICT.** ⎦

    I,   Dina Barnett   , a   midwife   , on oath state that I attended on Mrs.
Samuel Barnett   , wife of   Samuel Barnett   on the 16th   day of   July , 1903;
that there was born to her on said date a   male   child; that said child was living
March 4, 1905, and is said to have been named Lewis Barnett

her

Dina   Barnett

mark

Witnesses To Mark:

⎧ V. W. Snider
⎩ R. B. Webster

    Subscribed and sworn to before me this   13th   day of   June   , 1905.
(SEAL)

V. W. Snider

My Commission Expires Aug 17th 1908   Notary Public.

288

Applications for Enrollment of Seminole Newborn
Act of 1905   Volume II

W.F.
Sem. NB-178.

DEPARTMENT OF THE INTERIOR,
COMMISSIONER TO THE FIVE CIVILIZED TRIBES.

In the matter of the application for the enrollment of Evaline Barnett, Felix Barnett and Lewis Barnett as citizens of the Seminole Nation.

--: D E C I S I O N :--

It appears from the record herein that on <u>June 14, 1905</u> there were filed with the Commission to the Five Civilized Tribes applications for the enrollment of Evaline Barnett, Felix Barnett and Lewis Barnett as citizens of the Seminole Nation.

It further appears from the record herein and the records of this office that the applicants Evaline Barnett, Felix Barnett and Lewis Barnett were born January 18, 1900, January 14, 1902 and July 16, 1903, respectively, and are children of Betsie Barnett who, it appears from the record herein, is a citizen "by birth of the Seminole Nation; but who has never been identified upon the final roll of citizens of said nation, and Samuel Barnett, an alleged citizen of the Creek Nation.

The Act of Congress approved March 3, 1905 (Public No. 212) among other things provides:

"That the Commission to the Five Civilized Tribes is authorized <u>for ninety days after the date of the approval of this act</u> to receive and consider applications for enrollment of infant children born prior to March fourth, nineteen hundred and five, and living on said latter date, to citizens of the Seminole tribe whose enrollment has been approved by the Secretary of the Interior; and to enroll and make allotments to such children, giving to each an equal number of acres of land, and such children shall also share equally with other citizens of the Seminole tribe in the distribution of all other tribal property and funds."

I am of the opinion that, inasmuch as the applications for the enrollment of the said Evaline Barnett, Felix Barnett and Lewis Barnett were not filed with the Commission to the Five Civilized Tribes within the ninety days provided by law, the Commission to the Five Civilized Tribes Five Civilized Tribes was without authority to receive or consider such applications and that, therefore, I should decline to receive or consider the same, under the provision of law above quoted, and it is so ordered.

Tams Bixby Commissioner.

Muskogee, Indian Territory.
OCT 23 1905

Applications for Enrollment of Seminole Newborn
Act of 1905   Volume II

Seminole
NB-178   **COPY**
                        Muskogee, Indian Territory, October 23, 1905.

Samuel Barnett,
        Paro, Indian Territory.

Dear Sir:

        Inclosed herewith you will find a copy of the decision of the Commissioner to the
Five Civilized Tribes rendered October 23, 1905, declining to receive or consider the
application for the enrollment of Evaline Barnett, Felix Barnett and Lewis Barnett as
citizens of the Seminole Nation.

        The decision, with the record of proceedings in the case, is this day transmitted to
the Secretary of the Interior for review. The final decision of the Secretary will be made
known to you as soon as this office is informed of the same.

                                Respectfully,
                                SIGNED   *Tams Bixby*
Registered.   Commissioner
Incl. Sem. NB-178.

Seminole
NB-178   **COPY**
                        Muskogee, Indian Territory, October 23, 1905.

A. S. McKennon,
        Attorney for Seminole Nation.
                Wewoka, Indian Territory.

Dear Sir:

        Inclosed herewith you will find a copy of the decision of the Commissioner to the
Five Civilized Tribes rendered October 23, 1905, declining to receive or consider the
application for the enrollment of Evaline Barnett, Felix Barnett and Lewis Barnett as
citizens of the Seminole Nation.

        The decision, with the record of proceedings in the case, is this day transmitted to
the Secretary of the Interior for review. The final decision of the Secretary will be made
known to you as soon as this office is informed of the same.

                                Respectfully,
                                SIGNED   *Tams Bixby*
                                        Commissioner
Incl. Sem. NB-178.

Applications for Enrollment of Seminole Newborn
Act of 1905   Volume II

Muskogee, Indian Territory, October 23, 1905.

The Honorable,   **COPY**
  The Secretary of the Interior.

Dear Sir:

There is herewith transmitted the record of proceedings in the matter of the application for the enrollment of Evaline Barnett, Felix Barnett and Lewis Barnett as citizens of the Seminole Nation, including the decision of the Commissioner to the Five Civilized Tribes, rendered October 23, 1905, declining to receive or consider said application.

Respectfully,

SIGNED   *Tams Bixby*

Through the   Commissioner.
  Commissioner of Indian Affairs.
2 Incl. Sem. NB-178.

J.P.

DEPARTMENT OF THE INTERIOR,
WASHINGTON.   LLB.

I.T.D.   15272-1905.   December 7, 1905.
         16272-1905.

LRS.

D.C. 55271-1905.

Commissioner to the Five Civilized Tribes,
  Muskogee, Indian Territory.

Sir:

October 23, 1905, you transmitted the record in the matter of the application for the enrollment of Evaline Barnett, Felix Barnett, and Lewis Barnett as citizens of the Seminole Nation.

Reporting November 15, 1905, the Indian Office recommended that your decision, adverse to the applicants, be approved. A copy of its letter is inclosed.

The Department concurs in said recommendation and your decision dated October 23, 1905, is hereby affirmed.

Respectfully,
(Signed) Thos. Ryan,
First Assistant Secretary.

1 inclosure.

Refer in reply
to the
following:

Land
86482-1905.

COPY.

DEPARTMENT OF THE INTERIOR,
OFFICE OF INDIAN AFFAIRS,

WASHINGTON.

November 15, 1905.

The Honorable,
The Secretary of the Interior.

Sir:

I have the honor to enclose a report from the Commissioner to the Five Civilized Tribes, dated October 23, 1905, transmitting the record of the application, made June 14, 1905, for enrollment as citizens of the Seminole Nation for Evaline, Felix, and Lewis Barnett.

October 23, 1905, the Commissioner decided adversely to all the applicants.

The record shows that the applicants, Evaline, Felix, and Lewis Barnett, were born January 18, 1900, January 14, 1902, and July 16, 1903, respectively, and are children of Betsie Barnett, who is a citizen by birth of the Seminole Nation, but who has never been identified upon the final roll of citizens of that nation, and Samuel Barnett, an alleged citizen of the Creek Nation.

In view of the record and of the fact that the application for the enrollment of these minors was not made within ninety days after the approval of the Act of March 3, 1905 (33 Stats., 1071), the approval of the Commissioner's decision adverse to the applicants is recommended.

Very respectfully,
C. F. Larrabee,
Acting Commissioner.

MMM; WDW.

Seminole NB
\# 178

Muskogee, Indian Territory, December 20, 1905.

Samuel Barnett,
    Paro, Indian Territory.

Dear Sir:

You are hereby notified that the Secretary of the Interior under date of December 7, 1905, affirmed the decision of the Commissioner to the Five Civilized Tribes dated October 23, 1905, declining to receive or consider the application for the enrollment of Evaline Barnett, Felix Barnett and Lewis Barnett, as citizens of the Seminole Nation.

Respectfully,
                                Commissioner.

––––––––––––

Seminole NB
\#178

Muskogee, Indian Territory, December 20, 1905.

A. S. McKennon,
    Attorney for Seminole Nation,
        Wewoka, Indian Territory.

Dear Sir:

You are hereby notified that the Secretary of the Interior under date of December 7, 1905, affirmed the decision of the Commissioner to the Five Civilized Tribes dated October 23, 1905, declining to receive or consider the application for the enrollment of Evaline Barnett, Felix Barnett and Lewis Barnett, as citizens of the Seminole Nation.

Respectfully,
                                Commissioner.

Applications for Enrollment of Seminole Newborn
Act of 1905   Volume II

DEPARTMENT OF THE INTERIOR,

COMMISSION TO THE FIVE CIVILIZED TRIBES.

Muskogee, Indian Territory, June 17, 1905.

In the matter of the application for the enrollment of Dave Roberts as a citizen by blood of the Seminole Nation.

THOMAS JONES, being first duly sworn, testified as follows, through Jesse McDermott, Interpreter.

Examination by the Commission:

Q What is your name? A Thomas Jones.
Q What is your age? A About 52.
Q What is your post office address? A Melette[sic].
Q Are you a citizen of the Creek Nation? A Yes sir, I am.
Q What is the name of your wife? A Cindy Jones is her name.
Q What was her name before you married her? A Cindy Brown.
Q Do you know the name of the mother of Cindy Brown?
A Her Indian name--Yar-welle.
Q To what band did she belong? A Jimmie Johnson.
Q Do you know who Jimmie Johnson succeeded as Band Chief? A I do not know.
Q What is the name of the father of your wife, Cindy Jones? A Osahwa Harjo.
Q Was he ever known by the name of Crow? A Yes.
Q Has Cindy Jones any brothers or sisters? A She has a brother by the name of George Crow. She has a sister by the name of Sally.
Q How long have you been married to Cindy Brown? A About three years/
Q Were you lawfully married to her? A Yes sir.
Q Are you the father of Dave Roberts? A No sir.
Q Is Dave Roberts the child of your wife? A Yes, he is.
Q And this child was born before you married her? A Yes.
Q How many times has your wife been married.[sic] A She has been lawfully married once.
Q To whom was she married? A She was married to me.
Q Is that the only time she was awfully married? A Yes.
Q Are you acquainted with Noah Roberts, a Creek citizen? A Yes.
Q Is he the father of Dave Roberts? A Yes.
Q Was your wife ever married to Noah Roberts? A No.
Q By whom were you married to Cindy Brown A Luke McIntosh.
Q And were you married under the Creek laws or the United States laws? A Under the United States law.
Q Have you a marriage license? A Yes. I left it at home.
Q Was Dave Roberts living on March 4, 1905.[sic] A Yes sir.
Q Who was he living with? A He lives with me.
Q Where? What postoffice? A About two miles from Mellette.

Q Is his mother living? A Yes.
Q Where does she live? A She lives with me.
Q You and Cindy Jones are living together at this time? A Yes.
Q Did you make an application for the enrollment of this child as a Creek Citizen?
A Yes, that was my intention.
Q Did you make this application, or did Cindy Jones make this application? A Cindy made the application.

It appears from the records of the Commission that application was made for the enrollment of David Roberts as a citizen by blood of the Creek Nation on July 13, 1904, by his mother, Cindy Jones, Creek New Born Enrollment Case, No. 559.

Q How old is this child? A He will be five years the 6th day of next December.
Q Born December 6, 1901, was he? You mean four years old the 6th of December? A I may be mistaken, but I thought that the child would be five years old.
Q The mother of the child made affidavit that David Roberts was born on the 6th of December, 1901.

The mother of this child, Cindy Jones, is identified as Cindy Brown, No. 3 on Seminole card 518, approved roll No. 1698.
It further does not appear from the records of the Commission that any application has been made for the enrollment of David Roberts as a citizen by blood of the Seminole Nation prior to this date.

----oOo----

Kate DeBord, upon oath states that as stenographer to the Commission to the Five Civilized Tribes, she accurately recorded the testimony in the above entitled cause, and that the foregoing is a full, true and correct transcript of her stenographic notes thereof.

Kate D^{e}Bord

Subscribed and sworn to before me this 17th day of June, 1905.

Chas E Webster
Notary Public.

DEPARTMENT OF THE INTERIOR,
COMMISSION TO THE FIVE CIVILIZED TRIBES.
Mellette, I. T., July 13, 1904.

In the matter of the application for the enrollment of David Roberts as a citizen by blood of the Creek Nation.

CINDA JONES, being duly sworn, testified as follows:

Applications for Enrollment of Seminole Newborn
Act of 1905   Volume II

Through L. G. McIntosh Official Interpreter:

By Commission:

Q What is your name? A Cinda Jones.

Q What is your age? A About 30.

Q What is your post office address? A Mellette.

Q Are you a citizen of the Creek Nation? A No, sir.

Q Are you a citizen of the Seminole Nation? A Yes, sir.

Q Have you received an allotment as a Seminole? A Yes, sir.

Q For whom do you make application to the Commission for enrollment?
A David Roberts.

Q Do you make application for the enrollment of David Roberts as a citizen by blood of
the Creek Nation? A Yes, sir.

Q How old is David Roberts? A I don't know exactly but I have a record. I don't know
anything about dates.

Q Can you produce the record of the date of his birth? A My husband can.

Q Can you read and write in English or Creek? A No, sir.

Q Who made the record of the date of the birth of your child, David Roberts?
A A young man by the name of Jim Anderson, now in jail at Muskogee, made it.

Q How long after the birth of David before he put down the date of his birth?
A The day that the child was born.

Q Describe the book or paper upon which the record is made? A It is a small piece of
paper. It had a back but it is gone.

The witness presents a piece of paper, which appears to have been a leaf of a
memorandum book, upon which is written various notes, in Creek, which Official
Interpreter, L. G. McIntosh, states is the date of the birth. The note relating to the date of
the birth he translates as follows:
"I Jim Anderson write this letter. December 6, 1899 Dave was born."

Q Was that you child for whom application is now made to the Commission for
enrollment as a citizen of the Creek Nation? A Yes, sir, this is my child of which the
date of the birth is here written. I wish to have him enrolled as a Creek citizen.

Q Is David present here, your child? A Yes, sir.

The child is present and appears to be as old as the record presented tends to
show.

Q Who is the father of David Roberts? A Noah Roberts.

Q Is he living? A Yes, sir.

Q Is he a citizen of the Creek Nation? A Yes, sir, of the Kialigee Town.

Q Were you ever married to him? A I lived with him a while.

Q How long? A About six months.

Q Were you married to him? A We were not married. I suppose we were married
under the old Indian Rule.

Q Where is Noah Roberts living now? A He lives down in here in this neighborhood.

Q Was Noah Roberts living with you when David was born? A No, sir.

296

Applications for Enrollment of Seminole Newborn
Act of 1905   Volume II

Q Did he ever live with you after David was born? A No, sir. He deserted me in six months time.
Q Do you know whether Noah ever recognized David as his child? A Yes, sir.
Q Are you married now? A Yes, sir.
Q What is your husband's name? A Thomas Jones.
Q Was application ever made for the enrollment of your child, David Roberts, as a citizen of the Seminole Nation? A I don't know.

THOMAS JONES, being duly sworn, testified as follows:

Through L. G. McIntosh Official Interpreter:

By Commission:
Q What is your name? A Thomas Jones.
Q What is your age? A About 40.
Q What is your post office address? A Mellette.
Q Are you a citizen of the Creek Nation of Artussee Town? A Yes, sir.
Q Do you know whether application has ever been made for the enrollment of David Roberts, child of Cinda Jones, as a citizen of the Seminole Nation? A This child was enrolled and the child got per capita payment but this last year my wife went up there to draw for the child herself during the Seminole Council and to see about the per capita payment and stayed around there about three days and they decided there while in council that children of that age couldn't draw any annuity for they had not filed and having not filed were not citizens and could not receive any annuity and was put off the roll.
Q You mean the Seminole Trible[sic] Roll? A Yes, sir.
Q Then, as I understand it, up to that time David was considered a citizen of the Seminole Nation? A Yes, sir.
Q Do you know whether application was ever made to the Commission for his enrollment as a citizen of the Seminole Nation? A No, sir. We made application for his enrollment as a Creek Citizen. We made out an affidavit but we didn't have the record of the date of the birth and so we just made it out as we remembered it and the affidavit did not agree with this (referring to the record presented as evidence in this case) but this was found in the book that we keep our records in.
Q As I understand you then [sic] an affidavit was executed in the matter of his birth?
A Yes, sir.
                    CINDA JONES recalled:

By Commission:
     The records of the commission show that an affidavit in the matter of the application for the enrollment of birth of David Roberts was executed on June 14, 1904 and filed with the Commission. Said affidavit states that David Roberts was born on the 6th day of December, 1901.

Q The affidavit, executed by Cinda Jones and Hanna Bullett, states that Dave Roberts was born December 6, 1901, is that correct or is it an error? A It is an error.

                    THOMAS JONES recalled:

By Commission:
Q Do you know whether Cinda, the mother of David Roberts, lived with Noah Roberts a while? A Noah and her never lived together at his house but she was at home and Noah would go there and stay a while and go back and forth and pretend that he was going to live with her but he quit and didn't take her as his wife.

CINDA JONES recalled:

By Commission:
Q Did Noah Roberts ever contribute anything to your support? A Never did contribute anything.
Q Ever by you any cloths while he was living with you? a No, sir.
Q Ever contribute anything for you to eat? A He contributed some things after the birth of the child to sustain the child.
Q How long did he sustain the child? A About a month.
Q Did he provide for it for a full months time? A Yes, sir.
Q Did he bring it himself or send it by some one? A Himself.
Q What did he say about the child? A He didn't say anything about the child.
Q Did he say anything about the child being his? A Yes, he said it was his.

I, D. C. Skaggs, on oath state that the above and foregoing is a full, true and correct transcript of my stenographic notes as taken in said cause on said date.
D. C. Skaggs
Subscribed and sworn to before me this August 3, 1904.
Charles H. Sawyer
Notary Public.

DEPARTMENT OF THE INTERIOR,
COMMISSION TO THE FIVE CIVILIZED TRIBES.
Mellette, I. T., July 14, 1904.

SUPPLEMENTAL TESTIMONY in the matter of the application for the enrollment of David Roberts as a citizen by blood of the Creek Nation.

NOAH ROBERTS, being duly sworn, testified as follows:

Through L. G. McIntosh Official Interpreter:

By Commission:
Q What is your name? A Noah Roberts.
Q What is your age? A About 29 years.
Q What is your post office address? A Indianola.
Q Are you a citizen of the Creek Nation? A Yes, sir.
Q What town do you belong to? A Kialigee.

Applications for Enrollment of Seminole Newborn
Act of 1905   Volume II

Q Have you a child named David Roberts? A I think there is one living by that name.

Q Who is the mother of that child? A Cinda Jones.

Q Was she at any time your wife? A I lived with her a while.

Q Were you ever married to her? A Yes, sir.

Q Did you get a marriage license and certificate? A No, sir.

Q How were you married to her? A I lived with her a while but I didn't marry her according to any laws. I got me another wife.

Q Did she have a child by you? A Yes, sir.

Q What is the name of that child? A They called it David.

Q It is living is it? A Yes, sir. I haven't been there very lately but the last time I saw it it was still alive.

Q How long has it been since you saw it? A I haven't seen the child for two weeks.

Q Have you seen it within a month's time? A Yes, sir.

Q Do you know the date of its birth? A It was about December according to months and it is going on four years old.

Q How long did you live with Cinda, the mother of David? A I didn't live with her more than about two months.

Q Are you positive that David is your child? A I am not positive but they say it is my child and I suppose it is. The woman was not a straight woman and others delt[sic] with her but I lived with her about two months[sic] time and she threw the child on me and I suppose it is mine. I can't say positively that the child is mine.

Q Have you ever been told that it looks like you? A They say it is just like me. She started to throwing it upon other men but she fastened it upon me. I am no mullatto[sic] but people say that child's hair looks like he was a mullatto[sic].

Q How long before this child was born was it that you lived with Cinda two months?

A We were kind of staying together in the summer and that winter the child was born.

Q How long before this child was born was it that you first had sexual intercourse with Cinda? A I don't know exactly. A good many had that sort of deallings[sic] with her.

Q About how long? A I stayed with her about two months. I didn't pay much attention to it and I am not certain how long after it the child was born.

Q Was it as long as nine months? A I suppose it might have been that long.

Q Well was it that long to the best of your recollection? A It might have been that long but I don't know. I never paid any attention to it after I left her.

Q After David was born did you recognize him as your child? A No, sir.

Q Did you ever by anything for the child? A They throwed[sic] the child to me and I gave it a pair of shoes. And that is all I have given it. I might have recognized the child but she throwed[sic] it on several different ones and so I didn't recognize the child.

Q But you say people say it looks just like you? A I haven't heard any one particular say it but it is a rumor.

Q What time of the year was it you first took up with Cinda, in the early spring or summer? A It was in the summer. Hot about like it is now.

Q How long before you began living with her was it you first began doing business with her? A I never did live with her. I never did stay at the place but would go from my own home and stay with her may be a whole day and night and then come home.

Q Well how long before that was it you first began doing business with her? A Counting the whole I stayed around about two months time but heard that other men were getting in there and I wouldn't take her as a wife.

Q That is not an answer to my question? (The interpreter replies "I can't get him to answer either.")

Q Well do you know[sic] recognize David Roberts as your child? A No I don't because that I don't know that he is.

Q Was it your intention at the time you were going and staying with Cinda from the time to time to take her as your wife? A Yes, sir.

Q Well what I want to know is whether David is your child? A I don't know myself.

Q You went and stayed from time to time with Cinda and had sexual intercourse with her didn't you? A Yes, sir.

Q Well didn't you expect that a child would follow that? A It might have been. Again she might have already been pregnant but again it is something I don't know.

Q Well did you or did you not have that kind of dealings with her before you went to her home and stayed with her from time to time? A No, sir.

---oooOOOooo---

I, D. C. Skaggs, on oath state that the above and foregoing is a full, true and complete transcript of my stenographic notes as taken in said cause on said date.

D. C. Skaggs

Subscribed and sworn to before me this 4th day of August, 1904.

W^m.T.Martin Jr.

Notary Public.

I.D.

Cr.En.559.

DEPARTMENT OF THE INTERIOR,
COMMISSIONER TO THE FIVE CIVILIZED TRIBES.

In the matter of the application for the enrollment of David Roberts as a citizen by blood of the Creek Nation.

DECISION.

The record in this case shows that on July 13, 1904, Cinda Jones appeared before the Commission to the Five Civilized Tribes at Mellette, Indian Territory and made application for the enrollment of her minor child, David Roberts, as a citizen by blood of the Creek Nation.

Further proceedings were had July 14, 1904 and February 1, 1905.

A copy of the testimony taken June 17, 1905, in the matter of the application for the enrollment of said David Roberts as a citizen by blood of the Seminole Nation is made part of the record herein. Said latter application will be considered in a separate decision.

The evidence shows that said David Roberts was born December 9, 1899, and that he was living at the date of the application herein.

The evidence further shows that said David Roberts is an illegitimate minor child of Cinda Jones, who is identified on the approved roll of citizens by blood of the Seminole Nation, opposite No. 1698.

It does not appear from the evidence that said David Roberts is the child of a citizen of the Creek Nation.

It is, therefore, ordered and adjudged that there is no authority of law for the enrollment of said David Roberts as a citizen by blood of the Creek Nation and the application for his enrollment as such is accordingly denied.

Tams Bixby
Commissioner.

Muskogee, Indian Territory.
OCT 12 1905

GR FHE

DEPARTMENT OF THE INTERIOR,

I.T.D. 14930-1905   WASHINGTON. November 18, 1905.

Commissioner to the Five Civilized Tribes,
        Muskogee, Indian Territory.

Sir:

October 13, 1905, you transmitted the record in the matter of the application for the enrollment of David Roberts as a citizen by blood of the Creek Nation, including your decision of October 12, 1905, rejecting said application.

Reporting November 11, 1905, the Indian Office recommends that your decision be approved. A copy of its letter is inclosed.

The Department concurs in said recommendation, and your decision is hereby affirmed.

Respectfully,
Thos Ryan
First Assistant Secretary

1inclosure.

Refer in reply to the
following: Land
83799-1905   DEPARTMENT OF THE INTERIOR,
                            OFFICE OF INDIAN AFFAIRS,
                            WASHINGTON. Nov. 11, 1905.

The Honorable,
        The Secretary of the Interior.

Applications for Enrollment of Seminole Newborn
Act of 1905   Volume II

Sir:

I have the honor to enclose a report from the Commissioner to the Five Civilized Tribes, dated October 13, 1905, transmitting the record of the application for enrollment as a citizen by blood of the Creek Nation, of David Roberts.

October 12, 1905, the Commissioner decided adversely to the applicant.

The record shows that David Roberts was born December 9, 1899, was living at the date of the application, July 13, 1904 and is the illegitimate minor child of Cinda Jones, who is identified on the approved roll of citizens by blood of the Seminole Nation, at number 1698. It is not shown that David Roberts is the child of a Creek citizen.

In view of the record, the approval of the Commissioner's decision adverse to the applicant is recommended.

Very respectfully,

C.F. Larrabee
Acting Commissioner.

M M M NL

S.N.B. 179.

DEPARTMENT OF THE INTERIOR,
COMMISSIONER TO THE FIVE CIVILIZED TRIBES.
SEMINOLE DIVISION

In the matter of the application for the enrollment of David Roberts, as a citizen by blood of the Seminole Nation.

DECISION.

The record in this case shows that on July 13, 1904, Cinda Jones appeared before the Commission to the Five Civilized Tribes at Mellette, Indian Territory, and made application for the enrollment of her minor child, David Roberts, as a citizen by blood of the Creek Nation; that said application was, on October 12, 1905, denied by the Commissioner to the Five Civilized Tribes; that on November 18, 1905, said decision of the Commissioner to the Five Civilized Tribes was approved by the Secretary of the Interior.

Said application of July 13, 1904, is therefore now considered as an application for the enrollment of said David Roberts as a citizen by blood of the Seminole Nation.

Further proceedings were had June 17, 1905.

The evidence shows that said David Roberts was born December 6, 1901, and was living on March 4, 1905.

The evidence further shows that the said David Roberts is a son of Cindy Jones, and that the said Cindy Jones is identified as Cindy Brown, No. 3 on Seminole care No. 518, approved roll No. 1698.

The Act of Congress of March 3, 1905 (Public 212), provides:

302

Applications for Enrollment of Seminole Newborn
Act of 1905 Volume II

"That the Commission to the Five Civilized Tribes is authorized for ninety days after the date of the approval of this act to receive and consider applications for enrollment of infant children born prior to March fourth, nineteen hundred and five, and living on said latter date, to citizens of the Seminole tribe whose enrollment has been approved by the Secretary of the Interior; and to enroll and make allotments to such children, giving to each an equal number of acres of land, and such children shall also share equally with other citizens of the Seminole tribe in the distribution of all other tribal property and funds."

Tams Bixby Commissioner.

Muskogee, Indian Territory.
December 22, 1905

S N B 179

Muskogee, Indian Territory, January 9, 1906.

Cindy Jones,   **COPY**
        Mellette, Indian Territory.

Dear Madam:

Inclosed herewith you will find a copy of the decision of the Commissioner to the Five Civilized Tribes, rendered December 22, 1905, granting the application for the enrollment of David Roberts as a citizen by blood of the Seminole Nation.

The attorneys for the Seminole Nation have been allowed fifteen days from the date of this notice within which to file protest against his enrollment. If at the expiration of that time no protest has been filed the name of David Roberts will be placed upon the final roll of citizens by blood of the Seminole Nation to be submitted to the Secretary of the Interior for his approval.

Respectfully,

SIGNED Tams Bixby

Registered.   Commissioner.
Incl. S N B 179.

S NB 179   **COPY**

Muskogee, Indian Territory, January 9, 1906.

McKennon & Wilmott[sic],
        Attorneys for Seminole Nation,
                Wewoka, Indian Territory.

Gentlemen:

303

Applications for Enrollment of Seminole Newborn
Act of 1905 Volume II

Inclosed herewith you will find a copy of the decision of the Commissioner to the Five Civilized Tribes, rendered December 22, 1905, granting the application for the enrollment of David Roberts as a citizen by blood of the Seminole Nation.

You are hereby advised that you will be allowed fifteen days from the date of this notice within which to file protest against the enrollment of this child. If at the expiration of that time no protest has been filed his name will be placed upon the final roll of citizens by blood of the Seminole Nation to be submitted to the Secretary of the Interior for his approval.

Respectfully,

SIGNED *Tams Bixby*

Commissioner.

Registered.

S N B 179

En. 559.

DEPARTMENT OF THE INTERIOR,
COMMISSION TO THE FIVE CIVILIZED TRIBES.
Mellette, I. T., February 1, 1905.

In the matter of the application for the enrollment of David Roberts as a citizen by blood of the Creek Nation.

WILLIAM COOPER, being duly sworn, testified as follows:

Through Alex Posey Official Interpreter:

BY COMMISSION:

Q What is your name? A William Cooper.

Q How old are you? A I do not know.

Witness appears to be about twenty-two.

Q What is your post office address? A Mellette.

Q Are you a citizen of the Creek Nation? A No, sir, I am a citizen of the Seminole Nation.

Q Do you know Cinda Jones? A Yes, sir.

Q What relation is she to you? A She is my aunt.

Q Is she a citizen of the Creek Nation? A No, sir, she is a Seminole.

Q Do you know a child of hers named David Roberts? A Yes, sir.

Q How old is that child? A About four years old, I think.

Q Who is the father of that child? A Noah Roberts.

Q Were Noah and Cinda ever married? A They were married according to Indian custom.

Q How long did they live together? A I do not know how long they lived together.

304

Q Dow Noah Roberts recognize David as his child? A He claims that it is not his child but the mother claims that it is his child.

Q Is it the general opinion that David is Noah Roberts child? A Yes, sir, every body thinks so.

Q The child is living is it? A Yes, sir.

Q Is Noah Roberts a citizen of the Creek Nation? A Yes, sir.

Q To what town does he belong? A Kialigee.

Q How long have Cinda and Noah been separated? A They separated before the child was born.

Q How long before the child was born? A I do not know.

Q Do you know why they separated? A I know of no reason.

---oooOOOooo---

I, D. C. Skaggs, on oath state that the above and foregoing is a full and true transcript of my stenographic notes as taken in said cause on said date.

D. C. Skaggs

Subscribed and sworn to before me this 8 day of February, 1905.

Edw C Griesel
Notary Public.

Seminole NB-179.

Muskogee, Indian Territory July 19, 1905.

Chief Clerk,
    Creek Enrollment Division.

Dear Sir:

On March 4, 1905 there was listed for enrollment as a citizen by blood of the Seminole Nation David Roberts, about three or four years old alleged son of Noah Roberts, a citizen of the Creek Nation and Cindy Jones, who is identified as Cindy Brown upon the approved roll of citizens by blood of the Seminole Nation.

It appears from the record in this case that an application was made for the enrollment of said David Roberts as a citizen by blood of the Creek Nation on July 13, 1904 (NC-559).

You are requested to inform the Seminole Enrollment Division as to what disposition, if any, has been made of such application.

Respectfully,

Commissioner.

———————

HGH

REFER IN REPLY TO THE FOLLOWING:

Sem. N.B. 179

Cr. En. 559

**DEPARTMENT OF THE INTERIOR,
COMMISSIONER TO THE FIVE CIVILIZED TRIBES.**

Muskogee, Indian Territory, July 22, 1905.

Chief Clerk,
    Seminole Enrollment Division.

Dear Sir:

    Receipt is acknowledged of your communication of July 19, 1905, in which you inquire as to the status of the application for enrollment as a citizen of the Creek Nation of David Roberts, an alleged son of Noah Roberts, a citizen by blood of the Creek Nation, and Cindy Jones, who is identified as Cindy Brown upon the approved roll of citizens by blood of the Seminole Nation.

    In reply you are advised that a decision denying the application for the enrollment of said David Roberts as a citizen of the Creek Nation, has been prepared by the Creek Enrollment Division and is now pending before this office.

    When final action is had in the matter, you will be duly notified.

Respectfully,

Tams Bixby

Commissioner.

———————

Refer in reply to the
following: Land
83799-1905
DEPARTMENT OF THE INTERIOR,
OFFICE OF INDIAN AFFAIRS,
WASHINGTON. Nov. 11, 1905.

The Honorable,
    The Secretary of the Interior.

Sir:

    I have the honor to enclose a report from the Commissioner to the Five Civilized Tribes, dated October 13, 1905, transmitting the record of the application for enrollment as a citizen by blood of the Creek Nation, of David Roberts.

306

Applications for Enrollment of Seminole Newborn
Act of 1905   Volume II

October 12, 1905, the Commissioner decided adversely to the applicant.

The record shows that David Roberts was born December 9, 1899, was living at the date of the application, July 13, 1904 and is the illegitimate minor child of Cinda Jones, who is identified on the approved roll of citizens by blood of the Seminole Nation, at number 1698. It is not shown that David Roberts is the child of a Creek citizen.

In view of the record, the approval of the Commissioner's decision adverse to the applicant is recommended.

Very respectfully,

C.F. Larrabee
Acting Commissioner.

M M M NL

GR FHE

DEPARTMENT OF THE INTERIOR,

I.T.D. 14930-1905   WASHINGTON. November 18, 1905.
    LRS

Commissioner to the Five Civilized Tribes,
    Muskogee, Indian Territory.

Sir:

October 13, 1905, you transmitted the record in the matter of the application for the enrollment of David Roberts as a citizen by blood of the Creek Nation, including your decision of October 12, 1905, rejecting said application.

Reporting November 11, 1905, the Indian Office recommends that your decision be approved. A copy of its letter is inclosed.

The Department concurs in said recommendation, and your decision is hereby affirmed.

Respectfully,

Thos Ryan
First Assistant Secretary

1 inclosure.

HGH

REFER IN REPLY TO THE FOLLOWING:

En. 559

DEPARTMENT OF THE INTERIOR,
COMMISSIONER TO THE FIVE CIVILIZED TRIBES.

Muskogee, Indian Territory, November 27, 1905.

Chief Clerk,
    Seminole Enrollment Division.

Dear Sir:

There is herewith enclosed copy of the decision of the Commissioner to the Five Civilized Tribes of October 12, 1905, in the matter of the application for the enrollment of David Roberts, as a citizen by blood of the Creek Nation.

You are advised that under date of November 18, 1905, the Department affirmed said decision.

Reference is made to Seminole N.B. 179.

Respectfully,

Geo D Rodgers
Acting Commissioner.

En. 559.

————

S N B 179

Muskogee, Indian Territory, January 9, 1906.

Cindy Jones,
    Mellette, Indian Territory.   **COPY**

Dear Madam:

Inclosed herewith you will find a copy of the decision of the Commissioner to the Five Civilized Tribes, rendered December 22, 1905, granting the application for the enrollment of David Roberts as a citizen by blood of the Seminole Nation.

The attorneys for the Seminole Nation have been allowed fifteen days from the date of this notice within which to file protest against his enrollment. If at the expiration of that time no protest has been filed the name of David Roberts will be placed upon the final roll of citizens by blood of the Seminole Nation to be submitted to the Secretary of the Interior for his approval.

Applications for Enrollment of Seminole Newborn
Act of 1905   Volume II

Respectfully,

SIGNED *Tams Bixby*

Registered.
Incl. S N B 179.

Commissioner.

S NB 179

COPY

Muskogee, Indian Territory, January 9, 1906.

McKennon & Wilmott[sic],
    Attorneys for Seminole Nation,
        Wewoka, Indian Territory.

Gentlemen:

    Inclosed herewith you will find a copy of the decision of the Commissioner to the Five Civilized Tribes, rendered December 22, 1905, granting the application for the enrollment of David Roberts as a citizen by blood of the Seminole Nation.

    You are hereby advised that you will be allowed fifteen days from the date of this notice within which to file protest against the enrollment of this child. If at the expiration of that time no protest has been filed his name will be placed upon the final roll of citizens by blood of the Seminole Nation to be submitted to the Secretary of the Interior for his approval.

Respectfully,

SIGNED *Tams Bixby*

Registered.
S N B 179

Commissioner.

Copy

Sem NB 179
BIRTH AFFIDAVIT.

DEPARTMENT OF THE INTERIOR.
COMMISSION TO THE FIVE CIVILIZED TRIBES.

IN RE APPLICATION FOR ENROLLMENT, as a citizen of the   Creek   Nation, of
Dave Roberts   , born on the 6$\underline{th}$ day of Dec , 1901

Name of Father: Noah Roberts   a citizen of the   Creek   Nation.
Name of Mother: Cindie Jones   a citizen of the   Creek[sic]   Nation.

             Postoffice   Eufaula

Applications for Enrollment of Seminole Newborn
Act of 1905   Volume II

AFFIDAVIT OF MOTHER.

UNITED STATES OF AMERICA, Indian Territory, ⎫
    Western   DISTRICT. ⎰

    I, Cindie Jones   , on oath state that I am 35   years of age and a citizen by Blood   , of the   Creek   Nation; that I ~~am~~ was the lawful wife of   Noah Roberts , who is a citizen, by Blood   of the   Creek   Nation; that a   male   child was born to me on 6th day of   Dec , 1901; that said child has been named Dave Roberts, and ~~was living March 4, 1905~~. is now living

her
Cindie Jones x

Witnesses To Mark: mark
    ⎰ Geo Hubble
    ⎱ Maxey Bullet

    Subscribed and sworn to before me this 14th day of   June   , 1904.

(Seal)   Thos F Turner
                                        Notary Public.

AFFIDAVIT OF ATTENDING PHYSICIAN OR MID-WIFE.

UNITED STATES OF AMERICA, Indian Territory, ⎫
    Western   DISTRICT. ⎰

was present with

    I,   Hannah Bullett   , a   , on oath state that I ~~attended on~~ Mrs. Cindie Jones   , wife of   Noah Roberts on the 6th day of   Dec , 1901; that there was born to her on said date a   male   child; that said child ~~was living March 4, 1905~~, and is said to have been named Dave Roberts   is now living

her
Hannah Bullett x

Witnesses To Mark: mark
    ⎰ Geo Hubble
    ⎱ Maxey Bullet

    Subscribed and sworn to before me this 14th day of   June   , 1904.

(Seal)   Thos F Turner
                                        Notary Public.

(The above Birth Affidavit given again.)

Sem NB 180
BIRTH AFFIDAVIT.

DEPARTMENT OF THE INTERIOR.
COMMISSION TO THE FIVE CIVILIZED TRIBES.

IN RE APPLICATION FOR ENROLLMENT, as a citizen of the   Seminole   Nation, of
Manaynie Holbutta   , born on the 1st day of   September   , 1904

Name of Father: Jackson Holbutta   a citizen of the   Seminole   Nation.
                              enrolled as Louisianna Noble Care $^{#}$231
Name of Mother: Louisianna Holbutta   a citizen of the   Seminole   Nation.

Postoffice   Wewoka I.T.

AFFIDAVIT OF MOTHER.

UNITED STATES OF AMERICA, Indian Territory,
    Western   DISTRICT.

I, Louisianna Holbutta enrolled as Louisianna Noble   , on oath state that I am
don't know   years of age and a citizen by   blood   , of the   Seminole
Nation; that I am the lawful wife of   Jackson Holbutta   , who is a citizen, by
blood   of the   Seminole   Nation; that a   female   child was born to me on
1st day of   September   , 1904, that said child has been named   Manaynie Holbutta ,
and is now living.   her
                                            Louisianna x Holbutta
Witnesses To Mark: mark
    J.L. Gary
    Thomas McGeisy

Subscribed and sworn to before me this 4th day of   January   , 1907.

J.L. Gary
Notary Public.

AFFIDAVIT OF ATTENDING PHYSICIAN OR MID-WIFE.

UNITED STATES OF AMERICA, Indian Territory,
    Western   DISTRICT.

I,   Lucy Holbutta   , a   mid-wife   , on oath state that I attended on Mrs.
Louisianna Holbutta   , wife of   Jackson Holbutta   on the   1st day of September,
1904; that there was born to her on said date a   female   child; that said child is now
living and is said to have been named Manaynie Holbutta

311

her
Lucy x Holbutta
mark

Witnesses To Mark:
- J.L. Gary
- Thomas McGeisy

Subscribed and sworn to before me this 4<u>th</u> day of   January   , 1907.

J.L. Gary
Notary Public.

AFFIDAVIT OF ATTENDING PHYSICIAN OR MID-WIFE.

UNITED STATES OF AMERICA, Indian Territory,
Western   DISTRICT.

was present when I,   Martha Holbutta   , a   sister in law   , on oath state that I ~~attended on~~ Mrs. Louisianna Holbutta   , wife of   Jackson Holbutta   on the   1st   day of September, 1904; that there was born to her on said date a   female   child; that said child is now living and is said to have been named Manaynie Holbutta

her
Martha x Holbutta
mark

Witnesses To Mark:
- J.L. Gary
- Thomas McGeisy

Subscribed and sworn to before me this 4<u>th</u> day of   January   , 1907.

J.L. Gary
Notary Public.

(The testimony below is handwritten and typed as given.)

Seminole N.B. #180

Thomas McGeisey sworn as Interpreter

Testimony of Jackson Holbutta

Q What is your name A Jackson Holbutta
Q What is your age A Don't know A Your P.O.   Wewoka IT
Q Are you a citizen of the Seminole Nation A Yes sir
Q What band do you belong to A Jim Johnson
Q What is your mother's name A Lucy Holbutta
Q What band does she belong to A Jim Johnson
Q What is your father's name A He is dead
Q How long has he been dead A Long time

Q Are you a married man A Yes sir
Q What is your wife's name A Lousianna Holbutta
Q What was her name before you was married A Lousianna Noble
Q Was you at the Seminole land office last May with your wife to enroll a baby A No sir
Q Where was you A In Jail
Q Are you the father of that child (Pointing to a baby in a sofha patch)   Yes sir
Q When was that child born A Sept 1st 1904
Q What is the child name A Manaynie Holbutta Q Boy or girl A Girl

	his
Witness to mark	Jackson x Holbutta
	mark

J.L. Gary
Thomas McGeisy

Subscribed and sworn to before me this 4th day of January 1907

J.L. Gary
Notary Public.

———————

(The testimony below is handwritten and typed as given.)

Seminole N.B. #180
Testimony of Louisianna Holbutta
Thomas McGeisey sworn as Interpreter
Louisianna Holbutta being first duly sworn, testified as follows:

Q What is your name A Louisianna Holbutta
Q Are you a citizen of the Seminole Nation A Yes sir
Q Your age A Don't know A Your P O   Wewoka I.T.
Q On or about May 3, 1905 you appeared before the Enrollment Office at Wewoka to enroll your minor child. Did you enroll that child A No Q Why not A Dont know
Q Is that child still living A Yes here it is pointing to child. A When was that child born. A 1st day of September 1904. Who is the father of that child. A Jackson Holbutta. Q is he a citizen of the Seminole Nation. A Yes sir
Q Is he your legal Husband A Yes sir
Q What has become of your husband Albert Noble A He is dead Q How long has he been dead A About 5 years
Q What is that childs name A Manaynie Holbutta

	her
Witness to mark	Louisianna x Holbutta
J.L. Gary	mark
Thomas McGeisy	

Applications for Enrollment of Seminole Newborn
Act of 1905 Volume II

Subscribed and sworn to before me this 4th day of January 1907

J.L. Gary

Notary Public.

COMMISSIONERS:
TAMS BIXBY,
THOMAS B. NEEDLES,
C.R. BRECKINBRIDGE.

WM. O. BEALL
Secretary

DEPARTMENT OF THE INTERIOR,
COMMISSIONER TO THE FIVE CIVILIZED TRIBES.

REFER IN REPLY TO THE FOLLOWING:

Seminole

Card No. 231.

ADDRESS ONLY THE
COMMISSION TO THE FIVE CIVILIZED TRIBES.

Muskogee, Indian Territory, May 17, 1905.

Lousianna Noble,
Wewoka, Indian Territory.

Madam:

On or about May 3, 1905, you appeared before the Seminole Enrollment Office, at Wewoka, Indian Territory, and stated that your former husband, Albert Noble, was dead, and that you also desired to make application for the enrollment of a minor child, but left the office before making formal application for the enrollment of such child and proof of death of Albert Noble.

It will be necessary, therefore, for you to appear before this office prior to June 1, 1905, and make formal application for the enrollment of your child and also proof of the death of Albert Noble. It will be necessary to secure the appearance before this office of the physician or midwife attending you at the time of the birth of said child.

Respectfully,

Chas E Webster

Clerk in Charge.

A.P.

REFER IN REPLY TO THE FOLLOWING:

Sem-NB-180.

DEPARTMENT OF THE INTERIOR,
COMMISSIONER TO THE FIVE CIVILIZED TRIBES.

Muskogee, Indian Territory, April 16, 1907.

Lousianna Holbutta,
Wewoka, Indian Territory.

Dear Madam:

314

Applications for Enrollment of Seminole Newborn
Act of 1905 Volume II

You are hereby advised that on March 4, 1907, the Secretary of the Interior approved the enrollment of your minor child, Manaynie Holbutta, as a new born Seminole Indian, and her name appears on the final roll of such citizens of the Seminole Nation opposite No. 248.

Respectfully,

Tams Bixby

Commissioner.

Sem. N B 180

Muskogee, Indian Territory, December 29, 1905.

McKennon & Willmott,
Attorneys for the Seminoles,
Wewoka, Indian Territory.

Gentlemen:

On May 3, 1905, Louisianna Noble, whose name appears upon the approved roll of Seminole citizens opposite number 780, appeared at the office of the Commission to the Five Civilized Tribes in Wewoka, Indian Territory, and stated that her former husband, Albert Nolble[sic] was dead, and that she desired to make application for the enrollment of a minor child under the provisions of the act of Congress of March 3, 1905. She left the office, however, before making formal application for the enrollment of her child, since which time all efforts to secure proper evidence of the birth of the child referred to have proved ineffective. Albert Noble, deceased, has been identified upon the approved roll of Seminole citizens opposite Number 779.

It is desired that you secure the affidavits of the mother and attending physician to the birth of this child of Louisianna Noble, and the date of its birth, the names of its parents, and whether it is nor or was living on March 4, 1905. The post office address of Louisianna Noble appears as Wewoka, Indian Territory, but letters addressed to her at that place have been returned unclaimed.

Please give this matter your early attention, securing the required evidence, if possible, in order that the application for the enrollment of this child may receive proper consideration.

Respectfully,

Commissioner.

B C

315

A.P.

DEPARTMENT OF THE INTERIOR,
COMMISSIONER TO THE FIVE CIVILIZED TRIBES.

Muskogee, Indian Territory, December 29, 1906.

Lousianna Noble,
    Wewoka, Indian Territory.

Dear Madam:

    You are hereby advised that a representative of the Commissioner to the Five Civilized Tribes will be in Wewoka, Indian Territory, Friday and Saturday, January 4 and 5, 1907, for the purpose of hearing testimony in Seminole enrollment cases and you and the physician or midwife who was in attendance at the birth of your child_____
Noble, should appear at that place on one of those days, for the purpose of testifying relative to one of those days for the purpose of testifying relative to the right of said child to enrollment.

                    Respectfully,
                        Tams Bixby
                              Commissioner.

D.C.LL.

DEPARTMENT OF THE INTERIOR,
COMMISSIONER TO THE FIVE CIVILIZED TRIBES.

    In the matter of the application for the enrollment of Percilla Davis as a new born citizen of the Seminole Nation.

Sem. NB-181.

BIRTH AFFIDAVIT.

DEPARTMENT OF THE INTERIOR,
COMMISSION TO THE FIVE CIVILIZED TRIBES.

IN RE Application for Enrollment, as a citizen of the   Creek   Nation, of
Percilla Davis   , born on the   16   day of   April   , 1901

Name of Father: Bill Davis   a citizen of the   U.S.   Nation.
Name of Mother: Belily Davis   a citizen of the   Seminole   Nation.

Post-office: Holdenville I.T.

AFFIDAVIT OF MOTHER.

UNITED STATES OF AMERICA,
   INDIAN TERRITORY.
   Northern   District.

I,   Belily Davis   , on oath state that I am   26   years of age and a citizen by
Birth , of the   Seminole   Nation; that I am the lawful wife of   Bill Davis   , who is a
citizen, by   Birth   of the   U. States   Nation; that a   Female   child was born to me on
16   day of   April , 1901 , that said child has been named   Percilla Davis   , and is
now living.   her
                                      Belily x Davis
WITNESSES TO MARK: mark
   Dell Witherspoon
   G L Harjo

Subscribed and sworn to before me this   16   *day of*   May , 1901.

Chas Rider
NOTARY PUBLIC.

AFFIDAVIT OF ATTENDING PHYSICIAN OR MID-WIFE.

UNITED STATES OF AMERICA,
   INDIAN TERRITORY.
   Western   District.

I,   Jane James   , a   citizen   , on oath state that I attended on Mrs.   Belily
Davis , wife of   Bill Davis   on the   16   day of   April , 1901 ; that there was born
to her on said date a   Female   child; that said child is now living and is said to have
been named   Percilla Davis

Jane x James

317

WITNESSES TO MARK:
{ Dell Witherspoon
{ G L Harjo

Subscribed and sworn to before me this 16 *day of* May , 1901.

Chas Rider

NOTARY PUBLIC.

———————

Sem-NB-181

Muskogee, Indian Territory, January 25, 1906.

McKennon & Willmott,
    Attorneys for Seminoles,
        Wewoka, Indian Territory.

Gentlemen:

There are on file with the records of this office the affidavits of Belily Davis and Jane James to the birth of Percilla Davis, child of Bill Davis a United States citizen and Belily Davis a citizen of the Seminole Nation, April 16, 1901.

You are advised that it is impracticable from the information contained in these affidavits to identify Belily Davis as a citizen or freedman of the Seminole Nation and I have to request that you secure if possible information which will identify Belily Davis upon the rolls of the Seminole Nation and that you forward new affidavits to the birth of Percilla Davis, in order that if this child is entitled to enrollment as a citizen of the Seminole Nation proper disposition may be made of the application for her enrollment.

Respectfully,

Acting Commissioner.

———————

Sem. NB-181.

DEPARTMENT OF THE INTERIOR,
COMMISSIONER TO THE FIVE CIVILIZED TRIBES.

DCW

In the matter of the application for the enrollment of Percilla Davis as a new born citizen of the Seminole Nation.

-: D E C I S I O N :-

It appears from the record herein that on March 4, 1905, written application was made to the Commission to the Five Civilized Tribes for the enrollment of Percilla Davis as a new born citizen of the Seminole Nation.

It further appears from the record herein and from the records of this office that the applicant was born April 16, 1901 and is the child of Bill Davis, a non citizen and Belily Davis said to be a citizen of the Seminole Nation, but whose name cannot be identified upon the final roll of citizens of the Seminole Nation approved by the Secretary of the Interior or has an application pending for enrollment as such.

This office through its field parties operating in the Seminole and Creek Nation and its land offices and by interviews at this office of residents of the Seminole and Creek Nations of extensive acquaintance in said nations made every effort to ascertain the whereabouts of said applicant and the name and identification of her mother, but no information has been obtained.

I am, therefore, of the opinion that the application for the enrollment of Percilla Davis as a new born citizen of the Seminole Nation should be dismissed, and it is so ordered.

Tams Bixby Commissioner.

Muskogee, Indian Territory.
FEB 20 1907

(The letter of January 25, 1906, to McKennon & Willmott, above, given again.)